Advance Praise for *Get Up, Stand Up*

"*Get Up, Stand Up* is a powerful call to action that inspires us to take our country back. . . .This comprehensive analysis of how modern corporatocracy robber barons stole the US (and most of the world) is a must-read for all who resonate with Levine's belief that We the People have the power and the responsibility to overthrow the ruling elite."

—John Perkins, author of *Hoodwinked* and
Confessions of an Economic Hit Man

"As you read Bruce Levine's rousing *Get Up, Stand Up*, inevitably you will be reminded of Thomas Paine's *Common Sense*, which served as a rallying cry for the colonialists to take action against their British rulers. Today, Levine argues, Americans are ruled by a tyrannical 'corporatocracy'—i.e., government by big business and for big business—and his analysis of why the American people remain so passive in the face of such tyranny is smart, lucid, and passionate."

—Robert Whitaker, author of *Anatomy of an Epidemic* and *Mad in America*

"In an era when most political commentary has degenerated into self-satisfied carping and smug Monday morning quarterbacking, Bruce E. Levine breaks out of this intellectual paralysis with a clarion call for a new kind of politics. Levine offers a progressive user's manual for reclaiming our government from the stranglehold of corporate greed and rightwing paranoia. As an antidote to apathy, *Get Up, Stand Up* is worthy of Bob Marley, which is very high praise indeed. Read it, absorb it, act on it."

—Jeffrey St. Clair, co-editor of *CounterPunch*
and author of *Born Under a Bad Sky*

"With this book, Bruce Levine reinvents the old saw 'the personal is political.' Healthy people make up a healthy movement, and *Get Up, Stand Up* is full of both hope and practical solutions."

—Anya Kamenetz, author of *DIY U* and *Generation Debt*

"Over the years, I have been astounded at the way mainstream, hardworking, formerly self-sufficient Americans have meekly accepted being screwed

by big business, Wall Street, and their elected officials. I have wondered, why hasn't there been an uprising over the looting of mainstream America by big business and Wall Street, facilitated by Congress? Through his brilliant analysis, psychologist Bruce Levine explains the process by which mainstream America has become demoralized and docile, how those in power maintain that power, and what it will take to turn things around. Anyone who cares about the decline of mainstream America should read this book. Anyone who wants to do something about the decline of mainstream America *must* read this book."

—Jim Gottstein, president/CEO Law Project for Psychiatric Rights

"We are living in a land in which corporate power buys as many politicians as it needs, unjust laws shovel money to the rich, and media substitute entertainment for information. Yet Bruce Levine dares to show how we can reclaim our deadened souls, regain integrity and passion, and begin to change a political system we have let numb us into resigned helplessness."

—Rev. Davidson Loehr, author of *America, Fascism, and God*

"Bruce Levine attempts to wake us from our collective political stupor, our anesthetized resignation to corporate rule. *Get Up, Stand Up* inspires hope that together we can regain our self-respect and create the families, communities, and, perhaps, the country we once dreamed possible."

—Oryx Cohen, director of the National Empowerment
Center's Technical Assistance Center

"Bruce Levine's intriguing new book examines how emotional suffering is interwoven with political disempowerment. He has taken our discussion of mental health out of the doctor's office and put it back where it belongs: in the community."

—Will Hall, host of *Madness Radio* and co-founder of Freedom Center

"Feeling politically demoralized? You're not alone. In his latest book, *Get Up, Stand Up*, Bruce Levine provides not only the diagnosis for our country's seeming paralysis, but also a very strong antidote."

—Steve Clark, walking and bicycling program manager, Transit for Livable
Communities, Minneapolis

Get Up, Stand Up

Get Up, Stand Up

Uniting Populists,
Energizing the Defeated,
— and —
Battling the Corporate Elite

BRUCE E. LEVINE

CHELSEA GREEN PUBLISHING
WHITE RIVER JUNCTION, VT

Project Manager: Patricia Stone
Editorial Contact: Susan Warner
Developmental Editor: Jonathan Teller-Elsberg
Copy Editor: Laura Jorstad
Proofreader: Eileen Clawson
Indexer: Shana Milkie
Designer: Peter Holm, Sterling Hill Productions
Cover Designer: Evan Gaffney

Printed in the United States of America
First printing March, 2011
10 9 8 7 6 5 4 3 2 1   11 12 13 14 15

Chelsea Green Publishing is committed to preserving
ancient forests and natural resources. We elected to print
this title on 30-percent postconsumer recycled paper,
processed chlorine-free. As a result, for this printing, we
have saved:

11 Trees (40' tall and 6-8" diameter)
3 Million BTUs of Total Energy
1,026 Pounds of Greenhouse Gases
4,940 Gallons of Wastewater
300 Pounds of Solid Waste

Chelsea Green Publishing made this paper choice because
we and our printer, Thomson-Shore, Inc., are members
of the Green Press Initiative, a nonprofit program dedi-
cated to supporting authors, publishers, and suppliers
in their efforts to reduce their use of fiber obtained
from endangered forests. For more information, visit:
www.greenpressinitiative.org.

Environmental impact estimates were made using the Environmental Defense Paper Calculator.
For more information visit: www.papercalculator.org.

Our Commitment to Green Publishing

Chelsea Green sees publishing as a tool for cultural change and ecological stewardship. We strive to align
our book manufacturing practices with our editorial mission and to reduce the impact of our business
enterprise in the environment. We print our books and catalogs on chlorine-free recycled paper, using
vegetable-based inks whenever possible. This book may cost slightly more because we use recycled paper,
and we hope you'll agree that it's worth it. Chelsea Green is a member of the Green Press Initiative (www.
greenpressinitiative.org), a nonprofit coalition of publishers, manufacturers, and authors working to protect
the world's endangered forests and conserve natural resources. *Get Up, Stand Up* was printed on Nature's
Natural, a 30-percent postconsumer recycled paper supplied by Thomson-Shore.

Library of Congress Cataloging-in-Publication Data

Levine, Bruce E., 1956-
  Get up, stand up : uniting populists, energizing the defeated, and
  battling the corporate elite / Bruce E. Levine.
    p. cm.
  Includes bibliographical references and index.
  ISBN 978-1-60358-298-8
1. Democracy--United States--Citizen participation. 2.
Democracy--Psychological aspects. 3. Political participation--United
States. 4. Political participation--United States--Psychological
aspects. 5. Political culture--United States. 6. Free will and
determinism. 7. United States--Politics and government. I. Title.
  JK1759.L565 2011
  322.40973--dc22

                        2010052619

Chelsea Green Publishing Company
Post Office Box 428
White River Junction, VT 05001
(802) 295-6300
www.chelseagreen.com

CONTENTS

1. **The People Divided Versus the Corporatocracy in Control, 1**

   The Corporatocracy in Control, 4 • The People Divided, 8

2. **Are the People Broken?, 13**

   The 1999 Battle of Seattle, 16 • The 2000 US Presidential Election, 17 • The Wars in Afghanistan and Iraq, 21 • Wall Street Bailout, 24 • Health Care Reform, 27 • The Election of Barack Obama, 29 • Labor Unions and Demoralized Working People, 31 • The Tea Party Movement, 34 • Who, in Large Numbers, Is Fighting for Social Justice?, 38 • Light Resistance to Major Oppression, 40 • Demoralized, Disorganized, Broken, or What?, 43

3. **Prelude to Battle: Understanding How the People Learned Powerlessness, 47**

   Psychological Principles and Techniques for Breaking a Population, 48 • Television, Technology, and Zombification, 60 • Helplessness in the Age of Isolation, E-Relationships, and Bureaucratization, 65 • Broken by Fundamentalist Consumerism and Advertising/Propaganda, 69 • Student-Loan Debt and Indentured Servitude, 75 • The Normalization of Surveillance, 82 • The Decline of Labor Unions and the Loss of Power for Working People, 83 • Moneyism, Money-Centric Culture, and Weakness, 89 • How Schools Teach Powerlessness, 95 • Noncompliance as a Mental Illness, 100 • Elitism Training, 109 • Liars, Hypocrites, Egomaniacs, and the Corporate Media, 112 • The US Electoral System and Learned Helplessness, 115

4. **Energy to Do Battle: Liberation Psychology, Individual Self-Respect, and Collective Self-Confidence, 121**

   Critical Thinking and Morale, 122 • Energizing People: Morality and Other Fuels, 127 • Healing from "Battered People's Syndrome" and "Corporatocracy Abuse," 131 • Combating Social Isolation and Building Community, 136 • Individual Self-Respect and Empowerment, 140 • Focus on the Non-Fascist Family: Creating Respectful Relationships, 143 • Liberation Psychology, 145 • Forging an Alliance among Populists, 152 • Inspiration to Overcome Distrust, 158 • Collective Self-Confidence: Solidarity and Success, 161

5. **Winning the Battle: Solutions, Strategies, and Tactics, 166**

Lessons from the Great Populist Revolt, 166 • *Modern Electoral Politics: Wise or Unwise Battlefield?, 173* • *The Strategy and Tactics of Disruption, 176* • *Are Protest Demonstrations Effective?, 182* • *The Power of Divorce, 188* • *Twenty-first-Century Abolitionism: Ending Student-Loan Debt Servitude, 194* • *Workplace Democracy: Worker and Other Co-operatives, 200* • *Helpful and Harmful Small Victories and Compromises, 204* • *Crossing the Final Divide, 207*

Notes, 211
Acknowledgments, 233
Index, 235
About the Author, 246

The People Divided Versus the Corporatocracy in Control

How many Americans believe that their voice matters in determining whether giant banks, insurance companies, and other "too-big-to-fail" corporations get bailed out? How many Americans older than twelve believe that they have any influence over a decision by the US government to invade another nation?

There are a slew of books and articles out there providing analyses of the profound problems of American democracy and offering recommendations aimed at improving matters. However, these analyses and recommendations routinely assume that Americans have sufficient personal energy to take action. Instead, what if many Americans have lost confidence that genuine democracy is possible? When such fatalism sets in, truths about economic injustices and lost liberties are no longer enough to set people free.

While a charismatic politician can still garner a large turnout of voters who are angry with whichever party is in power, the majority of Americans appear resigned to the idea that they have no power over institutions that rule their lives. At least that's what I see. I was curious if what troubled me also was troubling others, so I wrote an article titled "Are Americans a Broken People?" It was republished on numerous Internet sites, and I read more than a thousand reaction comments (some of which are included in this book). I was swamped with e-mails and received several media interview requests to discuss the article, which had apparently touched a nerve among those who identify themselves as progressive, libertarian, or populist. They too wondered why so many Americans have remained passive in the face of attacks on their liberties and their economic well-being. Some of the questions that I first raised in that article and will answer more fully in this book are:

- Has "learned helplessness" taken hold for a great many Americans? Are many Americans locked into an abuse syndrome of sorts in which revelations about their victimization by a corporate-government partnership produce increased anesthetization rather than constructive action?

- What cultural forces have created a passive and discouraged US population? Have so-called right-wing and so-called progressive institutions both contributed to breaking people's resistance to domination?

- And most important, can anything be done to turn this demoralization and passivity around? Is it possible for people to rebuild their morale and forge the connections necessary to support a truly democratic populism that can take power away from elite control?

Elitism—be it rule by kings or corporations—is the opposite of genuine democracy. It is in the interest of those at the top of society to convince people below them that (1) democracy is merely about the right to vote; and (2) corporations and the wealthy elite are so powerful, any thought that "regular people" can achieve real power is naive. In genuine democracy and in real-deal populism, people not only believe that they have a right to self-government; they also have the individual strength and group cohesion necessary to take actions to eliminate top-down controls over their lives.

If people lose sight of what democracy really is, or if they lose hope of the possibility of attaining it, then they lose their energy to fight for it. The majority of us, unlike the elite, will always lack big money, so we depend on individual and collective energy to do battle. Without such energy, the elite will easily subdue us.

This book is, in large part, about regaining that energy. There exist solid strategies and time-tested tactics that people have long used to battle the elite, and these will be detailed. However, these strategies and tactics are not sufficient. For large-scale democratic movements to have enough energy to get off the ground, certain psychological and cultural building blocks are required. With these energizing building blocks, it then becomes realistic—and not naive—to believe that large numbers of people can take the kind of actions that will produce genuine democracy. The belief that their actions can be effective provides energy to take actions, taking actions strengthens the faith, and an energizing cycle is created.

Instead of this energizing cycle, there appears now to be a de-energizing cycle in which decreasing belief in the chance for success results in decreasing actions, and decreasing actions results in even less hope that genuine democracy is possible.

Historian Lawrence Goodwyn has studied democratic movements and written extensively about the Populist Movement in the United States that occurred during the 1870s through the 1890s, what he calls "the largest democratic mass movement in American history." Goodwyn concludes that democratic movements are initiated by people who are not resigned to the status quo or intimidated by established powers, and who have not allowed themselves to be "culturally organized to conform to established hierarchical forms." Goodwyn writes in *The Populist Moment*:

> Democratic movements are initiated by people who have individually managed to attain a high level of personal political self-respect . . . In psychological terms, its appearance reflects the development within the movement of a new kind of collective self-confidence. **"Individual self-respect" and "collective self-confidence" constitute, then, the cultural building blocks of mass democratic politics.** [emphasis added]

Without *individual self-respect*, people do not believe that they are worthy of power or capable of utilizing power wisely, and they accept as their role being a subject of power. Without *collective self-confidence*, people do not believe they can succeed in wresting power away from their rulers.

What today, culturally and psychologically, has destroyed individual self-respect and collective self-confidence? One goal of this book is to examine this question. The good news is that answers to it provide, within the ordinary daily events of people's lives, a road map of opportunities to regain individual self-respect, collective self-confidence, and real power.

The elite who maintain a hold on power are few; even with the support of some non-elites who share an ideology of hierarchical control, this group is a small minority. Those of us who believe in genuine democracy—of, by, and for the people—far outnumber the elitists, but we are divided. The elite's strategy of "divide and conquer" is one that routinely works, but not always. Their strategy fails when we recognize that the divides among us pale in significance compared with a common desire to have our fair share of power. And so this book is also about unifying people who oppose elite control so as to focus on our common desire for genuine democracy.

Is wresting power away from the corporate-government partnership a naive fantasy? If too many people believe this—and it's exactly what we're schooled by the corporate elite to believe—then it will remain just a naive fantasy. If, instead, enough people unlearn powerlessness and unify forces, then we can battle and beat the corporate elite. Describing how this can be done is the goal of this book.

The Corporatocracy in Control

A corporate-government partnership that governs society is a *corporatocracy*. In direct democracy, the people directly rule. In a republic, people have power through representatives, who actually represent them. In a corporatocracy, while there are elections, the reality is corporations and the wealthy elite rule in a way to satisfy their own self-interest.

In elections in a corporatocracy, it's in the interest of the governing class to maintain the *appearance* that the people have a say, so more than one candidate is offered up. It's in the interest of corporations and the wealthy elite that the winning candidate is beholden to them, so they financially support both Democrats and Republicans. It's in the interest of corporations and the wealthy elite that there are only two viable parties—this cuts down on costs. And it's in the interest of these two parties that they are the only parties with a chance of winning.

In a corporatocracy, corporations and the wealthy elite directly and indirectly finance candidates, who are then indebted to them. It's common for these indebted government officials to appoint to key decision-making roles those friendly to corporations, including executives from these corporations. And it's routine for high-level government officials to be rewarded with high-paying industry positions when they exit government. It's common and routine for former government officials to be given high-paying lobbying jobs so as to use their relationships with current government officials to ensure that corporate interests will be taken care of.

There are revolving doors of employment in what are now commonly called *industrial complexes*. Most famously, the term *military-industrial complex* was coined by Dwight Eisenhower, who devoted his Farewell Address in 1961 to its "grave implications." There is also the "energy-industrial complex," the "agriculture-industrial complex," and—as many Americans recently discovered—the "financial-industrial complex," with one of the most well-publicized door revolvers being George W. Bush's last Treasury secretary, Henry Paulson, who had previously been CEO of Goldman Sachs. However, this is not just a Republican thing. Prior to becoming President Barack Obama's chief economic adviser, Lawrence Summers in 2008 received $5.2 million from hedge fund D. E. Shaw; and Obama's number two man at Treasury, Neal Wolin, was previously an executive at the Hartford Financial Services Group. In 2010, *Mother Jones* magazine ("The Bankers on Obama's Team") listed nine other high-level members of the Obama administration who have been part of the corporate elite in the financial industry.

Owing to my involvement in mental health treatment reform, the industrial complex that I am most familiar with is the "pharmaceutical-industrial complex." Two high-profile politicians who have revolved between the doors of government and pharmaceutical corporations are Billy Tauzin and Mitch Daniels.

When in Congress, Billy Tauzin, a Democrat turned Republican, played a key role in shepherding the Medicare prescription drug law into passage in ways that it would become a financial bonanza for Big Pharma. Tauzin fought hard—and won—the battle to ensure that the federal government would be prohibited from negotiating discounts with drug companies. The law was signed by George W. Bush in December 2003. A few months later, Tauzin announced that he was retiring from Congress to take the job as director of Pharmaceutical Research and Manufacturers of America (PhRMA), a trade group representing giant pharmaceutical corporations. Through February 2010, Tauzin received an estimated annual salary of $2 million as head of PhRMA, where he became, essentially, Big Pharma's leading lobbyist.

In 2010, the national media began to discuss the possibility of Mitch Daniels, governor of Indiana, becoming a future Republican candidate for president of the United States. Mitch Daniels is a former vice president at Eli Lilly and Company, the giant pharmaceutical corporation headquartered in Indiana and best known for its blockbuster psychiatric drugs Prozac and Zyprexa. Prior to his career at Eli Lilly, Daniels had been Indiana senator Richard Lugar's chief of staff and also chairman of the National Republican Senatorial Committee. Daniels moved on to Eli Lilly in 1990, ultimately becoming senior vice president for corporate strategy and policy, where he served until leaving the company in 2001. He then became director of management and budget under George W. Bush.

The Bush family, Eli Lilly, and Mitch Daniels go way back. After George Herbert Walker Bush left his CIA director post in 1977, and before becoming vice president under Ronald Reagan in 1980, he was on Eli Lilly's board of directors and lobbied hard on behalf of Big Pharma (for example, for special tax breaks for Eli Lilly and other pharmaceutical corporations). In 1991, then Eli Lilly executive Mitch Daniels co-chaired a fund-raiser that collected $600,000 for the Bush-Quayle presidential campaign.

Along with being the director of management and budget in George W. Bush's administration, Daniels was also a member of the Homeland Security Advisory Council (as was Lilly's CEO, Sidney Taurel). In November 2002, *The New York Times* pointed at Lilly for tampering with the Homeland Security Act so as to include provisions aimed at protecting Eli Lilly and a few other big pharmaceutical corporations from lawsuits.

Eli Lilly received even more attention from the national media on January 15, 2009, when it pled guilty to charges that it had illegally marketed its blockbuster antipsychotic drug Zyprexa for unapproved uses to children and the elderly (two populations especially vulnerable to its dangerous side effects). Former Lilly sales representative Robert Rudolph, one of the eight whistle-blowers in this case, wanted jail time for executives, arguing, "You have to remember, with Zyprexa people lost their lives." Lilly pled guilty to a misdemeanor charge and agreed to pay $615 million to end the criminal investigation and approximately $800 million to settle the civil case. CBS reporter Sharyl Attkisson commented, "Eli Lilly has pled guilty to marketing the sometimes dangerous drug Zyprexa in ways never proven safe or effective . . . Lilly has agreed to pay $1.4 billion . . . Ironically, that's about as much as the company's Zyprexa sales in the first quarter last year."

While the mass media, at various times, has reported on each of the above details, the mass media does not connect the dots to reveal the corporatocracy. In fact, mass media is a major part of the corporatocracy: Much of it is owned by a handful of large corporations, and all of it is dependent on corporate advertising. Still, polls show that most people know government, corporations, and the wealthy elite work together to ensure their own self-interest, even if they don't know all the details of how.

The elites referred to in this book are those people who hold positions of authority in large corporations and in government and who have the power to directly or indirectly affect the lives of thousands or even millions of other people. Those running corporations answer to their board of directors instead of to their employees or citizens in general. Nearly all high-level government officials are elected with the help of money from corporations and the wealthy, and all face daily influence from corporate lobbyists and other wealthy campaign donors.

The problem of the corporatocracy will not be solved by replacing the current crop of CEOs with kindhearted men and women. Many elites give generously to charity and believe that they are acting in society's best interest. The problem of rule by a corporatocracy is that it creates disproportionate power, the antithesis of democracy. Such disproportionate power is intoxicating, and so it's no surprise that elites fiercely protect their positions and the institutions and systems that enable their power.

The corporatocracy is not a monolith, not a uniform bloc. The profits of one corporation can reduce the profits of another, and the profits of an entire industry can affect the costs of another. So, as is the case among organized crime families, there is certainly infighting within the corporatocracy. However, members have retained an effective unity when it comes to maintaining a system that benefits them as a whole. But just as the corporatocracy has divided and conquered the rest of us, it is not impossible for the corporatocracy itself to be divided and conquered.

The People Divided

I will provide evidence in chapter 4 that the majority of Americans are actually populists, in the sense that they are anti-elitists who trust the American people's judgment more than the corporate-government alliance. I will also describe differences among populists. I believe it is possible that populists can overcome their divides and together battle against elite control, and I will offer suggestions as to how to create this unity.

The corporate media routinely divides Americans as "liberals," "conservatives," and "moderates," a useful division for the corporatocracy because no matter which of these groups is the current electoral winner, the corporatocracy retains power. In order to defeat the corporatocracy, it's more useful to divide people in terms of "elitism" and "anti-authoritarianism"; and in order to unite anti-authoritarians, it's important to understand the psychological differences among them.

One example of an anti-authoritarian movement that I am personally familiar with is the mental health treatment reform movement, which comprises people who identify themselves as "on the left," others who identify themselves as "libertarians," and still others who disdain any political labels. I can tell you from my nearly two decades of working with these reformers that they certainly have different political views, but they all share a distrust for Big Pharma, a contempt for pseudoscience, and a belief that people deserve truly informed choice with respect to treatment. Most of these reformers respect Erich Fromm, the leftist psychoanalyst, along with Thomas Szasz, the libertarian psychiatrist, both passionate anti-authoritarians who have confronted mental health professionals for using dogma to coerce and control people.

Similarly, the education reform movement includes anti-authoritarians across the ideological spectrum, from libertarian educators such as John Taylor Gatto to left educators such as Alfie Kohn. While there are political differences among them, they agree that most standard schools are oppressive environments that more often encourage obeying orders, apathy, and dependence on authorities rather than nurturing curiosity and critical thinking.

Among anti-authoritarians, there are both the more "afflicted" and the more "comfortable," and it's important to understand their differing psychological realities in order to better unite them. This comfortable-afflicted continuum, at its most fundamental level, is based on the magnitude of frustration and other pains that one has in getting through the day. In our money-centric society, the capacity to pay bills significantly affects people's level of comfort, but there are other important nonfinancial variables that can either mitigate or exacerbate pain. Pain is reduced by having a platform in which one's voice can be heard by others; pain is increased when one feels completely voiceless, impotent, and powerless. Pain is reduced by having a meaningful job, even if it's not lucrative; pain is increased when one is working *only* for a paycheck. Pain is reduced by having other people in one's life who are joyful about one's joy and sad about one's sadness; pain is increased by isolation and an absence of caring. Pain is reduced by a feeling of connectedness with one's locale and natural world; pain is increased when one feels completely alienated from one's surroundings.

The afflicted are pained by some combination of their money worries, their employment, their unemployment, their isolation, and their alienation. In contrast, one is in the comfortable group if, all in all, the satisfactions of life outweigh the frustrations. One need not be financially well off to be in the comfortable group. It may be enough to have a platform, a meaningful job, and/or a non-alienating locale.

At different times in my life, I have been at different points on the afflicted-comfortable continuum. I have been overwhelmed by the pains of money worries, a stupid job, an alienating environment, and isolation. But I also know what it feels like to not have these pains. And I have come to understand how my level of pain about everyday life affects my receptivity to ideas, my energy level, and my capacity to take action.

Among "comfortable anti-authoritarians," many may know that there are millions of Americans working mindless jobs in order to hold on to their health insurance, or hustling two low-wage jobs to pay college loans, rent, and a car payment, or who may be unable to find even a poorly paying, mindless job and are instead helplessly watching eviction or foreclosure and bankruptcy close in on them. Many comfortable anti-authoritarians may intellectually understand the plight of the afflicted, but unless they have been part of that afflicted class—and remember what it feels like—they may not be able to fully empathize and respect the afflicted's emotional state. One major symptom of this lack of empathy and respect is the assumption that passive people are politically inert because they are ignorant; for example, that they lack knowledge of how they are being victimized. This assumption of ignorance as the cause of passivity is a great source of resentment for the afflicted, and this resentment is a great source of disunity.

I don't presume to know what everybody in the afflicted class needs, but I can tell you what would have engaged me when I was a member. I certainly didn't need lectures or other easy ego-tripping advice on what I should do. From the comfortable, I would have liked to hear some recognition that human beings often become passive not because they are ignorant, stupid, lazy, or immature but because they are overwhelmed by their pain, and their primary goal is to shut down or divert themselves in order to function at all. So when I found myself watching too much stupid television to divert myself from the pain of my life, I *knew* that watching stupid television was destructive for me. People *know* that alcohol, drugs, gambling, and other shutdowns, escapes, and diversion are not healthy; but they also know that without these shutdowns and diversions, their pain can be so overwhelming that they feel suicidal, homicidal, or psychotic. Comfortable anti-authoritarians need to respect the reality of the effects of overwhelming pain. The assumption that people's inactions are caused by ignorance sounds and smells elitist to many in the afflicted class who lack the energy to be engaged in any activism. Instead of lecturing to the afflicted, the comfortable might try respecting them and, if possible, sharing resources with them. Respect, resources, and anything that concretely reduces their level of pain is likely to be far more energizing than a scolding lecture.

Other divides among anti-authoritarians have caused disunity. It's natural for us to come to different conclusions as to the causes of passivity as well as to have different strategies for transforming it. Spirited debate is what democracy is all about. But when debate turns to mutual antipathy and divides anti-authoritarians, it plays into the hands of the elite. When advocates become so ego-attached to their analyses that they're unwilling to hear other explanations and other solutions, then they have forgotten the spirit of democracy. All of our experiences are limited, and so none of us has all the answers. The spirit of democracy is one of mutual respect and confidence that others can have truths and solutions that any one of us may not have yet considered.

Most of us understand the reality that we are governed by a corporatocracy, and for many of us it's a truth that triggers frustration and anger. Some of us are able to use that frustration and anger to energize constructive actions. However, there is a large group of anti-elitists who have been so worn down by decades of personal and political defeats, by financial struggles, by social isolation, and by daily interaction with impersonal and inhuman institutions that they no longer even feel the urge to act; for them, the truth of elitist control does not trigger resistance. Instead, their pain results in an ever-increasing withdrawal from the political sphere.

This is a different explanation for widespread political inaction by Americans than is routinely offered, and some activists struggling for democracy disagree. They insist that people are inactive because they are ignorant of what's going on, or that flawed organizations that should be channeling the desire for change are failing us. I am certainly in favor of getting truths out there and improved organizing efforts. However, I believe that missing from these oft-preached solutions is a vitally important piece of the puzzle—the problem of demoralization. The aim of this book is to deal with that piece so all who believe in democracy can have a better chance of achieving it.

• 2 •

Are the People Broken?

66So, how do you explain the absence of protest in the streets
today, the passivity in response to the fact that we have now
doubled the number of troops in Afghanistan that George W.
Bush had? How do you explain the apathy?99
—Bill Moyers (question to Howard Zinn), *Bill Moyers Journal*,
December 11, 2009

66Already the oil from the nightmare brought to us by BP
is making its way into these wetlands, into this natural para-
dise that belongs not just to the people of Louisiana but to
all Americans . . . The response of the Obama administration
and the general public to this latest outrage at the hands of a
giant, politically connected corporation has been embarrass-
ingly tepid. We take our whippings in stride in this country. We
behave as though there is nothing we can do about it.99
—Bob Herbert, *New York Times*, May 21, 2010

66'Apathy'?? Come on . . . Who cares about that?99
—Johnny2Bad, *Video Café*, December 23, 2009

People's spirit of resistance to domination cannot be definitively measured
in a scientific sense, and social scientists are often hesitant to study
phenomena that are not completely quantifiable and objective. There
are some quantifiable variables, however, that tell us something about
people's spirit of resistance.

What if polls show that a sizable number of people oppose a war, a
corporate bailout, or a disputed election, but they remain passive with
respect to public protest? When the majority of Americans disagree with
major public policies yet relatively few are on the streets demonstrating,
that says something, and so I will examine this.

13

There are other quantifiable variables worth examining. Anti-corporate voter turnout says something, although it can be argued that people inclined to vote for an anti-corporate political party, like the Green Party, are the people most likely to believe that it's futile to wage battle in a dice-loaded electoral process.

Today what's considered the "radical left populism" of the Green Party is really far closer to mainstream Democratic Party politics during Franklin Delano Roosevelt's time. And the Green Party, after peaking with 2.7 percent of the presidential vote in 2000, is today almost completely ignored by the mainstream press and hardly taken seriously even by much of the left-oriented alternative press. Libertarian, Labor, and all other "third" parties are similarly ignored. Contrast this with a previous era in the United States when political parties that were truly anti-hierarchical and/or called for radical economic and political transformations received sizable attention and votes. In the presidential election of 1892, the People's Party received 8.5 percent. And in the presidential election of 1912, the Socialist Party received 6 percent, while Teddy Roosevelt's Progressive Party—which, among other things, pledged to "dissolve the unholy alliance between corrupt business and corrupt politics" and promised a national health care system—garnered 27 percent of the vote (more than the incumbent president and Republican candidate, William Taft).

It's not surprising that the corporate-controlled media would assume the superiority of its economic system, thus ignoring more democratic possibilities. What is more troubling is the limited ideological range of the independent media. Even within the independent press, with a few exceptions, there is an acceptance of hierarchical governance and a push only for reforms to make the corporatocracy somewhat less dehumanizing.

Another way to measure America's hopelessness is to examine what politicians campaign on. Politicians constantly do their own private polling and examine focus groups to assess the mood of the public. It would have been expected that Barack Obama, as a Democrat running after eight years of a Republican president, would have run on "change." But Obama ran as much or more on the "hope" message. His "hope and change" campaign was so successful that he won both the 2008 presidential election and the 2008 *Advertising Age* "Marketer of the Year" award (he received 36.1 percent of the vote; Apple ran second at 27.3 percent). Obama loyalists and cynics can debate whether he cared about—or merely exploited—people's hopelessness, but his success at tapping into it tells us something.

People's resistance to domination versus their acquiescence can also be assessed by the magnitude and level of commitment. Voting takes little effort, participating in a demonstration takes more, and participation in ongoing protests or organizing efforts represents even more devotion. Historically, the most significant and serious kind of activism involved a willingness to sacrifice and risk. Risks can be economic, such as participating in a labor strike that might cost a person his or her job. They can be legal, like civil disobedience that results in jail or prison. And risk at the extreme is the willingness to put one's life on the line for a cause, such as in the case of a hunger strike. As part of assessing the state of morale among Americans, I am interested in the current magnitude and level of resistance and activism in the United States compared with that of other nations and with other periods in American history.

There are other subjective ways to get at the mood of people. In informal conversations, I have compared the fighting spirit of retired postal workers who participated in their 1970 wildcat strike with the beaten-down state of current postal employees (who have good reasons for feeling insecure and expendable). I also regularly talk to college students, a demographic that once had a relatively high spirit of resistance. Today politically active college students almost always tell me that they feel fairly alone on campus, as the overwhelming majority of their peers care mostly about partying and their future moneymaking potential, which is easy to understand given the huge debts that they are accruing. Again, these informal conversations are not proof of anything but are not irrelevant.

I don't ignore the fact that resistance to domination continues to exist. There remain American workers each day fighting for a fairer and more humane deal. There remain community organizers and activists, including approximately fifteen thousand of them who gathered in Detroit,

Michigan, in June 2010 for the second United States Social Forum. There continue to exist small, intelligent activist groups such as City Life/Vida Urbana who are quite effectively fighting against home foreclosures and evictions. And there even remains civil disobedience on the part of people such as pediatrician Margaret Flowers, a member of Physicians for a National Health Program, willing to be jailed for the cause of genuine health care reform. However, the plain truth is that overall there is less resistance to elite rule.

But what of the protests that have occurred in recent times? How do they fit into the situation I describe of widespread political passivity? Let's look at recent major examples of protest uprising against corporate-government policies and power.

The 1999 Battle of Seattle

The close of the twentieth century gave some promise that a grassroots and activist populism might be reawakening. In late November 1999 in Seattle, estimates ranged from forty to one hundred thousand people turned out to protest against the World Trade Organization (WTO), which was meeting there. It became known as the "Battle of Seattle."

The protesters included diverse groups ranging from labor unions to student organizations, religious groups, and anarchists. While the corporate media tried to label this as an anti-free-trade demonstration, it was not. The protesters did not oppose international trade per se but opposed the model of free trade that favored the corporatocracy and shafted the rest. The Battle of Seattle was a protest against the WTO and corporate-dominated globalization—and it was a protest for genuine democracy.

The size and the energy of the protest was especially heartening because the WTO at that time was by no means a well-known institution, and globalization was a relatively abstract idea. While the Battle of Seattle did not stop the tide of corporate-controlled globalization, in one sense it was a success. Prior to it, the mainstream media almost never explained why anyone would be upset with global organizations such as the WTO, the World Bank, or the International Monetary Fund (IMF). The Battle of Seattle forced the mainstream media to identify these globalization institutions and explain why people might be protesting against them.

The Battle of Seattle was followed in April 2000 by additional large protests in Washington, DC, against the World Bank and IMF. Some of those attending had been in Seattle; others were inspired by the events in Seattle to keep the movement strong. Whether it was an accident of circumstance or a lack of sustained motivation, the World Bank/IMF protests drew a much smaller crowd, estimated at between ten and fifteen thousand.

The Battle of Seattle certainly energized me. In particular, I was inspired to protest against the TransAtlantic Business Dialogue (TABD), which met in my hometown of Cincinnati in November 2000. There were only three hundred demonstrators, but having lived in conservative Cincinnati since 1978, I was surprised to see anybody at all protesting against this little-known corporate-globalization conference. Of course, the small number of protesters made it easy for TABD Conference co-chair Bertrand Collomb (chairman of the Lafarge Corporation) to joke, "Not having protesters at an international meeting means you are not important." The size of the demonstration was accurately reported by the area's major newspaper, *The Cincinnati Enquirer*, which included a photograph that actually made the crowd look larger than it was. The *Enquirer* mentioned the banners and signs with the slogans OUR DEMOCRACY—NOT FOR SALE and TABD—TRULY AWFUL BUSINESS DEALS, and it included a quote by protester Eric O'Neil, a member of Laborers Local 256: "The TransAtlantic Business Dialogue is making a global sweatshop out of the economy of the world."

So what with the Battle of Seattle, the DC protests, and the fact that *anyone* in a decidedly nonradical city such as Cincinnati would even be aware of a TABD meeting, much less protest it, I was hopeful about a democracy surge in the next decade. My hopes soon began to fade.

The 2000 US Presidential Election

More than a hundred million Americans voted in the 2000 presidential election, and the corporate media reported enough key facts that many of them believed the election was illegitimate. In fact, even by August 2003, *The New York Times* reported that since the election, "a fairly consistent 38 percent of respondents in The New York Times/ CBS News Poll have said that Mr. Bush was not legitimately elected president."

Following the 2000 election, the corporate media widely reported that Al Gore received approximately five hundred thousand more votes than George W. Bush. It widely reported that the Florida Supreme Court's order for a recount of the disputed Florida vote was overruled by the US Supreme Court in a politicized 5–4 decision. And the corporate press even reported the remarkable dissenting comment of Justice John Paul Stevens: "Although we may never know with complete certainty the identity of the winner of this year's presidential election, the identity of the loser is perfectly clear. It is the nation's confidence in the judge as an impartial guardian of the rule of law."

Even with this mass media exposure of the nondemocratic nature of the election, only a handful of US citizens immediately took to the streets to protest following the Supreme Court's December 12, 2000, ruling to hand the election to Bush. The vast majority of us seemed resigned to accepting the official election results. On Bush's Inauguration Day, January 20, 2001, approximately sixty thousand Americans did protest, with about a dozen even getting arrested. However, for the elite, this posed no threat. Despite the fact that many of the fifty-one million Gore voters believed they had been disenfranchised, and that many millions of Americans believed Bush was not legitimately elected, and despite organizers having more than a month to get the crowd out, only sixty thousand people showed up to demonstrate. Actually, it was the perfect number of demonstrators for the elite: large enough to provide evidence of American "democracy"—allowing free speech for losers—and small enough to make clear to the world how few people were upset. For the entering Bush-Cheney administration, that relatively small number of demonstrators may have told them that they could get away with just about *anything* without much protest, and that may well have been the message that they received.

Contrast the disputed 2000 US presidential election with disputed presidential elections in Iran in 2009, in Mexico in 2006, and in Ukraine in 2004. In all cases, the more progressive candidate was initially defeated. However, unlike Americans, those Iranians, Mexicans, and Ukrainians who believed that the election had been stolen from them were not so passive.

In 2009, there was a highly prominent, disputed presidential election in Iran. The official state results showed that Mahmoud Ahmadinejad, backed by the Islamic fundamentalist establishment, won with 62 percent of the votes cast and that the reformist candidate Mir-Hossein Mousavi received 34 percent of the votes cast. Mousavi, a former prime minister, was a reformer on many social and economic issues, but like all official candidates, Mousavi had to be first vetted by the Iranian Guardian Council, which consisted of establishment clerics and lawyers. Following the report of the official results, demonstrations immediately broke out. Just three days after the election, *Time* magazine reported that "although the Interior Ministry kept broadcasting a communiqué warning that no permit had been issued for the rally, 2 million to 3 million Iranians from a broad cross section of society converged on Freedom Square to demand a recount." Though most independent observers agree that there was election fraud in Iran in 2009 and that Ahmadinejad did not receive 62 percent of the vote, three months after the election World Public Opinion (affiliated with the University of Maryland) reported that 55 percent of Iranians polled said they had voted for Ahmadinejad. So it is actually possible that the 2009 Iranian election, though fraudulent, was more democratic than the 2000 US presidential election.

In the disputed Mexican presidential election held on July 2, 2006, the official results showed that Felipe Calderón of the right-of-center National Action Party won by a difference of 243,934 votes (or 0.58 percent) over Andrés Manuel López Obrador of the left-of-center-center Coalition for the Good of All (PRD, PT, Convergence). In response to official election results, Obrador and his supporters claimed that there had been voting irregularities and demanded a recount. When the government refused, Obrador's supporters staged several large protests, with one estimated to be attended by as many as three million Mexicans. In addition to peaceful protests, there was some civil disobedience, including demonstrators surrounding and blocking offices of foreign-owned banks and government offices, but in the end Obrador was defeated.

Were Iranian and Mexican demonstrators naive romantics, or is it in fact possible for a fully energized, large, and persistent citizenry to actually right an election wrong? In the disputed presidential election in Ukraine in November 2004, Viktor Yanukovych was initially declared the winner over Viktor Yushchenko, but Yushchenko's supporters staged what came to be known as the "Orange Revolution." In addition to large and sustained demonstrations, there were sit-ins, general strikes, and some civil disobedience, which were successful at getting the election results annulled. A revote ordered by Ukraine's Supreme Court for December 26, 2004, was intensely monitored by international observers, who declared it to be fair. The final results gave the victory to Yushchenko, who received 52 percent of the vote, compared with Yanukovych's 44 percent, and Yushchenko was inaugurated as president of Ukraine on January 23, 2005. The Orange Revolution was successful.

In watching the civil unrest in Iran in 2009, in Mexico in 2006, and in Ukraine in 2004, some Americans felt superior, taking pride in our "orderly transition of power." However, if one believes that a transition of power is an illegitimate one, as many millions of Americans believed following the 2000 election, and one remains orderly, does that make one superior or broken?

The US presidential election in 2000 is also significant both for the rise of an anti-corporate third party and a resulting demoralization over anti-corporate, third-party politics. In the 1996 presidential election, the anti-corporate Green Party presidential candidate Ralph Nader received less than 1 percent of the total vote. In 2000, however, with increasing disgust for pro-corporate agendas of both the Democrats and Republicans, Green Party presidential candidate Ralph Nader received 2.7 percent of the total vote, almost three million votes. This was the first time that an anti-corporate candidate had a significant showing since 1948, when Progressive/American Labor Party candidate Henry Wallace garnered

2.4 percent of the vote. Since World War II, third-party candidates who received sizable percentages have not run against the corporatocracy (billionaire Ross Perot in 1992 and 1996 ran against bad government; John Anderson in 1980 was a pro-business moderate Republican; and George Wallace in 1968 ran on pro-segregation and law-and-order).

The Green Party candidacy of Nader in 2000, however, was ultimately more demoralizing than energizing. While Nader may or may not have cost Gore the election, the perception by many progressive Americans is that Nader contributed to the victory of the villainous Bush. What's not debatable is that Nader and the Green Party lost their luster. In the 2004 and 2008 elections, even if one combines the percentage of the Green Party presidential candidate and Ralph Nader (who ran as an independent), the total for each election was less than 1 percent of the turnout.

The Wars in Afghanistan and Iraq

The Afghanistan War was launched by the United States on October 7, 2001. By the spring of 2010, it had surpassed the Vietnam War as the longest official war in US history (though unofficially the Vietnam War remains longer). This milestone passed with virtually no protests, despite polls showing widespread opposition to the Afghanistan War.

In early December 2009, Barack Obama announced an increase of thirty thousand to the more than seventy thousand US troops already in Afghanistan, raising the number of US troops to approximately one hundred thousand (when Obama became president in January 2009, there were roughly thirty-four thousand US troops in Afghanistan). While the American people evidenced trust in Obama's belief that a troop increase was necessary, by mid-December 2009 two polls showed that the majority of the American people actually opposed the war. Specifically, Americans were asked this question in both polls: "Do you favor or oppose the US war in Afghanistan?" In a CNN poll, 55 percent opposed the war and 43 percent favored it. In an AP/GFK poll, 57 percent opposed the war and 39 percent favored it.

Despite the large number of Americans opposed to this war, recent protests against it have been remarkably small. Indeed, these recent protests have been much smaller than the twenty thousand people who demonstrated in Washington, DC, on September 29, 2001, against the impending invasion of Afghanistan—this at a time when the overwhelming majority of the American people (more than 80 percent) actually favored taking military action in Afghanistan. (Osama bin Laden and al-Qaeda, which had taken credit for the September 11, 2001, attack on the World Trade Center, were believed to be in Afghanistan, and the American public wanted action against them.)

Unlike Vietnam War protests, which started modestly when that war was popular but dramatically increased with its decline in popularity, American protests against the Afghanistan War have actually declined as this war's popularity has declined. While it's no surprise that Vietnam War protests, given the then draft and the higher number of casualties, provoked far larger protests than those against recent unpopular wars, the current decline remains remarkable.

There was far more protest by Americans against the imminent invasion of Iraq, which ultimately occurred on March 20, 2003. This second Iraq War was also initially favored by the majority of Americans. However, it was quickly established that the Bush-Cheney argument that Iraq's dictator Saddam Hussein was in partnership with al-Qaeda was ludicrous (as Saddam Hussein and al-Qaeda were more rivals than allies), and many Americans doubted—and were soon proven right—that Iraq had "weapons of mass destruction," which became Bush's primary rationale for the invasion. So when Bush, already seen to be an illegitimate president by 38 percent of Americans, pushed the United States toward what seemed by many to be an illegitimate war, there was every reason to believe that there would be massive demonstrations. And there were.

On February 15, 2003, there were between six and eight hundred sizable demonstrations in cities around the world. In New York City, where the largest demonstration in the United States occurred, organizers claimed half a million people attended, while the police estimated the crowd at closer to one hundred thousand.

The largest of the worldwide demonstrations on February 15, 2003, against the impending invasion were not in the United States but in Europe. Police in London estimated a crowd of 750,000, and organizers estimated over 2 million, the largest demonstration ever in the British capital. In Spain, there were demonstrations in fifty-five cities with the largest occurring in Madrid, where the government estimated 660,000 and organizers reported 2 million; and in Barcelona estimates ranged from 350,000 to more than a million. Perhaps the largest crowds of all were in Rome, Italy, where police estimated 650,000 and organizers reported over 3 million people.

Once the Iraq War commenced, the US and worldwide protests never again achieved that kind of magnitude, though there continued to be significant protests around the world. As late as 2007, demonstrations in Washington, DC, saw numbers ranging, depending on who did the estimating, from "tens of thousands" to more than a hundred thousand, but reporters observed that crowds were nowhere near the size of earlier demonstrations. On March 20, 2010, on the seventh anniversary of the Iraq invasion, a demonstration in DC against the war drew "thousands," but was, according to estimates, significantly smaller than 2007. Also on that seventh anniversary in New York City, there were reports of a "few dozen enthusiastic protesters" attending a rally. One of these New York City protesters, Kathy Hoang, said, "It's sad that a lot of people did not come out for this protest. People are getting used to the war and don't bother even to think about it anymore."

Kathy Hoang was exactly right. Again like the Afghanistan War, as the Iraq War became increasingly unpopular in the polls, the size of demonstrations has actually diminished.

Recall Bill Moyers's pained questions to historian Howard Zinn in December 2009, quoted at the beginning of this chapter, about an absence of protest in the streets in response to still another US troop increase in Afghanistan at the same time that the majority of Americans opposed the war. Zinn responded:

> Let's put it this way—I don't think people are apathetic about
> it. I believe most people in this country do not want us to be in

Afghanistan. But they're not doing anything about it, you're right. We're not seeing protests in the street. And I think one of those reasons is that the media—the major media, television, and newspapers—they have not played their role in educating the public about what is going on.

The problem with blaming the corporate media for the recent lack of Americans' protest against US wars is that polls show the American people know enough to oppose these wars. Lack of information can't be the explanation for inaction in the face of widespread, conscious dissatisfaction. This requires a different explanation.

Wall Street Bailout

The official name of the original bailout was the Emergency Economic Stabilization Act of 2008. It was enacted in October 2008, creating the $700 billion Troubled Assets Relief Program to purchase failing or "toxic" bank assets, especially mortgage-backed securities, and to make capital injections into banks.

How did Americans initially feel about the Wall Street bailout? In one September 2008 poll, the Pew Research Center reported that the American public supported the bailout, but most other polls showed that the nation was opposed.

> **Los Angeles Times/Bloomberg Poll, September 19–22, 2008**
> "Do you think the government should use taxpayers' dollars to rescue ailing private financial firms whose collapse could have adverse effects on the economy and market, or is it not the government's responsibility to bail out private companies with taxpayers' dollars?"
> | | |
> |---|---|
> | Use Taxpayers' Dollars | 31% |
> | Not Government's Responsibility | 55% |
> | Unsure | 14% |

CBS News/New York Times Poll, September 21–24, 2008

"Do you approve or disapprove of the federal government's plan to provide money to financial institutions to help them get out of their financial crisis?"

Approve 42%

Disapprove 46%

Unsure 12%

USA Today/Gallup Poll, September 17, 2008

"Do you favor or oppose the Federal Reserve's decision to make the loan to AIG?"

Favor 40%

Oppose 42%

Unsure 18%

By 2009, not only did the majority of Americans disapprove of providing government assistance to ailing giant financial institutions, but polls showed that they were "resentful" about this. A March 2009 CBS poll reported that "only 37% of Americans approve of the government giving money to banks and financial institutions as a way of trying to fix the nation's economy. More than 53% disapprove." Beyond simple "disapproval," CBS reported, "Nearly half of Americans are now mostly resentful that President Barack Obama's policies toward the nation's banks and financial institutions could benefit irresponsible managers and bankers." While the main bailout program was crafted by Bush's Treasury secretary and signed into law by Bush, Obama (who at the time of the CBS poll had been president for less than two months) never had any qualms about maintaining that program despite strong public opposition. The CBS poll reported that 75 percent of Americans believed that bank problems were caused by "management decisions"; only 17 percent felt that bank problems were caused by "conditions beyond companies' control." In contrast, Americans were in favor of providing help to homeowners. While only 37 percent approved of government assistance to bankers, 71 percent approved of such help for homeowners.

Yet even though a good number of Americans—likely the majority—opposed the Wall Street bailout, what did they do? There was opposition to the bailout by self-identified Tea Partiers—a group that I will detail later. There were also protests from progressive groups across the United States in September 2008, but all of them were very small. The largest progressive group demonstration was in New York City, organized by labor unions, near the New York Stock Exchange. Protesters held signs such as NO BLANK CHECKS FOR WALL STREET and cheered populist speeches by Reverend Jesse Jackson, United Federation of Teachers president Randi Weingarten, and AFL-CIO national president John Sweeney, who drew cheers when he stated, "We want our tax dollars used to provide a hand up for the millions of working people who live on Main Street and not a handout to a privileged band of overpaid executives." However, in 2008 this was the left's best-organized and largest demonstration against the bailout, and it drew maybe a thousand protesters (Reuters estimated "several hundred").

On April 29, 2010, the progressive online magazine *AlterNet* reported on an AFL-CIO-led protest against Wall Street excesses by "more than 5,000 union members and others." Bruce Vari, an unemployed electrical worker with Local 3, worried that there wasn't enough pressure from below: "There should be more people here. This is a start, but we're hurting more than we're showing."

In late 2010, Americans discovered that the Federal Reserve had loaned far more money to "too-big-to-fail" corporations than we had been originally led to believe. *The Wall Street Journal* reported on December 1, 2010, "The US central bank on Wednesday disclosed details of some $3.3 trillion in loans made to financial firms, companies and foreign central banks during the crisis." In addition to America's banks and insurance companies, the Federal Reserve also bought short-term debt from General Electric and several other giant corporations at the same time that "too-small-to-care-about" businesses could not get bank loans. Though millions of American were upset by this, they appeared resigned to the reality that the US government had become, in effect, an insurance company for giant corporations.

Health Care Reform

Despite the fact that several polls showed that, overall, Americans actually favored a "single-payer" or "Medicare-for-all" health insurance plan, it was not even on the table in the Democrat-Republican 2009–2010 debate over health insurance reform legislation. Polls showed that an even larger majority of Americans favored the government providing a "public option" to compete with private health insurance plans, but the public option was quickly pushed off the table in the Democrat-Republican debate.

A July 2009 Kaiser Health Tracking Poll asked, "Do you favor or oppose having a national health plan in which all Americans would get their insurance through an expanded, universal form of Medicare-for-all?" 58 percent of Americans favored it, and only 38 percent opposed this Medicare-for-all universal plan. And a whopping 77 percent favored "expanding Medicare to cover people between the ages of 55 and 64 who do not have health insurance."

A February 2009 CBS News/New York Times Poll reported, "Americans are more likely today to embrace the idea of the government providing health insurance than they were 30 years ago. 59% say the government should provide national health insurance, including 49% who say such insurance should cover all medical problems."

A December 2009 Reuters poll concluded that "most Americans would like to see a 'public option' in health insurance reform . . . Just under 60 percent of those surveyed said they would like a public option as part of any final healthcare reform legislation."

The Time Magazine/ABT poll on July 27–28, 2009, also showed that Americans favored a single-payer/Medicare-for-all plan and, even more strongly, a public option. Specifically this poll asked:

> "Would you favor or oppose a health care bill that creates a national single-payer plan similar to Medicare for all, in which the government would provide health care insurance to all Americans?"

Favor 49%
Oppose 46%
No answer/don't know 5%

"Would you favor or oppose a health care bill that creates a government-sponsored public health insurance option to compete with private health insurance plans?"

Favor 56%
Oppose 36%
No answer/don't know 8%

This poll also reported that 55 percent believed the US health care system needed "major reform," not just "minor adjustments." Only 11 percent rated US health care as "excellent" (31 percent called it "good"; 33 percent called it "only fair," and 22 percent called it "poor"). With respect to how good a job private health insurance companies are doing, only 7 percent reported "excellent" (28 percent said "good"; 36 percent said "only fair," and 24 percent said "poor").

While Americans believe the United States needs health care reform, public protests for the kind of reform they favor were small. The largest health care reform rally in 2009 occurred in July in Washington, DC, and had organizational support from Health Care for America, the National Physicians Alliance and other progressive health care professional organizations, the AFL-CIO, and several other unions, including the Service Employees International Union, the Communications Workers of America, and the American Federation of State, County and Municipal Employees. The thrust of the rally was to pass legislation of *any kind* that would provide insurance for the millions of Americans who were uninsured and under-insured. Even with the efforts of multiple organizations, this rally drew only ten thousand people.

So, given Americans' support for both a single-payer/Medicare-for-all plan and a powerful public option—neither of which was achieved— what could be said about the final health insurance reform legislation?

Progressive economist Robert Reich, the former secretary of labor under Bill Clinton, favored the passed legislation—but quite soberly:

> So don't believe anyone who says Obama's health care legislation marks a swing of the pendulum back toward the Great Society and the New Deal. Obama's health bill is a very conservative piece of legislation, building on a Republican rather than a New Deal foundation. The New Deal foundation would have offered Medicare to all Americans or, at the very least, featured a public insurance option.

Reich notes that Obama's legislation has its roots in the Eisenhower administration, which locked in the tax break for employee health benefits, as well as in the Nixon administration, which pushed competing health plans and urged a requirement that employers cover their employees. Obama actually applied Nixon's ideas and took them a step farther by requiring all Americans to carry health insurance, giving subsidies to those who need it. With this bill, Americans did gain certain insurance-coverage rights; but because of its mandatory requirement, insurance companies have been handed millions of new customers.

The Election of Barack Obama

> 66 Obama represented a rising up against the system . . . In voting for Obama, most people were rising up against the forces of oppression. But the media deceived them and the Democratic leadership betrayed them . . . our efforts are being dissipated by our media and our leadership, which have betrayed us completely. Obama alone has neutralized or destroyed any number of progressive goals. 99
> —Perry Logan, *AlterNet*, December 13, 2009

I read several reaction comments to my article arguing that the large turnout for Obama was, as Perry Logan put it above, "a rising up against the system" and evidence that Americans are not broken. Was Barack Obama a populist candidate and support for him truly evidence of a populist revival, and did President Obama really then betray those who voted for him? Or was the Barack Obama phenomenon not so much evidence of a people rising up against the system but rather evidence of how marketers could tap Americans' hopelessness and sell a package tied to hope?

In reality, Senator Obama's voting record and candidate Obama's campaign were very assuring to corporate America. Not only did Senator Obama vote in favor of the Wall Street bailout on October 1, 2008, but a week earlier he and Republican presidential candidate John McCain put out a joint statement in support of it.

Did candidate Obama threaten the military-industrial complex? While candidate Obama said that there should be a "fixed timeline" for withdrawing combat troops from Iraq and his opponent did not, candidate Obama was good news for the military-industrial complex. The military-industrial complex has now grown beyond longtime defense industry manufacturers such as Lockheed Martin, Boeing, and Raytheon to also include the newer "service industries" such as Blackwater/Xe, DynCorp, and Triple Canopy; as of 2010, there were between 200,000 and 250,000 contractors on the ground in the wars in Iraq and Afghanistan. Candidate Obama indicated that he would not diminish defense spending but merely shift or even increase it; and in 2010, President Obama asked Congress to hike defense spending the following year 2.2 percent to $708 billion—that's 6.1 percent higher than peak defense spending during the Bush administration. Candidate Obama repeatedly made it loud and clear that the United States must shift its defensive resources to Afghanistan, where he promised to escalate the American military effort. He kept his promise.

Senator, candidate, and ultimately President Obama also made the energy-industrial complex smile. As a senator, as a candidate, and as president, Obama has supported "a new generation of safe, clean nuclear power plants," "new offshore areas for oil and gas development," and "clean coal technologies," labeling all of these "clean/green energy sources/jobs"— music to the ears of corporate interests.

Did President Obama betray any of candidate Obama's promises? *Washington Post* columnist Ezra Klein pointed out that Obama did betray his campaign pledge on the public option to compete with private health insurance plans, as Obama never fought for the public option as president. The Obama White House, using legalistic hair splitting, claims that he never really committed to the public option in his campaign.

While President Obama is perhaps guilty of some betrayal, the reality is that he made it loud and clear in his campaign that what was paramount for him was corporate interests in major areas such as the financial-industrial complex, the military-industrial complex, and the energy-industrial complex, and he was vague on just how hard he would fight for the kind of health care reform that would have truly upset health insurance or pharmaceutical corporations.

It is understandable that people can become so desperate, they actually fantasize that a candidate who as senator and throughout his presidential campaign curried favor with corporate America would then, when he became president, dedicate himself to fighting the corporations on behalf of common folk. In retrospect, it is much clearer to many Americans that the election of Barack Obama was evidence not of people rising up against the system but of how marketers could exploit Americans' hopelessness to sell a candidate.

Advertising—be it for a car or candidate—works best exploiting strong emotional needs and pains such as hopelessness and anger. Following Obama's election and increased skepticism about an elected politician's ability to provide an antidote for hopelessness, politicians have increasingly exploited anger to sell themselves, this especially so for Tea Party candidates. However, when a candidate who exploits hopelessness and anger gets elected and then doesn't satisfy the need of supporters to feel more positively, a numbing apathy can emerge.

Labor Unions and Demoralized Working People

On January 8, 2010, the US Department of Labor reported an unemployment rate of 10.0 percent, which represented 15.3 million people.

These numbers were up from December 2007, the official start of the recession, when the unemployment rate had been 5.0 percent, amounting to 7.7 million people. Not included in the official 10 percent unemployment totals were 9.2 million "involuntary part-time workers" (they want but can't find full-time work) and about 2.5 million people "marginally attached to the labor force" (individuals not in the labor force but who want and are available for work; they are not counted as unemployed because they did not actively search for work in the past four weeks). Among the marginally attached were 929,000 "discouraged workers" (persons not currently looking for work because they believe no jobs are available for them). The bottom line is that while 10 percent were officially counted as unemployed, closer to 18 percent of Americans would have labeled themselves as unemployed or significantly underemployed.

In the last third of 2008 and most of 2009, Americans were inundated with staggering monthly job loss totals, routinely over half a million per month. We heard about the huge numbers of job losses from the corporate media, and almost all of us saw it happening around us to neighbors, friends, family, or co-workers—or we were being laid off ourselves. For quite some time previously, we'd been hearing about and feeling the permanent loss of well-paying manufacturing jobs, the decrease in real wages, the increasing inequality between the rich and poor, and the disappearance of the middle class.

So why didn't more working people take to the streets? That's what Bill Moyers asked Richard Trumka, president of the AFL-CIO, on January 29, 2010.

> *Bill Moyers*: I'm curious, Rich, about why we haven't been seeing more public demonstrations from people who have lost their job? I mean, we covered a story early last year in Chicago of workers who sat in, when it looked as if their factory was going to be closed down. Why has there been so little of that?
>
> *Richard Trumka*: Well, you know what? I think some of it is people have been so beat down, that they—we sort of

plucked the hope out of them. And what we have to do is restore that hope. They don't think that there's anything that they can do. They feel hopeless. Corporations are so powerful, and they control the political process so much that there's nothing we can do. They're wrong, of course. And we're getting more and more people that are willing to start coming out now.

Bill Moyers: So, what's happened that unions don't seem to be fighting back the way they did in the 1930s?

Richard Trumka: Well, I don't think that's so. I think we are fighting back.

The story about the Chicago workers that Moyers mentioned was covered by CNN and other corporate media. These workers staged a five-day sit-in protest in December 2008 at Republic Windows and Doors when it became clear that their factory was going to be closed down. These workers sought neither a pay raise nor even to get their jobs back—merely severance pay and a guarantee that their last paychecks would not bounce. Generally, Bill Moyers was correct in his observation that there had been no great outpouring of demonstrations by distressed workers and their supporters in the United States.

In 2009, in contrast, outside the fifty United States, in US territories and in other nations around the world, there were huge protests against job losses. In October 2009 in Puerto Rico, several thousand (organizers claimed a hundred thousand) union members gathered in the financial district outside San Juan to protest the government's plan to lay off more than twenty thousand workers. In February 2009 in Ireland, when unemployment was less than 6 percent, 120,000 Irish workers protested, led by employees from SR Technics and Waterford Crystal, two companies that were facing serious problems. In Scotland in 2009, "More than 20,000 Take to Streets to Protest Johnnie Walker Plant Closure" read a *Telegraph UK* headline. And in other parts of the world—India, for example—there were even larger protests by workers.

In October 2010, in response to the French government's plan to raise retirement age from sixty to sixty-two, there was a nationwide strike by major French unions that canceled all flights and train travel and disrupted daily life. There were ongoing huge demonstrations, including one, according to police estimates, of 1.2 million people. If the US government was about to raise the Social Security retirement age (there has been some talk of this), it is difficult to imagine that Americans would take actions similar to those taken by the French.

On October 2, 2010, in Washington, DC, there was an "umbrella demonstration" that covered virtually every major progressive cause—jobs, peace, the environment, and justice—which was supported by virtually every progressive organization. *The Washington Post* reported, "Tens of Thousands Attend Progressive 'One Nation Working Together' Rally in Washington," and *The New York Times* reported, "Tens of thousands of union members, environmentalists, and peace activists rallied at the Lincoln Memorial on Saturday, seeking to carry on the message of jobs and justice." One Nation Working Together claimed newspaper estimates were low and that 175,000 people attended. In this demonstration, there were more than three hundred participating groups, including the AFL-CIO, many other union groups, National Council of La Raza, the NAACP, the Sierra Club, People for the American Way, the National Gay and Lesbian Task Force, and virtually the entire range of progressive, liberal, and left organizations. Given the array of causes and number of organizations involved, the size of the protest was relatively small, at least too small to have any impact on the elite.

One Nation Working Together and 2011 state workers protests, however, makes it clear that there are some Americans still willing to actively demonstrate their displeasure with governmental policy. The Tea Party movement makes this point as well.

The Tea Party Movement

Today the Tea Party phenomenon appears to be the most energized political movement in the United States. There is a great deal of debate about its funding and the different motives of its leaders versus its followers, but what virtually all Tea Party critics and supporters alike agree on is that, at the grass roots, Tea Partiers are *angry*.

Anger, as a stage of grief, most often precedes depression. Angry Tea Partiers all feel a loss, but there are differences among them as to what that loss is. For some self-identified Tea Partiers, the most painful loss is that of power to Democrats, liberals, and African Americans; others are pained by their perceived loss of freedom and liberty. Some Tea Partiers have rage with legal abortion and illegal immigrants, but others have only a hatred of taxes and what they consider a tyrannical, socialist government.

Many of those who have become Tea Partiers were once angered by Democrat Bill Clinton, helped elect Republican George W. Bush, and then moved from "political anger" to "political depression" when they saw Bush and the Republicans expand government spending. This dynamic is psychologically similar to many on the left who were enraged by George W. Bush, helped elected Barack Obama, and then became politically depressed when they saw Obama appease large corporations.

Among the several organizations that identify with the Tea Party movement is one called Tea Party Patriots: Official Home of the American Tea Party Movement. Its mission statement reads as follows: "The impetus for the Tea Party movement is excessive government spending and taxation. Our mission is to attract, educate, organize, and mobilize our fellow citizens to secure public policy consistent with our three core values of Fiscal Responsibility, Constitutionally Limited Government and Free Markets." The grassroots Tea Partiers whom I have spoken with agree with this mission and these values.

By January 2010, more Americans had a positive view of the Tea Party movement than either of the major parties, with 41 percent of Americans looking favorably at the Tea Party versus only 35 percent for the Democratic Party and only 28 percent for the Republican Party. In August 2010, CBS reported that 29 percent of those polled "supported" the Tea Party. An April 2010 New York Times/CBS poll found "18 percent of Americans who identify themselves as Tea Party supporters," and on September 30, 2010, Fox News reported that 13 percent of registered voters consider themselves "part of" the Tea Party movement.

On April 15, 2009, there were about 750 Tea Party demonstrations, with most crowds under a thousand at each. On September 12, 2009, their protest Taxpayer March on Washington drew "in excess of 75,000" according to the Washington, DC, Fire Department. This demonstration, also called the 9/12 Demonstration, drew people not simply to protest "big government"; many were also there to praise America and God and to rage against Barack Obama, abortion, and undocumented workers. Drawing on a similar combination of people, on August 28, 2010, organizers claimed their DC event Restoring Honor drew three to five hundred thousand people, while CBS News (which commissioned AirPhotosLive.com to estimate crowd size via aerial photographs at the height of the rally) estimated eighty-seven thousand people.

When it comes to cultural issues, there are major differences between those who attend Tea Party demonstrations and those who identify themselves as left populists. Still, many people in both groups believe that elite forces do not care about ordinary people. Both groups opposed the Wall Street bailout, and many grassroots Tea Partiers, like left populists, are opposed to the kind of corporate globalization measures—such as the North American Free Trade Agreement (NAFTA)—that have resulted in the outsourcing of US jobs overseas. At the grass roots, many Tea Partiers hold anger for both Democrats and Republicans, with some grassroots Tea Partiers having even more contempt for Republicans, whom they view as more hypocritical about "limited government" and "fiscal responsibility" than are Democrats. The Tea Party movement includes a large number of grassroots members with a genuine belief in liberty and freedom but also, like any movement, includes opportunists.

Tea Party Nation, another Tea Party organization, organized the National Tea Party Convention in February 2010. The convention was essentially a sellout of grassroots Tea Partiers to the Republican Party, as high-profile Republican Sarah Palin (who, in her vice presidential run in 2008, supported running mate John McCain's strong advocacy of NAFTA and the Wall Street bailout) was the keynote speaker. The National Tea Party Convention charged $549 for admission, which helped pay Palin's $100,000 speaking fee. Palin then gave a speech in which she used the terms *elite* and *elitists* pejoratively to a group of a thousand people who could afford to pay $549 to listen to a politician. The Tea Party movement is heavily supported by right-wing corporations such as Koch Industries, the second-largest private company in America, and by front groups like Americans for Prosperity. In April 2009, *The Atlantic* asked, "The Tea Party Movement: Who's in Charge?" and concluded that, in addition to Americans for Prosperity, two other national-level conservative groups were primarily responsible for guiding it: Don'tGo, a tech savvy free-market action group and FreedomWorks, the conservative action group led by Dick Armey, former Republican Congressman and strong advocate of NAFTA. There are many grassroots Tea Partiers quite cynical of such Republican Party opportunists who in fact promote corporatocracy-controlled globalization at the expense of US jobs.

Following the financial crisis of 2008 and losses—sometimes catastrophic—of home, savings, or job for many, and following the controversial Republican-Democratic bipartisan Wall Street bailout, it would be expected that some kind of angry political movement would form.

What is remarkable is not that the Tea Party movement came into being but just how relatively tame it is. In other periods of American history when corporate-government policies have led to economic disaster, there was civil unrest, and the corporatocracy truly felt threatened. Contemporary Tea Partiers' anger has been almost exclusively funneled into peaceful demonstrations and electoral politics, relatively timid actions compared with those taken by Americans during other periods of major economic crisis. While contemporary Tea Partiers identify with the colonial Tea Partiers, there is among contemporary Tea Partiers virtually no civil disobedience, which was widespread among "anti-taxers" in 1773 and routine in American history during periods of economic injustices. Leaders of this modern "anti-government-spending" movement continue to dutifully pay their federal taxes, instead of not only refusing to pay but publicizing their tax resistance with a willingness to go to jail for their beliefs. Anti-taxer Tea Party businesspeople should be embarrassed by their own relative timidity next to anti-taxer Iranian shop owners who in July 2010, after Iranian president Mahmoud Ahmadinejad increased taxes on businesses, struck Tehran's Grand Bazaar, shutting down their enterprises.

The corporate elite on Wall Street—especially those responsible for bundling subprime mortgages into mortgage-backed securities and creating other "financial weapons of mass destruction" that resulted in the worst financial crisis since the Great Depression in the 1930s—must have breathed a sigh of relief upon seeing how timid American reaction has been. The corporate elite must be especially delighted that of all the very tame reactions that have occurred, the largest has been the one directed not against Wall Street itself but at its junior partner, the federal government.

Who, in Large Numbers, Is Fighting for Social Justice?

On March 25, 2006, in Los Angeles, five hundred thousand people protested against crackdowns on illegal immigrants. The specific target of the protest was a piece of legislation known as HR 4437, passed by the House on December 16, 2005, which if enacted into law would have raised penalties for illegal immigration and classified illegal immigrants as felons, classified those who helped them enter or remain in the United States as felons, imposed more penalties on employers who hire illegal immigrants, and erected fences across one-third of the US-Mexican border. Protesters wanted not only a rejection of HR 4437 but also a more just "path for US citizenship" for undocumented immigrants.

While Los Angeles, with its large Latino population, produced this historically huge demonstration of half a million people, there were other protests across the United States on that same day. Denver saw more than fifty thousand demonstrators. In Phoenix, there were twenty thousand, one of the largest demonstrations in that city's history. In Charlotte, North Carolina, between five and seven thousand people demonstrated, some carrying signs with slogans such as AM I NOT A HUMAN BEING?

Millions more Latino Americans—legal and illegally in the United States—demonstrated across the nation the following month, April 2006, culminating in the National Day of Action with five hundred thousand protestors in Dallas alone.

"It's a good feeling that we are finally standing up for ourselves," said Robert Martinez at the rally in Dallas. Martinez, who had crossed the Rio Grande illegally twenty-two years before and eventually became an American citizen, said, "For years, we never say nothing. We just work hard, follow the rules and pay taxes. And they try to make these laws. It's time people knew how we felt."

Juan Gomez, who had arrived in Dallas from Peru ten years before and is now vice president of United Voices for Immigrants and a teacher of English to immigrant adults, said, "We are here to support American values. America was built with immigrants."

On that same day in San Diego, twenty thousand demonstrators gathered at Balboa Park and marched downtown to a rally, with many carrying signs proclaiming WE ARE AMERICANS AND WE MARCH TODAY, WE VOTE TOMORROW. And in Miami, Orlando Fernandez, fifty-one, who had arrived in Miami twenty-six years earlier on the Mariel boat lift and who now works for a nonprofit organization that helps the poor, believed that politicians would take seriously these kinds of numbers: "This is a year of elections, and politicians want to gain popularity with this problem."

Orlando Fernandez was correct. After the immigration crackdown legislation HR 4437 passed the House in late 2005, the US Senate never even took a vote on it—and so it never became law. But Latino activists and their supporters weren't satisfied. On March 21, 2010, they rallied in Washington, DC, for legislation to give legal status to millions of illegal immigrants. *The New York Times* reported that "the crowd, overwhelmingly Latino immigrants," was in the "tens of thousands" and organizers reported that two hundred thousand turned out. On May 1, 2010, fueled by a new anti-illegal-immigrant law in Arizona, there were significant rallies and vigils in seventy cities across the United States with police estimates of crowds of fifty thousand in Los Angeles, twenty-five thousand in Dallas, ten thousand in Chicago and Milwaukee, and in the "thousands" in other US cities.

It is worth noting that in this case, the people who are most active in pursuing social justice make up a group that has been least socialized by American institutions and culture. That's not really anything new in American history.

Light Resistance to Major Oppression

While there is certainly some resistance going on in the United States, compared with many other nations and many other periods in American history, the resistance is so light that it's difficult to imagine the corporatocracy feels threatened in any serious way.

Compared with most of the industrialized world, can the people of the United States be considered an oppressed group? What exactly are Americans' hard work and taxes getting them next to the rest of the industrialized world?

Take something very obvious and concrete—time off work. In the United States, unlike most other countries in the industrialized world, there is actually no federal law mandating that companies pay employees for time off. Looking at US companies of all sizes and workers of all tenures, a study by the Center for Economic and Policy Research found that American workers on average received nine days' paid vacation with six days of paid holidays and that almost one in four US workers do not get any paid days off at all. All nation members of the European Union (EU) *must* provide workers with a minimum of twenty paid vacation days a year plus public holidays. In Finland, law guarantees workers a minimum of thirty days' paid vacation plus up to fourteen paid holidays a year. Germans have six weeks of federally mandated vacation; on average in 2007 Americans were working 1,804 hours per year versus 1,436 hours for Germans—the equivalent of nine extra forty-hour weeks per year. And those European statistics are just minimums, as the average number of paid days off in the EU is even higher.

The Work, Family, and Equity Index reports that the United States stands out in its failure to guarantee paid sick leave. In 136 other countries, employers are required to provide a week or more of paid sick leave annually. According to the Bureau of Labor Statistics and the Institute for Women's Policy Research, forty-six million private-sector employees in the United States do not have a single paid sick day at work, while eighty-six million workers do not have paid leave to care for sick children or dependent adults. Some form of paid leave to new parents is guaranteed in 169 other countries around the world; the United States joins Liberia, Papua New Guinea, and Swaziland on the short list of nations that fail to provide paid time off when a child is born.

Fear breaks human beings, and America's health care system creates fear for the unhealthy and the healthy alike. When people get sick throughout almost all the industrialized world except the United States, they and their loved ones only have to be concerned about their return to health—not whether illness might financially destroy them. Throughout most of the industrialized world, when you lose your job, you only have to worry about finding another one—not about also having no health care. Thousands of Americans die each year because their health is tied to their wealth, including those who die simply because they can't afford health insurance. Twenty-five percent of Americans say they have not gone to the doctor because of the cost. Health care premiums, adjusting for inflation, have increased 78 percent since 2001, with average employees contributing 143 percent more to their company-sponsored health insurance than in 2000.

Even the recently passed health insurance reform will not change the fact that the only health insurance that many Americans (including myself) can afford is one of those catastrophic plans with an extremely high deductible and large co-payments, with ever-increasing premiums that eventually make even it unaffordable. While reform will create millions of new customers and hundreds of billions of dollars more income for insurance companies, it will not change the fact that when many Americans get sick, we will continue to think more than twice before seeking health care. While Americans hear propaganda about bad health care and long waits in foreign hospitals, I hear just the opposite from Canadian and other foreigners who are proud of their nations' universal and affordable health care systems. Contrary to the urban myth, researchers in Canada have found that a mere 0.1 percent of Canadians actually choose to cross the border to seek care in the United States. In fact, the myth isn't just wrong, it's backward: Americans go abroad for health care at a rate four times higher than the rate of Canadians coming to the United States, and "a lack of health insurance" is the most common factor cited by those Americans traveling to other countries for medical care.

Compared with the rest of the industrialized world, Americans get shafted not only in time off work and health care but also in terms of higher education. Higher education in most of the industrialized world is heavily subsidized by government and is far less expensive if not free, and graduates from much of the rest of the world are not routinely entering the work world with crushing debt. While Americans do get something in return for the taxes that they pay for Social Security and Medicare, unlike the rest of the industrialized world, Americans get damn near nothing for the rest of their federal income taxes except unnecessary wars. It goes on and on.

- The average hourly earnings of American workers, adjusted for inflation, fell from 1972 to 2008.
- Since 1960, while tax rates have remained pretty much unchanged for average Americans, the highest-income households have seen the sharpest *decrease* in tax rates (those in the top hundredth of 1 percent have seen their tax rate reduced by almost half).
- The income gap in the United States between the top 1 percent and everyone else hasn't been so large since the Roaring Twenties.
- Of the thirty industrialized nations in the Organization for Economic Cooperation and Development (OECD), the income spread between the wealthy and everyone else is the highest in the United States—twice the OECD average.
- Six banks—Goldman Sachs, Morgan Stanley, JPMorgan Chase, Citigroup, Bank of America, and Wells Fargo—have assets equivalent to 60 percent of our gross national product.

Though some Americans may not be aware of how badly they are faring compared with the rest of the industrialized world, damn near all Americans know that what's happening to them compared with the corporate elite is economically unfair, yet for the most part they are subdued. While one kind of logic tells us that the worse things get, the more resistance people will put forth, a "psycho-logic" appears to trump this.

Demoralized, Disorganized, Broken, or What?

> 66There was hardly a peep when Bush the Lesser stole the 2000 election while everybody watched. Now Obama trashes his promises to stop useless wars and make the health insurance Congress enjoys available to everyone, and no more than a few hundred people protest.99
>
> —pzbrawl, *AlterNet*, December 13, 2009

Virtually all readers commenting on my article agreed that Americans were not resisting anywhere near to the extent called for given the loss of their liberties and the assault on their economic well-being. But not all agreed that Americans were "broken," "demoralized," or "dispirited."

Les Leopold, executive director of the Labor Institute and the Public Health Institute and author of *The Looting of America*, in an article he wrote responding to mine, sees the relative passivity as a failure of organizations, activists, leaders, and political parties.

> While [the abuse syndrome] may describe individuals Levine has encountered, I can't buy it as a political justification. I believe we can find more compelling reasons by looking at our own political infrastructures—our activists and leaders, our political parties—and not by analyzing "US citizens" at large . . . So rather than looking for the problem in the "American People" we should examine our failure to create and mobilize progressive infrastructures that have the wherewithal to organize large-scale protests.

Organization is clearly important to any democratic movement, and throughout history, people enduring domination have been accused of being apathetic or stupid when they really were lacking the proper organizational vehicles. I don't ignore this, and I will discuss strategies and tactics for organized resistance. However, I do believe that without a large enough number of people regaining individual self-respect and collective self-confidence, even the best organizers will fail.

Others, while also agreeing that the system is corrupt and anti-democratic, commented that this is a situation of "people getting the government they deserve." They are disgusted with their fellow Americans, seeing them as "lazy," "stupid," or "spoiled." Many in this camp feel that any psychological explanation for people's passivity is simply an excuse, and that Americans should instead be condemned.

> "Broken? Or rather stupid and lazy? Every once in a while the left notices that it is in a state of complete failure. Quickly it devises a new excuse, in this case that we are "broken" . . . Get over yourselves. You aren't rape victims or turned out whores . . . Stop the crybabying and learn how to fight and develop the courage to do it."
>
> —Razumov, *AlterNet*, December 16, 2009

> "My own interpretation is that we have really been too economically 'spoiled' (yes, even now) in this Country, for far too long, and had it too good, historically, for most of the population to realize anything more than the materialistic creature comforts. We have been lulled . . . we are not abused or 'broken' enough! . . . [It is] psychobabble to call the fence-sitters 'victims of abuse dynamics.'"
>
> —bloominblacksheep, *AlterNet*, December 13, 2009

> "Yes, Americans are pussies for allowing the government that is supposed to represent their interests to be bought off and paid for in the name of corporate interest and outland-

ish greed. America is a festering shithole of selfishness and stupidity where the populace have sadly replaced Democracy with Capitalism Run Amok."

> —daveydudely, *Reddit*, January 25, 2010

By far the largest number of comments, however, were from people who believed that the American people are passive not because they are poorly organized, spoiled, or stupid, but because they are dispirited. While they might use different terms—broken versus demoralized versus hopeless, and so forth—they can say from experience either that they themselves are dispirited or that they see a great deal of demoralization around them.

> "I live in a small PA town that was once a part of the steel-making powerhouse of this country. I worked in a 'small' steel plant of 5,500 employees. It shut down 20 years ago as did most other industry in Western PA. I can see the deterioration happening before my eyes. People walk kinda hunched over. Sunken eyes. Young men standing around idle or giving scary stares at strangers and who could care less. Demoralized? Damn right . . ."
>
> —Lonzie, e-mail, December 11, 2009

> "The Masters are Corporation and Media. They don't need an army to fight civil wars or whips to put the rebels under leash. There are no rebels left in the US."
>
> —Loya, *Information Clearing House*, December 15, 2009

> "It's absolutely true, we're demoralized, broken . . . What was once the exclusive province of bums, loiterers and addicts, the most hopeless seams of our society are now the growing encampments of people and families who have reached the end of their rope. Broken? Yes, broken and possibly broken beyond repair."
>
> —Checkerboard Strangle, *Capital Hill Blue*, December 15, 2009

"Yes, we are broken. I have long since given up any hope of really changing the system. No one that can get elected in this country should get elected."
—Stephan Goodwin, *AtheistNexus*, December 14, 2009

"It's hard not to feel hopeless but one can persist without hope, we do it all the time. I have Obama's phone # on my cell, when I get really angry I call his office. Real people answer, eventually, and most agree with what one is saying. See, everything is hopeless."
—nancykeiler, *AlterNet*, December 14, 2009

"Ok, let's start a revolution—you go first! . . . In the end, the state always gets its way. The state always wins. People are always oppressed. There may be periods of reprieve, but in the end, schmoes like me either die, get maimed, have a bit of glory then go to jail, or give up and go home."
—dan10opa, *AlterNet*, December 13, 2009

"I returned to the US from living in a Third World country . . . How shocked I am now to see the people of the US going down the same sad path . . . In a Third World country, people accept government control, corruption, disconnection from power over their finances or themselves. Poor people in these countries accept that they are poor and will always be poor. The middle class just gets poorer as the rich take more and more. And the rich live in big walled compounds and lock themselves in so they can have their fabulous lives and ignore what is going on in the streets. And no one complains because they feel it will do no good, they feel hopeless and helpless."
—seashore, *AlterNet*, December 13, 2009

In the next part, I explain how people's ability to resist domination has been worn down.

Prelude to Battle

Understanding How the People Learned Powerlessness

> 66All our things are right and wrong together. The wave of evil
> washes all our institutions alike. 99
>
> —Ralph Waldo Emerson

What forces have created a passive, unengaged, and demoralized US population? What culturally and psychologically has destroyed the *individual self-
respect* and *collective self-confidence* necessary for democratic movements?

In examining societal causes for Americans' passivity, it is often difficult to distinguish between the *evidence* for passivity versus the *cause* of
it. For example, is watching television five hours a day a sign of passivity
and brokenness, or the cause?

In this section, I will first examine the basic psychological principles
and techniques for pacifying and breaking a population. In the remainder
of chapter 3, I'll apply this theoretical understanding to the actual experience of Americans, examining how these principles and some of these
techniques play out—sometimes subtly and sometimes more obviously—
in American culture and in major US institutions.

While this may disappoint some conspiracy theorists, I do not believe
that the elite have orchestrated every aspect of a system that helps break
people's resistance. For example, the ultimate impact of television could
not have been clear to the corporatocracy at the onset of the television
era. However, when it became clear that television could be used to help
cement rather than challenge the values of industrialization, moneymaking, and consumerism, the corporatocracy ensured that television viewing
increased. The elite also could not have known at television's onset that it
would lead to decreased attention spans and create fertile ground for the
invention of a new mental disorder called attention deficit hyperactivity
disorder, which would ultimately lead to the normalization of psychiatric drugs for children, including the normalization of heavily subduing

antipsychotic drugs for nonpsychotic disruptive behavior, which would create astounding profits for giant pharmaceutical corporations, which would give these corporations even greater power and influence. There is no single maniacal dictator or even oligarchy consciously crafting all the phenomena that ultimately pacify people. If a phenomenon creates more wealth and power for the corporatocracy, it becomes a part of society and culture, and many of these phenomena, including television, do in fact pacify a population.

Psychological Principles and Techniques for Breaking a Population

> 66 we've learned to be helpless. we are very carefully schooled in countless ways to see ourselves as helpless . . . you quickly learn that there's absolutely NOTHING you can do to change your situation . . . what choices are we told we DO have? what options are we given to exercise our personal power? . . . the spending and the act of acquiring become synonymous in our minds with exercising our personal power—spend, acquire, appear powerful. 99
>
> —profmarcus, *AlterNet*, December 13, 2009

Learned Helplessness

Throughout much of human history, people have needed no experiments to confirm what we now call *learned helplessness*, but in modernity people are taught to trust scientific studies more than their own common sense and experience.

In one well-known learned helplessness experiment, there were three groups of dogs, two of which were electroshocked. Group 1 was not shocked. Group 2—the "escape group"—received shocks but could stop them by pressing a panel with their noses. Group 3 was given electric shocks of identical intensity and duration to Group 2's, but no actions by Group 3 dogs could stop this. Thus, Group 3, in contrast with Group 2, had no control over shocks.

The first part of this study revealed that both Group 1 (unshocked) and Group 2 (control over shocks) had, for the most part, no ill effects from this experiment. However, as common sense would predict, Group 3 (who had no control over ending their electric shocks) became increasingly passive, with symptoms associated with depression.

In the second part of this study, the three groups of dogs were given a task. They could escape from electric shocks by jumping over a low barrier. Common sense would tell you that Group 3—who had previously learned that nothing they did had any effect on stopping their electric shocks—would be less likely to attempt jumping over the barrier to escape the shocks. Common sense proved to be right. Although escaping from the electric shocks was relatively easy, significantly fewer of these "learned helplessness" Group 3 dogs jumped over the low barrier to escape the shock, with many Group 3 dogs simply lying down and crying. Group 3 dogs had been conditioned to powerlessness and had learned helplessness.

Learned helplessness is one commonsense explanation for depression and immobilization. Specifically, when people have been conditioned to believe that no action they take will stop their suffering, they learn helplessness and powerlessness and sink into an immobilized state.

Abuse Syndrome

Abuse is, at bottom, about control. Some abusers may get a rush from inflicting pain, but all abusers are addicted to control. Abusers seek to gain complete control over their victims. When the abuse starts, the victim may have the strength to identify the abuse, confront it, and— if necessary, and if the option exists—end the relationship. If this does not happen and the abuse continues, a vicious weakening cycle—what's commonly called the *abuse syndrome*—takes hold.

How does one gain complete control over other human beings? One reduces their self-worth, self-respect, and self-confidence, ultimately creating the belief that without their abuser, they cannot survive.

There are several forms of abusive behaviors, all imparting the message: *You are not worthy of respect and caring.* Physical abuses such as beatings and rape are the most obvious communication to the victim that *You are not a person to be cared about, but an object to be used to meet needs.* Verbal and emotional abuse can be obvious ("you are a worthless bitch") but also subtle. Nonverbal emotional abuse—a look of disgust or contempt, a mocking tone of voice, or a dismissive shrug—can be insidious and lethally damaging to self-respect. Neglect is also a form of abuse, as it is yet another communication to the victim that *You are not worthy of respect and caring.* Abuse victims get the message that all or a significant part of their being is less than human, evil, or diseased.

The trauma and shame of chronic abuse can be emotionally extremely painful. One normal reaction to overwhelming pain is immobilizing depression, which has parallels to political apathy. A useful clinical model of depression is to see it as a "strategy" for shutting down overwhelming pain. By depressing one's being, one feels less pain. However, by depressing one's being, one also becomes passive and immobilized, less capable of addressing the source of the pain.

Whether one is abused by a spouse or the corporatocracy, the pain of that humiliation can be anesthetized by depression, apathy, drugs, and a wide range of other diversions. However, all anesthetizations can be addictive, which means people get into the habit of using them to shut down their pain, which in turn means that they will need to increasingly depress their being to continue to dull their pain; and each time one does this, one feels weaker. Immobilization and passivity in the face of an oppressor routinely produce shame, which itself is painful and can thus result in more shutdowns and immobilization. This is the vicious cycle of depression and apathy.

As the abuse syndrome cycles downward, victims of abuse lose so much self-worth and become so weak that they can become psychologically dependent on their abusers. Even in those cases when abusers are actually economically dependent on their victims, these victims can still come to believe that they will not be able to survive without their abusers, and so they actually live in fear that the abuser will leave.

To deny the pain of humiliating acquiescence, victims of abuse may defend and even express positive feelings about their abuser. This extreme stage of the abuse syndrome has been called the *Stockholm syndrome.* This term is derived from the events of a 1973 Swedish bank robbery case in which hostages became emotionally attached to their bank-robber captors, defending their captors during and after their six days of captivity. Despite the fact that their captors had held them hostage and actually jeopardized their lives, the captors became seen by the victims as protectors from the police. One explanation for the Stockholm syndrome is that victims believe it is more likely that they will be harmed if they defiantly hate their abusers. Thus, since compliance feels safer, there is an incentive for victims to convince themselves that their abuser is a protector whom they *should* have affection for. This justifies their compliance.

Cognitive Dissonance

For most abused people, there is an unpleasant tension produced by the reality that they are abused but do nothing to end the abuse. This unpleasant tension is called *dissonance*. The term *cognitive dissonance* simply refers to the tension of having two conflicting or contradictory cognitions (thoughts, ideas, beliefs, attitudes, or opinions) at the same time.

Common sense tells us that human beings dislike dissonance and tension and will try to reduce it by creating consistency and harmony. They can reduce this dissonance and tension in more than one way. They can change their actions to be more consistent with their thoughts—for example, victims can leave abusers; or they can remain passive in the face of abuse and change their thoughts—utilizing justifications, rationalizations, and denial of certain facts. These justifications ("I deserve it"), rationalizations ("he beats me for being bad, which shows me how much he really loves me,") and denials ("he only pushed me down once, and it was an accident") render one's lack of rebellion consistent with one's other beliefs ("abuse is wrong").

Most people would prefer the harmony of consistency rather than the disharmony of inconsistency, and it is often easier to alter one's cognitions than one's actions so as to create that consistency. Thus, it should be no surprise that people may sacrifice the truth—the truth that they are being abused, or that they are abusive—for such harmony. This is the *theory of cognitive dissonance*, which was big stuff in psychology when it was "discovered" in the late 1950s. But this was really less of a new discovery than a recycling of common sense. Long before modern psychological research, Aesop, a storytelling slave in Greece who lived around 620 to 560 BC, told the fable called "The Fox and the Grapes," which provided us with pretty much all we need to know about cognitive dissonance. Here's one version of the fable:

> Once upon a time there was a fox strolling through the woods. He came upon a grape orchard and spotted a bunch of beautiful grapes hanging from a high branch. "Boy, those sure would be tasty," he thought to himself. He backed up and took a running start, and jumped, but he did not get high enough. He tried again and again but just couldn't get high enough to grab the grapes. Finally, he gave up. As he walked away, he put his nose in the air and said: "I am sure those grapes are sour."

Social Isolation and Surveillance

Throughout much of recorded human history, there have been tyrants, tyrannical institutions, gangsters, and gangster nation-states that have used various methods to break populations. It's not all that difficult to get people to convert their political or religious beliefs, or to even confess to crimes that they haven't committed.

One method of breaking individuals and populations is social isolation. When people are kept isolated from one another, they will not have their doubts about authority validated. They are less likely to consider that there are others such as themselves who could potentially band together, achieving greater strength and enough power to overthrow a tyranny. Even more powerful is to keep people both isolated and without privacy and thus incapable of reflecting on their situation. This can be done with constant surveillance—keeping people always under somebody else's observation so that they're not doing anything they're "not supposed to."

So-called cult leaders indoctrinate new members by both isolating and surveilling the new recruits so as to first break them down and then build them up with allegiance to the group. New recruits are routinely cut off from the outside world, not allowed to talk to other new recruits, constantly watched, and thus prevented from discussing the process of indoctrination. New recruits may only be allowed to speak with already indoctrinated members, and often the group leader becomes the only person providing feedback. This denies new recruits any validation of their concerns about the group itself and the nature of indoctrination.

The less free time that recruits have to reflect, reconsider, analyze, and think about what they are exposed to, the more successful the indoctrination. Recruits who question are made to feel rude or stupid. The goal is to establish complete dependency on the group and the leader.

Fear, Punishment, and Bribes

In George Orwell's *1984*, the totalitarian state uses surveillance to discover people's fears. When Winston Smith's forbidden relationship with Julia is discovered by the state, he is sent to Room 101, where prisoners are threatened by their greatest fear so as to prepare them for political "re-education." Winston's greatest fear, the state has learned through surveillance, is rats. A wire cage holding hungry rats is fitted to his face and is pushed on him. Right before his face is inserted inside the cage, Winston shouts: "Do it to Julia!" Winston's fear, the state knew, can kill even love. Winston is broken, accepts the doctrines of the state, embraces Big Brother, and is re-integrated into society.

> 66The fact is millions of us in this country are fully and painfully aware that this society does not permit us to live as human beings . . . It seems that you don't seem to get the fact that the SOLE REASON americans aren't being physically tortured and killed en masse is because they ACCEPT THEIR OPPRESSION. You show me a new american revolution, and I'll show you a population crushed by a tank.99
>
> —goodyweaver, *AlterNet*, December 14, 2009

Draconian punishments can not only break the victim but also create an overwhelming fear designed to break potential rebels from attempting any opposition. While there was resistance against the Nazis by Jews, most famously in the Warsaw Ghetto, and resistance by other underground movements, some people still wonder why there wasn't more. Nazi retaliation for sabotage consisted of randomly rounding up dozens of hostages and executing them. For the killing of a German soldier, Nazis would execute one hundred civilians or kill all the men in a nearby village and then burn the village to the ground. Thus, individual resistance not only jeopardized one's own life but guaranteed death for one's own people. In breaking a population's resistance, reprisal tactics are a staple.

In modern therapeutic boarding schools, a common tactic to break "anti-social" young people is to punish the entire group if one member breaks the rules. The use of peer pressure is quite effective, at least temporarily. Also temporarily effective is rewarding young people for "ratting out" their peers. From my experience, these methods may work in the short term but create enormous resentment, hostility, and loss of self-respect, and this causes many of these young people to become even more anti-social when they are free from such institutions.

Economic reprisals can also break the resistance of rebels and terrorize anyone else considering rebellion. The US government-corporate partnership's response to Cuba is an example of reprisals that have actually cost businesses money in lost financial opportunities in Cuba itself. But these reprisals have continued because it was deemed more important to send a threatening message to the world, which helps to ensure that labor and resources in the rest of the Americas, Africa, and Asia remain inexpensive and accessible to US corporations. For decades now, the American people have actually favored normalizing relations with Cuba. An April 2009 CBS News/New York Times Poll asked Americans, "Do you think the United States should or should not re-establish diplomatic and trade relations with Cuba?" A solid majority of 67 percent of Americans said we should reestablish such relations versus only 20 percent who said we should not. But as Noam Chomsky points out:

Ignoring the will of the population is normal, but more inter-
estingly in this case is that powerful sectors of the business
world also favor normalization . . . Their interests in this case
are overridden by a principle of international affairs that does
not receive proper recognition in the scholarly literature of
international relations: what we may call the "Mafia principle." The Godfather does not tolerate "successful defiance,"
even from a small shopkeeper who fails to pay protection
money. It is too dangerous. It must therefore be stamped out,
and brutally, so that others understand that disobedience is
not an option.

In addition to fear and punishment, bribes for compliance can also
break people. After a spouse has been beaten and verbally degraded and
may be sullen or even considering leaving, the abuser might give a present, which in effect communicates, *You have so little self-respect that you
can be treated without respect or caring, then bought off.*

When people do things that they do not respect in return for money
or other rewards, they lose integrity. When a building loses its structural
integrity, it loses strength, and when people lose their ethical integrity,
they lose psychological strength. No intelligent abusers want their victims
to have the strength of integrity, and it can sometimes be more efficient to
bribe rather than beat people so that they act in ways they don't believe in.
Historically, the US corporate-government partnership has, both domesti-
cally and internationally, used both bribes and bullets to subdue trouble-
some populations. Self-respect keeps us from accepting those bribes that
reward us for violating our integrity; but taking that first bribe reduces our
self-respect and weakens us so that it makes it more difficult to resist future
bribes, and so a vicious weakening cycle takes hold.

Drugs

Just as people themselves can abuse drugs, abusers can use drugs to abuse
and break people. Psychotropic drugs can disconnect people from their
unpleasant emotions but also disconnect them from other feelings that

inform them of their very being—their cares, concern, beliefs, values, and aspirations. The totalitarian state in Aldous Huxley's science fiction *Brave New World* pressures everyone to use the psychotropic drug *soma*, a kind of antidepressant hallucinogenic.

A piece of American history sounds like science fiction—or the rant of a crackpot conspiracy theorist—but was confirmed decades later by congressional investigations and *The Washington Post* and *The New York Times*. Ewen Cameron, ultimately president of the American Psychiatric Association in 1953 and later the first president of the World Psychiatric Association, was at one point in his career curious to discover powerful ways to break down patient resistance, and he experimented with LSD (as well as with electroshock and sensory deprivation). Dr. Cameron was often able to produce severe delirium as patients lost their sense of identity, even forgetting their own names and how to eat. The CIA, under a project code-named MKULTRA, eager to learn more about Dr. Cameron's techniques, funded him as well as other renowned psychiatrists in the 1950s and 1960s to conduct brainwashing experiments.

In modern society, certain psychotropic drugs are illegal, but psychotropic drugs that make giant pharmaceutical corporations money are encouraged. Amphetamines such as Adderall are used by mainstream medicine on children who have been labeled with attention deficit hyperactivity disorder (ADHD). Such amphetamines can sometimes make these children more manageable and attentive to authorities (with respect to these goals, children and parents report varying degrees of effectiveness). Whether or not recipients see their drug as effective, they often report that these drugs disconnect them from their emotions and from their sense of who they are. Cocaine and ADHD drugs affect the neurotransmitters dopamine, serotonin, and norepinephrine, and antidepressants used in combination affect the same neurotransmitters.

Not only are illegal psychotropics and prescription psychotropics chemically similar, but they are used by people for the same reason: to take the edge off their pain so as to function. When using any kind of psychotropic drug, sharp emotional edges can be rounded out so that people can also be less troubled by things that *should* trouble them. The hypocrisy surrounding illegal and prescription psychotropic drugs breaks Americans in at least two ways.

At one level, because people are being misinformed by the pharmaceutical-industrial complex about the realities of prescription psychotropic drugs, they are more likely to gulp them down and give them to their children; and we are more likely to have a population that will be less bothered by *all* pains, including those caused by dehumanization and injustice.

At a second level, by criminalizing and incarcerating people who are using psychotropics illegally, authorities control a potentially rebellious population. It has been my experience that many illegal drug users are some of society's most rebellious members. While some rebel against societal rules for their own selfish ends, others rebel more than the typical American does against societal hypocrisy and injustice, but their use of illegal drugs makes them easy targets for authorities. By reducing the social status of illegal drug users to that of "criminal" and removing them from society in the form of prison terms, they are separated from other people who might otherwise be inspired by their anti-authoritarianism.

Labeling and Objectification

People can be broken by their acceptance of others' labels, especially by the labeling of a natural aspect of their humanity as sinful, shameful, or pathological. If one believes, for example, that one's natural sexuality is sinful or pathological, then one loses wholeness and strength. Historically, sexuality has been a favorite target of both religious and psychiatric authorities (for example, homosexuality was an official mental illness in US psychiatry until the 1970s). While today's state, religious, and psychiatric authorities are relatively more tolerant of various kinds of sexuality than in the past, people are told that other aspects of their humanity are pathological.

Not too long ago in the United States, there was nothing pathological about a kid who hated school. Those days are gone. There are now millions of American children who are not complying and conforming to school systems who are being labeled, diagnosed, and drugged.

There are also many naturally introverted kids who are increasingly being labeled, diagnosed, and drugged. Not too long ago, many of these shy kids would eventually overcome their life-restricting shyness, and some of them would utilize their introversion to do great creative things. But today parents of these children increasingly accept diagnoses such as social anxiety disorder and medicate their children, especially with Paxil. How did "social anxiety" become a commonplace mental disorder?

In 1999, the maker of Paxil, GlaxoSmithKline, actually hired the public relations firm Cohn & Wolfe to convince people that they or their shy children had social anxiety disorder. Cohn & Wolfe created a campaign called "Imagine Being Allergic to People," recruited celebrities and paid them to give interviews about their own social anxiety disorder, as well as hiring psychiatrists to lecture in the top twenty-five media markets about social anxiety disorder. By 2001, Paxil (which is also used for depression and other diagnoses) had become the seventh most profitable drug in America, and today social anxiety disorder is one of the most commonly diagnosed mental illnesses. Cohn & Wolfe won public relations awards, as nowadays skilled propagandists are allowed to publicly take pride in their work.

Lies/Propaganda

Lies control people in a variety of ways. To the extent that people are controlled by lies, not only do they comply with the liar's version of reality, but by losing connection with reality, people lose a certain wholeness and the strength to resist. Or people can so overreact to liars that they distrust everyone, which makes it impossible to form democratic movements.

Today in polite society, lies are told about lies. A century ago, the burgeoning corporatocracy was actually comfortable with the term *propaganda*. Today, however, the term is reserved for the "bad guys"—whoever the bad guy might currently be.

Although rulers have used propaganda for quite some time, it was not until 1914 and the need to manufacture enthusiasm for World War I that governments systematically utilized a wide range of propaganda to provoke their populations to hate their enemies and die for their country.

Mark Crispin Miller points out in his introduction to Edward Bernays's classic *Propaganda*: "Here was an extraordinary state accomplishment: mass enthusiasm at the prospect of a global brawl that otherwise would mystify those very masses, and that shattered most of those who actually took part in it."

Walter Lippmann (1889–1974), influential journalist and adviser to US presidents, personified an elite who were quite open in their belief that the people were incapable of self-governing, and that it was the job of the more responsible elite to create what Lippmann called "the manufacture of consent" of the public. Molding public opinion via propaganda is still seen by the elite as responsible, though it is no longer politically correct to state this publicly in the fashion that Bernays and Lippmann did.

An especially insidious kind of lie that breaks a population or an individual is "co-opting and bastardization." Specifically, this means labeling an institution with a positive ideal or goal but ensuring that the institution actually promotes the opposite. Remember *1984*'s "Ministry of Peace," which in reality was the War Department? And *1984*'s "Ministry of Truth" was actually a ministry of lies that developed slogans such as "War is peace," "Freedom is slavery," and "Ignorance is strength."

Communist Party was a great Orwellian name for an institution used by Soviet elitists intent on depriving their population of any decision-making power. Similarly, what better name than *Republican Party* for a political party headed by elitists who would recoil at the idea of a real republic? And what better name than *Democratic Party* for elitists terrified of genuine democracy?

People have long known about learned helplessness, the abuse syndrome, cognitive dissonance, and the use of social isolation, surveillance, fear, punishment, bribery, psychotropic drugs, and propaganda to break an individual or a population. Common sense tells us that when human beings feel powerless to take actions to stop their pain, they sink into helpless passivity. Common sense tells us that when people remain in abusive relationships, they can eventually deceive themselves, including the self-deception that their abuser is their protector. Common sense tells us that when people are being physically and emotionally abused, they lose self-respect and strength if they remain in that relationship, and that people will use all kinds of rationalizations to justify their inaction. Common sense tells us that isolation and surveillance reduce people's ability to resist domination. Common sense tells us that people are broken by fear, punishments, and bribery, as well as by drugs that disconnect them from their being; and we know that bastardizing noble ideas will cause them to lose their power. Common sense tells us that if we feel a natural part of our being is sinful, shameful, or diseased, then we will be less whole and weaker. And common sense tells us that we can get to such a point of weakness, the truth of our oppression no longer sets us free but can in fact shame us, creating even more pain, and deepening the self-destructive cycle.

How do these basic psychological principles and techniques for pacifying and breaking a population play out in American culture and in major US institutions? That is what I will examine in the remainder of this chapter.

Television, Technology, and Zombification

In 2009, the Nielsen Company reported that TV viewing is at an all-time high if one includes the following "three screens": a television set, a laptop/personal computer, and a cell phone. Nielsen reported that the average American is viewing television 151 hours per month, or close to 5 hours per day. This increase, according to Nielson, is part of a long-term trend attributable to greater availability of screens, increased variety of different viewing methods, more digital recorders, DVR, and TiVo devices, and a tanking economy creating the need for low-cost diversions.

For several years, I've asked children and adolescents what they do each day. For a school day, the average is: seven hours in school; one to two hours' homework; six to nine hours' sleeping; two hours' eating/personal hygiene; four to six hours' television and video games; and one to three hours on the Internet, cell phone, iPod, or other technology. Researchers report that children in North America average eight hours a day on television, video games, movies, the Internet, cell phones, iPods, and other technologies (not including school-related use).

While many young people are passionate about their friends, I have found that after school, they often do not go outside with other kids in non-organized activity. During weekends, there may actually be an increase of television and video game activity. There are young people who are *not* passive, incommunicative "zombies," and who actually know how to interact with others, create things that they are proud of, and think clearly; these young people are almost always the ones who are not spending much of their free time watching television and playing video games.

In 1950, about 10 percent of American homes had television sets; now it's more than 99 percent. The number of TVs in the average US household is 2.24, with 66 percent of households having three or more sets. The TV set is turned on in the average US home for seven hours a day. Two-thirds of Americans regularly watch TV during dinner. About 40 percent of Americans' leisure time is spent on television. Husbands and wives spend three to four times more time watching television together than they do talking to each other.

How does the United States compare to the rest of the world in TV viewing? There aren't many cross-cultural studies, and precise comparisons are difficult because of different measurements and different time periods.

NOP World, a market research organization, interviewed more than thirty thousand people in thirty countries in a study released in 2005. In this study, average TV viewing was significantly lower than most other studies because certain kinds of TV viewing were excluded. The United States was one of the highest TV-viewing countries (along with Thailand, Egypt, and Turkey). Americans watched approximately 63 percent more television than Mexicans, who watched the least of all those surveyed; and Americans watched 54 percent more than Swedes, 43 percent more than Indians, and 36 percent more than Argentinians. Another cross-cultural comparison, reported on NationMaster.com more than a decade ago, examined only the United States and European countries and found that the United States and the United Kingdom were the highest-viewing nations at twenty-eight hours per week, with the lowest-viewing nations being Finland, Norway, and Sweden at eighteen hours per week.

The majority of what Americans view on television is through channels owned by six corporations: General Electric (NBC, MSNBC, CNBC, Bravo, and Syfy); Walt Disney (ABC, the Disney Channel, A&E, and Lifetime); Rupert Murdoch's News Corporation (Fox, Fox Business Channel, National Geographic, and FX); Time Warner (CNN, CW, HBO, Cinemax, Cartoon Network, TBS, TNT); Viacom (MTV, Nickelodeon/Nick-at-Nite, VH1, BET, Comedy Central); and CBS (CBS Television Network, CBS Television Distribution Group, Showtime, and CW, a joint venture with Time Warner). In addition to their television holdings, these media giants have vast holdings in radio, movie studios, and publishing.

While many progressives are concerned about this concentrated control by the corporate media, the major anti-democratic aspects of television may actually not be in its content. Specifically, the mere act of watching television—regardless of the programming—is the primary pacifying agent.

One of my first experiences of how powerful television is at keeping me locked in was when color television became popular. I remember going to department stores with my parents and immediately leaving them to find my way to the television section, and then becoming so transfixed by this thing called "color television" that I would have stayed forever glued to it rather than get back to real life. It didn't matter what the program was; it was this extraordinary technology that kept my attention. Thankfully, my parents couldn't afford a color television until I was much older. With today's high-definition (HD) televisions, real life must contend with even stiffer competition, and real life is routinely getting defeated.

Whatever the content of the program, television watching is an isolating experience. Most people are watching television alone, but even when watching it with others, they are routinely glued to the television rather than interacting with one another. Television keeps us from mixing it up in real life. Television keeps us indoors. People who are watching television are isolated from other people, from the natural world—even from their own thoughts and senses. Television produces isolation, and because television also reduces our awareness of our own feelings, when we start to feel lonely we are tempted to watch more television so as to dull the ache of isolation.

Who among us hasn't spent time watching a show we didn't actually like, or found ourselves flipping through the channels long after we've concluded that there isn't anything worth watching on the air? Television results in a kind of zombification—not a great thing for a genuinely democratic society. Researchers confirm that regardless of the programming, viewers' brainwaves slow down, transforming them closer to a hypnotic state. That's part of the explanation for why it's so hard to turn the television off even when it's not enjoyable—we have become pacified by it. People literally lose their will, mindlessly continuing to watch television.

Television viewers are mesmerized by what television insiders call "technical events"—quick cuts, zoom-ins, zoom-outs, rolls, pans, animation, music, graphics, and voice-overs, all of which lure them to continue watching even though they have no interest in the content. Television insiders know that it's these technical events (in which viewers see and hear things that real life does not present) that hypnotize people to watch. So it's not just through the content of programming and advertising that viewers are being manipulated—the very nature of television is a constant manipulative assault to keep a viewer watching.

Television is actually used by various authorities in our society to quiet potentially disruptive people—from kids to prison inmates. Managers in both public and private-enterprise prisons have recognized that providing inmates with cable television can be a more economical method to keep them quiet and subdued than it would be to hire more guards.

In a truly democratic society, one is gaining knowledge directly through one's own experience with the world, not through the filter of an authority or what television critic Jerry Mander calls a *mediated experience*. Mander is a "reformed sinner" of sorts who left his job in advertising to ultimately write the underground classic *Four Arguments for the Elimination of Television*. Television-dominated people ultimately accept others' mediated version of the world rather than discovering their own version based on their own experiences.

For a variety of technical reasons, Mander explains that authoritarian-based programming is more technically interesting to viewers than democracy-based programming. War and violence may be unpleasant in real life; however, peace and cooperation make for "boring television." And charismatic authority figures are more "interesting" than are ordinary citizens debating issues.

Television is of course financed by advertising, which is the engine of the consumer culture. For former advertising insiders such as Mander, television is the "delivery system's delivery system." It's an ideal medium for getting products—and the desire to buy them—inside people's heads. Television can make products seem more appealing than they really are. The hypnotic nature of television watching diminishes one's critical thinking. Television keeps people from focusing on their own thoughts and relationships; and this makes for inactive and passive people more likely to take seriously what is being sold to them.

Television is a "dream come true" for an authoritarian society. Those with the most money own most of what people see. Fear-based television programming makes people more afraid and distrustful of one another, which is good for an authoritarian society depending on a "divide and conquer" strategy. Television isolates people so they are not joining together to govern themselves. People become broken through both isolation and sensory deprivation, and television creates both. Television puts one in a brain state that makes it difficult to think critically. Television quiets and subdues a population. And spending the majority of one's free time isolated and watching television interferes with the connection to one's own humanity and thus makes it easier to accept an authority's version of society and life.

A genuinely democratic society needs people who are connected to one another, who respect and have confidence in themselves and others, who know themselves, who actively experience life and gain wisdom from it, who can think critically, and who can reject exploitative manipulations. Television watching creates pretty much the opposite kinds of people from those who can make genuine democracy work.

The good news is that television is something that one still has the legal right to reduce or eliminate from one's life and one's family. There are people who have simply given away their televisions. Others have restricted its use to one hour a day, or a couple of specific programs a week. Some parents have ensured that no televisions are in bedrooms and that there is no television watching during family meals. Some parents watch together with their young children and teach them a certain "sensory cynicism" by discussing the manipulative components of television. My experience is that adults teach best not by their lectures and rules but by what they model, which means parents should be watching as little television as possible. All of us should keep in mind that television, similar to psychotropic drugs, has enormous adverse effects, and so we may want to think long and hard about just what benefits we are receiving from any particular program content.

Helplessness in the Age of Isolation, E-Relationships, and Bureaucratization

> "What if the problem is not so much with being 'beaten down' as with being socially isolated? There are few settings where most USAers can hold a safe, honest, face-to-face, substantive discussion about politics and government . . . People are encouraged by being part of a group of like minded people, less afraid to say what is on their mind because they have been validated to some extent by sharing with others. Isolation leads to fear of standing out and then being 'beaten down' . . . Without a tribe we are more-or-less in the role of outcasts and that's not a situation that encourages much of anything other than suicide or desperate attempts at survival or joining a cult."
>
> —iforgetwho, *AlterNet*, December 13, 2009

The 2000 US census reported that approximately 25 percent of Americans were living alone, compared with only 7 percent one-person households in 1940. Some social scientists were unconcerned because living alone does not necessarily mean a lack of social connectedness. However, in 2006, a major study in the *American Sociological Review* delved deeper into this issue. The study, "Social Isolation in America: Changes in Core Discussion Networks Over Two Decades," examined Americans' core network of *confidants* (those people in our lives we consider close enough to trust with personal information and whom we rely on as a sounding board). The study examined data gathered through both the 2004 and the 1985 General Social Survey. This survey had a high response rate and utilized detailed face-to-face interviews in which respondents were pressed to confirm that what they said was what they meant.

The results? In 1985, 10 percent of Americans said that they had no confidants in their lives. But by 2004, 25 percent of Americans stated they had no confidants in their lives. The authors reported that "in addition to the large proportion of respondents who have no one to talk to, we find that the percentage of people who depend totally on a spouse for such close contact has increased from 5.0 to 9.2 percent." Both family and nonfamily confidants were lost in the past two decades, but there has been an even greater decrease in nonfamily confidants.

This study confirmed the continuation of US trends that first came to public attention in sociologist Robert Putnam's book *Bowling Alone*, published in 2000. Specifically, Putnam had reported a decline, especially since the 1970s, in *social capital* (his term for social connectedness) in virtually every area people have historically found community. Active involvement in face-to-face voluntary organizations and civic organization such as Parent Teacher Associations has plummeted. Americans have less face-to-face contact with friends and neighbors. There has been a steady erosion in informal contacts such as card playing and bowling. There has been a decline in membership and participation in the kind of progressive religious groups that have been at the center of major American social movements (such as the abolition of slavery, the fight for civil rights, and anti-war activism). And work life has decreasingly become a place where we find community, as the decline of labor union membership and increased job instability has brought a loss of fellowship.

In a now classic 1998 study examining changes in the mental health of Mexican immigrants who came to the United States, public policy researcher William Vega found that assimilation to US society was associated with three times the rate of depressive episodes for these immigrants. Vega also found major increases in substance abuse and other harmful behaviors. He noted, "Mexicans are coming from a much more integrated family system. There are tremendous benefits of that in terms of everyday psychological resilience . . . They are much more likely to be in a situation where people help each other out." Vega concluded that while these immigrants were focused on gaining more money and greater freedom, they had discovered the great cost was a "loss of reciprocal support."

One of the few areas that have seen an increase in face-to-face contact is in self-help groups such as Alcoholics Anonymous. So if one is willing to declare oneself "diseased," society provides a relatively easy way to have face-to-face contact with others, and I have met some people so desperate for friendship that they labeled themselves with a disease without compelling evidence for it.

How about the Internet? While some people may have hundreds of "friends" on Facebook or MySpace, that's different from having confidants. John T. Cacioppo, a neuroscientist at the University of Chicago and coauthor of *Loneliness: Human Nature and the Need for Social Connection*, concludes that so-called social-networking sites such as Facebook and MySpace may provide people with a false sense of connection. Cacioppo says, "It feels good immediately, but it doesn't give you the same sustenance." There has been a recent dramatic increase of Facebook users, as clearly millions of people are starving for social connectedness. The use of Internet social networking to help start the 2011 Egyptian revolution caused Facebook critics to rethink its potential for political impact, at least with a population that has not lost the strength and courage required to challenge oppressive institutions.

Texting and tweeting? Michael J. Bugeja, a professor of communications at Iowa State University and author of *Interpersonal Divide: The Search for Community in a Technological Age*, says that digital communication can increase feelings of isolation. Bugeja believes that texting or tweeting in the presence of another person sends the message to that person that someone else is more important. For Bugeja, "The human heart is suffering from lack of authentic interaction."

My personal experience—as well as the research—shows that e-mail is often a bad medium to sort out differences. When one is disagreeing, one needs to see and feel the other person's goodwill, affection, and respect, or such disagreements can easily feel like ego trips, hostility, and disrespect and can create needless antagonism that can end relationships. Even in business transactions, a Stanford study found that compared with face-to-face or telephone negotiation, e-mail negotiations are more likely to break down. Without the interpersonal glue that comes from a face-to-face encounter (and, to a lesser extent, a phone conversation), one must take special care in e-exchanges so as not to create conflict that can easily be misinterpreted. If one is excessively cautious, relationships never fully develop; if one is not so cautious, relationships end.

There is nothing more important in breaking people from their capacity to resist oppressive forces than creating a society of isolated people. With social isolation, people stop sharing information, there is an absence of mutual validation about the source of their misery, and they are much more likely to believe that it is their personal weakness that has allowed them to be victimized. With social isolation, people lack the bonds necessary to provide the collective self-confidence that they can overcome oppression. In chapter 4, I will provide specific strategies for transforming social isolation and loneliness in a way that creates more self-respect, collective self-confidence, and potential for greater democracy.

One of many causes of increased social isolation is an increasingly bureaucratized society, and bureaucratization in and of itself can break people. What does it do to us when we spend thirty minutes on the phone shouting answers to a programmed machine that responds in a monotone machine voice, "I don't understand," only to finally discover that the "machine menu" does not include what we need? What happens to our self-respect and dignity when we start speaking gibberish in the hope that this will trick the machine into giving us an actual person? I've done all of this. And this is only one part of a dehumanizing process of bureaucratization.

Have you done any air travel in the last decade? I avoid it as much as possible, but I cannot avoid it completely. A few years back, I tried to have a discussion with a Transportation Security Administration (TSA) security guard about how much sense it made taking away my few drops of suntan lotion in a clear eight-ounce bottle when ten times that amount in a three-ounce bottle was permitted. The guard made clear to me that my points, especially if made passionately enough, might jeopardize my chances of traveling—and maybe even get me arrested. Nowadays, as soon as I enter the airport terminal, I begin saying to myself, *Don't think, don't feel. Don't think, don't feel. Don't think, don't feel. Don't think, don't feel.* I wonder how much air traveling it will take before "don't think, don't feel" becomes my permanent condition.

Many Americans work jobs that meet the needs of machines and bureaucracies but satisfy none of their human needs for meaningfulness and social connectedness. In old-fashioned capitalism, human beings were simply dehumanized by the demands of profit, and the demanders of profit were flesh-and-blood bosses and owners. In old-fashioned capitalism, one could do or say something to actual people. Such assertions may not improve one's lot, but at least one could imagine having an emotional impact on another person. How does one have an impact on a machine menu? So we sink into even more helplessness and powerlessness.

Broken by Fundamentalist Consumerism and Advertising/Propaganda

Fundamentalist capitalism and communism both narrow human beings to their financial and material needs. Fundamentalist capitalism focuses on selfishness, greed, and competitiveness and excludes the reality that human beings are also cooperative, altruistic, and capable of love. Fundamentalist communism—in its Soviet Union form—was pretty much "ask not what your country can do for you, but rather do what your country demands," and it excluded people's need to work for themselves and their family. Religious fundamentalists are attached to their literal interpretations of their particular scriptures, and they exclude all facts that contradict their dogma. Fundamentalist consumers are attached to "stuff," including stuff that is unnecessary for survival and stuff that may be bad for their health. Fundamentalist consumers may be so attached to desired stuff that they disregard life, including human life—as the surviving friends and family of Jdimytai Damour will attest.

Damour, a temporary maintenance worker at a Long Island, New York, Walmart, was killed by a mob of fundamentalist consumers in 2008 on "Black Friday" (so named because retailers hope that on this, the day after Thanksgiving, a horde of consumers will begin turning their financial red ink into black ink). Damour was trampled to death by shoppers who were intent on buying one of a limited number of fifty-inch plasma HDTVs on sale. In the predawn darkness, approximately two thousand shoppers impatiently waited outside the Walmart where Damour worked, chanting, "Push the doors in." According to Damour's fellow Walmart worker Jimmy Overby, "He was bum-rushed by 200 people. They took the doors off the hinges. He was trampled and killed in front of me." Witnesses reported that Damour, thirty-four years old, gasped for air as shoppers continued to surge over him. When police instructed shoppers to leave the store after Damour's death, many refused, some yelling back, "I've been on line since yesterday morning!"

The mainstream media covering Damour's death focused on the mob of crazed shoppers and, to a lesser extent, irresponsible Walmart executives who failed to provide security. However, absent in the corporate press was anything about a consumer culture in which marketers, advertisers, and media promote fundamentalist consumerism.

In a fundamentalist consumer society, what is it "reasonable" to pay money for? Drinking water. Exercise. Meeting other people. Communicating with other people. Health. Sleep. Energy. Death. It is also now "reasonable" for parents to pay to make their children more manageable and thereby not create tension for authorities. In fundamentalist consumerism, one buys anything that makes one feel good and not feel bad. When one is living in a society in which virtually nothing is considered taboo to buy and sell, one is living in a fundamentalist consumer society.

The essence of fundamentalist consumerism is that one must purchase something in order to have pleasure, eliminate pain, and survive. Fundamentalist consumerism tells us that relying on something other than money—ourselves or community—is often an inefficient use of time compared with using one's time to make money and then paying others who can more quickly and expertly meet one's needs. Fundamentalist consumerism teaches, for instance, that it is inefficient to use one's time to grow one's own fruits and vegetables when one could have more money by working at a decent-paying job and paying for produce. Fundamentalist consumerism instructs us to view not just food growing but *everything* in this manner.

Fundamentalist consumerism permeates the entire economy and culture, and so there is no one person or even one group that we can overthrow to end it. While people certainly can resist the cheap-stuff propaganda and not worship at Walmart, IKEA, and other big-box cathedrals—and stay out of the path of a mob of fundamentalist consumers—it is difficult to protect oneself from the slow death caused by a consumer culture. Fundamentalist consumer culture creates passivity, invites depression, and destroys individual self-respect and collective self-confidence in a variety of ways.

Obliteration of Self-Reliance

The loss of self-reliance creates a loss of individual self-respect. In modern society, an increasing number of people—women as well as men—cannot cook a simple meal. They will never know the self-respect and the anti-anxiety effects of being secure in their ability to prepare their own food, grow their own vegetables, hunt, fish, or gather food necessary for survival. Many cannot fix a leaky faucet or change the oil in their car. In a consumer culture, such self-reliance makes little sense. But at a deeper level, believing that you are totally dependent on others undermines your sense of self, as though you are a child in an adult's body. People who feel completely dependent on others are likely to turn over decision-making power to those others, the precise mind-set that corporate and government elites most love to see. People who lack the confidence of even a small amount of self-reliance know that should they lose their incomes, they have no ability to survive. This creates enormous fear, which breaks people.

Alienation from Humanity

Another powerful way that people become broken is when they are disconnected from their own humanity. The priests of consumer culture—advertisers and marketers—know that fundamentalist consumers will consume more if they are alienated from their normal reactions (such as boredom, frustration, sadness, and anxiety). If these priests can convince people that a given emotional state is shameful or evidence of a disease, then people will be more likely to buy not only drugs but also other products to make them feel better. While, as I stated earlier, I don't believe that the elite have consciously engineered every aspect of a system so as to break people, high-level advertisers are quite aware of people's insecurities and take advantage of them, including creating and promoting new insecurities—as with the campaign mentioned earlier to promote the use of Paxil for social anxiety disorder. Advertisers quite consciously attempt to manipulate people to redefine the nature of their humanity in a way that will create greater dependence on what they are selling. Such a redefinition can be a complete lie or an extreme narrowing of the nature of humanity. When people buy into a narrowed definition of humanity, they become disconnected from their full humanity and are no longer whole; they become weaker and much more easily controlled, not simply by an advertisement but ultimately by any totalitarian individual, institution, system, or government-corporate partnership. This narrowing is the essence of all fundamentalism, which ignores or shames the multiple dimensions of life that fall outside what it can provide.

Promotion of Self-Absorption

Self-respect is quite different from self-absorption. With self-absorption, people actually lose self-respect and the capacity to work together. But self-absorption is exactly what a consumer culture demands. Self-absorption makes it more difficult to form friendships and other significant human relationships, and loneliness is good news for a consumer economy that thrives on increasing numbers of "buying units." More lonely people means selling more televisions, DVDs, et cetera.

How did fundamentalist consumerism come into existence? Certainly not naturally. It was quite consciously manipulated via advertising by the burgeoning financial elite in the late 1800s and early 1900s. While advertising had previously existed, a different kind of advertising was necessary in order to sell things to people that they really didn't need. This kind of advertising needed to be more psychologically astute. Far less important than the intrinsic value of the product was what psychological need it could satisfy (for example, the need to be modern, cool, young, hip, attractive, and so forth).

Prior to these new manipulations, most Americans chose leisure time rather than working for things that were not necessities. However, in a short period of time, this new kind of advertising transformed the United States into a nation of consumer debtors. By the 1920s, 60 percent of radios, automobiles, and furniture were purchased on credit. Later, with the advent of television and the normalization of fundamentalist consumer culture, advertisers were granted license to manipulate young minds, and these advertisers zealously targeted children so as to grab their "brand loyalty" for life.

What are the differences among *advertising, public relations,* and *propaganda?* There actually are no substantive differences, and at one time these terms were used interchangeably among the American elite and the corporatocracy.

A century ago, businesspeople were so impressed with how effective World War I propaganda campaigns were in the United States and around the globe at short-circuiting resistance to this war that they became enthusiastic about perfecting propaganda techniques for the products that they sold. If an unnecessary war could be sold, certainly it would be easy to sell unnecessary products.

Enter Edward Bernays, who came to be the most famous public relations/ advertising propagandist in American history. In his 1928 book *Propaganda,* Bernays was essentially trying to sell propaganda as a good thing. Bernays was proud of his craft of propaganda, and he would have preferred not to be forced to use euphemisms such as *public relations* for it. Bernays was an unabashed elitist, but he tried to convince others—and perhaps even himself—that he actually believed in democracy. He, for example, said:

> The conscious and intelligent manipulation of the organized habits and opinions of the masses is an important element in democratic society. Those who manipulate this unseen mechanism of society constitute an invisible government which is the true ruling power of our country . . . Ours must be a leadership democracy administered by the intelligent minority who know how to regiment and guide the masses.

This of course is an Orwellian, upside-down view of democracy. Bernays had the gift to make propaganda/advertising/public relations seem benign, grand, and even "democratic" to the audience he cared most about. This audience was the corporatocracy, which had the money to spend on him and his craft. His clients included Procter & Gamble, General Motors, General Electric, and a long list of other major corporations. He was a pioneer packager of presidents, specifically Calvin Coolidge. Bernays was also paid to improve the image of John D. Rockefeller and other elitists and institutions with public relations problems. And in the 1950s, Bernays was employed by the United Fruit Company, which used the CIA to overthrow the democratically elected leadership of Guatemala; this was replaced by a dictatorial oligarchy that was friendly to United Fruit and ensured that fruit would continue to be picked by an inexpensive native labor force.

Bernays popularized many propaganda/advertising/public relations techniques that are still used today. Most famously, Bernays, on behalf of the American Tobacco Company, had a group of attractive debutantes march in a New York City parade while smoking cigarettes. Bernays had instructed these young women to tell the press that they were a women's rights group who were lighting "Torches of Freedom"— cigarettes. These women were photographed and covered by the press exactly the way

Bernays had wanted—connecting freedom-loving women with cigarettes, and making it cool for women to smoke in public. All this advertising/public relations/propaganda made for selling more cigarettes, which made the American Tobacco Company happy.

Bernays was a pioneer not simply of propaganda/advertising/public relations but also of propagandizing the reasonableness of such manipulativeness. While the ruling class has always tried to propagandize its subjects, the "genius" of the American ruling class is to utilize people such as Bernays to propagandize the normality of propaganda. In American culture and in those societies that ape it, there is no shame for politicians to have public relations/advertiser propagandists. In the United States, it is "normal" for its population—including its children—to be increasingly assaulted by sophisticated psychological techniques aimed at manipulating and controlling them. In American culture, for example, there is no shame in being a person who manipulates children into pestering their parents into buying things that they don't need.

The practices of fundamentalist consumerism weakens and disconnects people by obliterating self-reliance, alienating them from their humanity, and promoting self-absorption. What perhaps is most troubling is how effectively Americans have been propagandized to accept that propaganda is okay. When we accept that it is okay for politicians, corporations, and other institutional authorities to use all manners and means to manipulate people, we give lies a legitimacy, and this "lie legitimacy" sneaks into our entire lives, including family life. We become a society of manipulators and liars, and this breaks integrity and destroys self-respect and the capacity to trust one another.

Student-Loan Debt and Indentured Servitude

> 66 In America today there are 70 million people—about one quarter of the US population—who owe a collective $700 billion in student loans. 99
>
> —David Brancaccio, *NOW* ("Student Loan Sinkhole?"), June 19, 2009

I met Jason Douglass in March 2010 when he came from Texas to Cincinnati to shoot some footage for his filmmaker boss. While his team set up lighting and checked sound, we chatted about student-loan debt. I wondered whether student-loan debt had become another important reason why many people in his age group—in their twenties and thirties—feel dispirited. Jason told me about his own student-loan debt and gave me permission to publish it. Below is an edited version of Jason's tale, along with a couple of others.

> 66 When I got the acceptance letter [from New York University] and subsequent price tag, I was saddened to realize that there was no way I could afford to attend. Luckily, or at least at the time I believed I was lucky, President Clinton pushed legislation that allowed a student to take out loans for the entire amount of tuition, including cost of living. Of course, I happily signed my name on the promissory note for $40k. I believed that my hard work would lead to great rewards . . . Now that I am out of college, my obligation has doubled to over $80k and looms over my head like a guillotine threatening to lop off my head. I have no dreams about owning a home, retirement, or properly taking care of my family. Those parts of the American Dream are dead to me. If I get a pay increase, then my loan payment amount will also increase—therefore there is no reason to aspire to anything. 99
>
> —Jason Douglass, e-mail, March 9, 2010

> 66 I owe nearly $200,000 in student loans. It was $140,000, but interest over 5 years has caused it to increase. I can't stop the interest or fees. It may as well be a million dollars. I make $27,000 a year working full-time. I can't even begin to make the nearly $2,000 per month payment. My credit is shot. I send each student loan company what I can, but it's a drop in a bucket. If I were a weaker person, I'd slit my wrists. Luckily, I own no property (not even a car) and I have nothing for them

to take from me. They could garnish my wages, but they'd get only a little bit more than they are getting from me now. . . . I wonder every day what will happen to me if I lose my job, which today, is VERY likely."

—terradea42, *AlterNet*, November 12, 2008

"I am 58 years old, and still owe $80,000 in student loans. I will go to my grave with this massive debt always over my head, even though I make timely monthly payments! . . . My credit has long ago been ruined; I can never get a mortgage loan, or even a loan to buy a used car . . . During the 1980s, when I divorced and became a single parent, I could only earn in the low $20,000s at mental health centers. I therefore decided to go for the doctorate. Unfortunately, I have never been able to earn more than $40,000; and this is WITHOUT any type of health insurance, sick/vacation time or any other benefits."

—therese kovach, *AlterNet*, November 12, 2008

Of the 3.2 million American youths who graduated from high school in 2008, 68.6 percent attended college, but about half of all college students don't graduate. About 30 percent of Americans eventually get a four-year college degree.

College tuition and administrative fees have inflated more than three times the rate of general inflation in the last thirty years. During this time period, while the general cost of living increased roughly threefold and medical costs have increased sixfold, college tuition and fees have increased almost tenfold. The cost, on average, for four years at a public university is more than 25 percent of the median American household income, up from 18 percent in 2000. For the poorest one-fifth of Americans, public university tuition costs 55 percent of their income.

Not surprisingly, the amount of outstanding student loans has increased sharply, even after accounting for inflation. In 1993, less than one-half of graduating college seniors had loans; by 2008, 66.4 percent of graduating seniors at four-year colleges had student-loan debt, including 62 percent of public university graduates.

The average amount of undergraduate student debt in the United States is now more than $22,000, according to the US Department of Education ($23,200, according to the Project on Student Debt), with many having far larger debt. For those with a master's degree, the average cumulative debt is over $40,000; for a PhD, it is better than $57,000; and for a professional degree, it is over $87,000. The American Medical Association reports that the average educational debt of graduates of medical school is more than $154,000, with 79 percent of all graduates carrying at least $100,000 in debt. Half of college students have four or more credit cards, their average total balance over $3,000; and the average total balance on graduate students' credit cards is around $9,000.

> **"**Indentured Servitude? I can only feel duped by the dream of obtaining the highest level of education in America . . . I'll be paying for my student loans for the rest of my life . . . A large portion of my earnings goes to the Wall Street elites that have commoditized and securitized my loans . . . I knew at the time I signed the student loans (again and again) that I would be responsible . . . what I didn't figure was the cost to my children.**"**
>
> —JeffVincent, *AlterNet*, November 12, 2008

Is it an exaggeration to say America is retuning to indentured servitude? In "Student Debt and the Spirit of Indenture," Jeffrey Williams, English professor at Carnegie Mellon University, concludes, "College student-loan debt has revived the spirit of indenture for a sizable proportion of contemporary Americans." Williams points out that college-loan debt, like indentured servitude, "looms over the lives of those so contracted, binding individuals for a significant part of their future work lives."

Historians estimate that between one-half and two-thirds of white immigrants to colonial America (three to four hundred thousand people) arrived as indentured servants. While indentured servitude had been common practice in England, the Americanization of the institution meant an increase in the length of servitude. Indentured servants in England were in servitude typically for a year (and this was closely regulated by law), while indenture in America was typically four to seven years (because of the cost of transit and a brokerage system). While student-loan debtors do not have to suffer the daily physical indignities of many indentured servants (many of whom were treated no differently from slaves), today in the United States student debt is an even longer debt commitment than colonial indentured servitude. The standard Stafford federal loan is, for example, fifteen years, and with waivers and refinancing, it is not uncommon for Americans to be paying off student loans well into middle age.

Similar to students signing their college loan papers, indentured servants also "freely chose" their servitude. While the elite in colonial times saw indentured servitude as a freely chosen, fair economic deal, the servants themselves routinely saw it as an exploitative system of labor, a form of time-limited slavery. Like colonial indentured servants who "freely chose" to sign papers agreeing that they would pay off their debt directly in labor, modern student-loan debtors "freely choose" to sign papers agreeing to pay off their debt. However, this is a "choice" that the elite do not have to make. No indentured servants and few student-loan debtors are in the elite or privileged classes.

In a legal sense, both the indentured servant and the student debtor have freely chosen their deal, but in reality indentured servants were and student debtors are *compelled* to agree to sacrifice future freedom to pay off their debt. Like colonial indentured servitude, the student-loan contract is virtually unbreakable. In the United States, student loans are enforced by garnishing wages, and, unlike most other forms of debt, student debt is almost never forgiven even in personal bankruptcy.

Similar to some indentured servants, some student-loan debtors do go on to prosper. The statistical argument for taking on student-loan debt is that over the course of a career, college graduates—on average—make significantly more money than nongraduates (according to some studies, as much as $1 million more). However, half of those who attend college don't graduate. And while the average college graduate makes significantly more money than nongraduates, in reality there are many college graduates who do not get high-paying jobs and who struggle to make debt payments for much of their adult lives.

Do citizens of all nations have high college tuition resulting in crippling student debt? English-speaking nations generally pay the most. In contrast, as I write this, there remains no tuition for public universities in Finland, Brazil, and Chile, and public universities in France are tuition-free with low administrative fees (historically, when the French government considers making even small increases, students and others demonstrate both peacefully and violently). Until recently, Germany, Austria, and Denmark had free tuition, and costs there continue to be minimal compared with American tuition and fees. In Iran, public university tuition as well as much of room and board is paid for by the government.

South of the US border in Mexico, the "flagship" of the public university system is called the National Autonomous University of Mexico (UNAM), with nearly three hundred thousand students. Immediately after NAFTA, the Mexican economy collapsed, and in 1999 the government raised tuition at UNAM from the US equivalent of 20 cents per year to $150 per year. The Mexican elite were increasingly sending their children to private universities, and other Mexicans sensed that the elite were in the process of abandoning UNAM, which was one of the largest and most respected universities in Latin America. In response to the tuition hike, there was a massive student protest and a lengthy shutdown of UNAM; more than one hundred thousand people marched through Mexico City. The government offered a compromise $85-per-year tuition. In addition to UNAM, there are other Mexican public federal and state universities, to which there is less resistance when tuition is raised. As of 2009, tuition and fees at Mexican public universities ranged in US dollars from $125 to $400 per year. In Mexico, student loans are virtually nonexistent for those attending public universities.

Between 1973 and 1977, I went to Queens College of the City University of New York. I paid no tuition and commuted from home and so incurred no debt. I could afford not to have a job during the school year; summer jobs provided me with enough income not only to cover my expenses during the school year but to actually save $3,000 by the time I graduated (which I used to backpack around Europe afterward). I entered graduate school in the fall of 1978, and between 1978 and 1985 I worked toward a master's and then a doctorate from another public institution, the University of Cincinnati, where I again paid no tuition. Between a small scholarship and graduate assistant positions, I graduated with no debt. So in ten years of higher education, getting a BA, an MA, and a PhD, I accrued no debt.

As a graduate student I had concerns about making a living after graduation, but knowing that I would graduate debt free reduced my fear. With no looming debt, I was not compelled to spend my time in graduate school currying favor with authorities and networking with people whom I would rather have nothing to do with. If I had been carrying significant debt when I began my practice, I doubt I would have done anywhere near the amount of writing that I have done; I would have worried far more about using my time to make a sure buck. Also, had I been carrying significant debt, I would have thought twice about voicing the kind of opinions that might economically marginalize me. In short, debt, at least for me, would have reduced both my time and capacity to take risks.

Even for those whose higher-education student loans turn out to be a "good investment" in terms of lifetime earnings, they may still lose out on a big part of what makes life worth living. During the time in one's life when it should ordinarily be easiest to resist authority because one does not yet have family responsibilities, it is sad to see so many young people burdened by debt. They worry, far more than I had to, about the cost of bucking authority, losing their job, and being unable to pay an ever-increasing debt. Even if the ledger eventually shows that the financial benefits of higher education are more than the debt accrued for it, the subduing effects of that debt still exist. In a vicious cycle, student debt has a subduing effect on activism, and political passivity makes it more likely that students will accept such debt as a natural part of life.

The Normalization of Surveillance

Tyrants have always used spies for surveillance. What's different today is the power and ubiquity of surveillance technology. And what is especially scary about surveillance today is just how "normal" it has become.

Control freaks want to know exactly what their subordinates are doing and what they're thinking about. While the information gained is useful for control, simply the *fear* of being surveilled makes a population easier to control. There are fewer and fewer places in our lives today where we can be confident that no one is peering in on our actions.

While the National Security Agency (NSA) has received publicity for monitoring American citizens' e-mail and phone conversations, it no longer matters, in one sense, whether this has stopped. The fear that it could easily happen is enough to make people communicate less about what they really think. Without critical thinking and mutual validation of lies and truths, there can be no democracy.

While government surveillance made the biggest headlines when the NSA's illegal program was revealed, it is employer surveillance that is now most common in Americans' lives. Employers read employees' e-mails, listen to their phone calls, monitor their Internet use, and videotape them with cameras. Lewis Maltby, author of the 2009 book *Can They Do That?* and founder of National Workrights Institute, reports that worker surveillance is increasing because of inexpensive technology. Some workers carry company-issued cell phones equipped with GPS, and Maltby reports that the cost now of tracking an employee twenty-four hours a day, seven days a week is only $5 per month. Even scarier than company-issued cell phones are company-issued laptops that employers "allow" employees to use for personal purposes. Maltby points out, "What employers don't tell you is that some company's computer technicians look at your private documents when the computer comes in for upgrading or repair." Heidi Arace and Norma Yetsko were fired by PNC Bank for forwarding off-color e-mail jokes to co-workers, and Nate Fulmer was fired by chemical supplier Environmental Express because he made fun of a local church sermon in a podcast he and his wife created at home. A survey in 2009 found that 27 percent of employers have policies restricting what employees are allowed to post on personal blogs. All of these employer surveillance practices, says Maltby, are legal, and workers are at the mercy of them unless they have union protection—which the vast majority of workers in the United States do not have.

What's most frightening is that the day is coming—and perhaps is already here—when surveillance feels as normal as traffic lights because people will be accustomed to it from birth. Up until a decade ago, many adolescents I saw in my practice could "screw around" in school for most of the semester, then "ace a final" and manage to get a passing grade; their parents would be none the wiser to their kid's close brush with failure. Now parents routinely check Web sites for their children's latest test grades and completed assignments, and parents start worrying early. This early monitoring often leads to family strife, which can result in these kids screwing up more—out of resentment for being surveilled. There is a big difference between helping kids stay on task versus distrusting and surveilling them. Parents, just like employers, are monitoring their children's computers, and some parents use the GPS in their children's cell phones to track their whereabouts. Often these controlling behaviors don't prevent what parents are frightened of but instead create two things: resentment and normalization of surveillance.

Surveillance not only creates fear that breaks resistance but can also destroy the capacity to trust others. Surveillance is now creating resentment even at the family level. It is a goal of tyrants to have a population terrified, without self-respect, without group support, and without a family to fall back on. It is the dream of all control freaks to have those whom they wish to control be completely dependent on them.

The Decline of Labor Unions and the Loss of Power for Working People

Over the last generation in the United States, there has been a steady decline in union fellowship. This has resulted in lower wages, increased worker surveillance, fewer workers with health insurance, diminished fraternity, and increased powerlessness for a huge segment of American society.

Union members make more money, are more likely to have health insurance, and are more likely to have an employer-based retirement plan than similar workers who lack union representation. Among full-time wage and salary workers in 2009, union members had a median weekly earnings of $908, while those in non-union jobs had median weekly earnings of $710. Nearly 80 percent of union members have employer-provided health insurance, compared with 50 percent of non-union workers, and these union and non-union percentages are nearly identical for employer-sponsored retirement plans. Union members also have shop stewards to whom they can lodge complaints about illegal or inappropriate actions by management, as well as other union assistance to help defend them from unfair treatment. And unions provide fellowship, without which increasing numbers of US employees are isolated from one another and thus deprived of the sense of power and hope that comes from union fraternity.

Many Americans cannot remember or even imagine a time when union workers felt the strength and courage to stand up both to industry bosses and their own union bosses if they were "selling them out."

In the middle of the Great Depression, even with extremely high rates of unemployment, autoworkers in Flint, Michigan, had the courage to stage a sit-down strike, occupying a General Motors factory so as to earn recognition for their United Auto Workers union as a bargaining agent. These autoworkers locked themselves in their factory and protected their jobs from being taken by scabs (strike breakers). This sit-down strike began on December 30, 1936, and lasted forty-four days. It was victorious.

Through a good part of the 1940s and 1950s, more than 35 percent of American employees were union members. By the end of 2009, only 12.3 percent of employees (15.3 million) were union members. Today union membership in the private sector has plummeted to 7.2 percent (7.9 million). Union membership has increased in the public sector to 37.4 percent (7.4 million); however, in the United States there are five times more employees in the private sector than there are in the public sector. Within the public sector, local government workers have the highest union membership rate, 43.3 percent (this includes workers such as teachers, police officers, and firefighters). Union membership rate is highest among workers fifty-five to sixty-four years old (16.6 percent); the lowest rate is among those sixteen to twenty-four (4.7 percent).

Of the 107.5 million nonmanagerial wage and salary workers in 2009, 15.9 million (14.8 percent) were represented by a union. This group includes both union members (14.5 million) and workers who report no union affiliation but whose jobs are covered by a union contract (1.4 million). This means that more than 91.6 million nonmanagerial US employees in 2009 were completely on their own in terms of negotiating pay and benefits and dealing with other workplace issues.

There are several reasons for the decline of union membership. Often mentioned as the "beginning of the end" was the passage of the Taft-Hartley Act in 1947, which restricted certain union activities and prohibited certain kinds of strikes such as "wildcat" or unauthorized strikes as well as strikes that the federal government deemed "imperiling the national health or safety." The Taft-Hartley Act also made it more difficult for politically radical union members to move into positions of union leadership.

Most labor observers agree that Ronald Reagan's 1981 firing of more than eleven thousand striking members of the Professional Air Traffic Controllers Organization had a chilling effect on unions. Also, most agree that the loss of manufacturing jobs due to the decimation of industries that are strongly unionized (for example, automobile-related industries) is another reason for union decline. And another nail driven into the coffin has been globalization agreements such as NAFTA (signed into law by Bill Clinton in December 1993), which have given corporations a great deal of leverage to break unions, as corporations can more easily relocate their factories overseas for more inexpensive labor. Often the mere threat that jobs will move overseas is enough to undermine unionization efforts.

Still another reason for the decline is offered by David Macaray, president and chief contract negotiator of the Association of Western Pulp and Paper Workers, Local 672, from 1989 to 2000. Macaray notes that government has co-opted some of what union contracts traditionally did.

He argues, "Government has assumed custody of key union provisions" such as safety issues. The creation of the Occupational Health and Safety Act is one of Macaray's examples. He points out that the 1970 passage of OSHA makes employers accountable to a federal safety code, and so it is a government agency that employees now can complain to.

There are many other reasons for the decline of union membership and power, such as businesses simply violating labor law to prevent unions from gaining a foothold in their turf, and governments failing to enforce labor law to halt these criminal practices. But there are two important causes that are often neglected. First, the effectiveness of the corporatocracy's anti-union public relations campaign cannot be underestimated. Second, union leaderships' cooperation with the corporatocracy's basic values has sucked the energy and vitality out of the union movement, a workers movement that had previously been energized by its quest for genuine democracy.

For many Millenniums, GenXers, and even some Baby Boomers, the face of a union leader—if there is any face at all—is that of Jimmy Hoffa, president of the International Brotherhood of Teamsters from 1958 to 1971. Hoffa was convicted in 1964 of jury tampering, attempted bribery, and fraud. After his release from prison, he was last reported seen in July 1975, and he was declared "legally dead" in 1982. While some young people know about Jimmy Hoffa—at least Jack Nicholson's 1992 movie portrayal of him—how many can mention one noncorrupt union leader? There are actually many noncorrupt twentieth-century labor leaders who achieved great gains for their members. A short list includes: A. Philip Randolph (African American civil rights leader and founder of the Brotherhood of Sleeping Car Porters), Walter Reuther (a leader in the Flint sit-down strike who later headed the United Auto Workers), and César Chávez (United Farm Workers founder).

While there have been corrupt union leaders and nonproductive workers protected by unions, it seems to have become increasingly acceptable to characterize all union leaders as corrupt and all union members as slackers. People such as myself who grew up in a union family are not naive to the reality of corrupt union leaders such as Hoffa, but we see them in much the same way as African Americans see the criminal element of their communities—as embarrassing exceptions that are exploited by bigots to justify their bigotry. While it is now politically incorrect in the United States to negatively stereotype African Americans, women, and homosexuals, it appears that it is not so politically incorrect to nega-tively stereotype union leaders and members. Perhaps this occurs because increasing numbers of Americans do not come from union families and do not have union member neighbors or friends. For most union members, their families, and their friends, unions mean social and economic justice, dignity, and an antidote to political impotence.

While the illegal corruption of unions by Jimmy Hoffa–type mobsters has been harmful, perhaps even more problematic have been the quite legal compromises by union leaders with the corporatocracy. Specifically, union leadership has often sold out rank-and-file workers so as to become "junior partners" to management in controlling the rank and file. It was once far more routine for rank-and-file union members to revolt not only against management but also against their union leadership.

In the 1960s and 1970s, there were many unauthorized "wildcat" strikes, approximately two thousand in 1969 alone. In 1970, there were two highly publicized major wildcat strikes in the United States. The Teamsters defied their union leadership and trucking bosses and went on a wildcat strike. So too did postal workers.

In 1970, my father, a postal clerk and union activist, along with more than two hundred thousand fellow employees went out on strike for two weeks. Postal workers achieved a sense of power that they never before or after were able to duplicate. At the time, postal employees were forbid-den by law from engaging in collective bargaining; wages were extremely low, and benefits were poor. This 1970 postal strike was a wildcat strike, not called for by national union leadership. It was fired up at the grass roots. Members from New York City locals walked off the job, and the strike spread. President Nixon ordered nearly twenty thousand National Guard and other military personnel to post offices to handle the mail, but this was an abysmal failure. Nixon and governmental officials underesti-mated the skills required for successful mail delivery. The strikers won.

Though it was not a complete victory, the postal workers gained the right to negotiate, and they secured a contract that improved pay and working conditions.

I talk to postal clerks and mail carriers working today, and I routinely get two reactions to that 1970 strike. One is an appreciation and almost awe about the courage and accomplishments of that previous generation of postal union workers, which gave current workers a decent-paying job. The second, especially after Reagan's firing of the striking air traffic controllers, is one of impotence—a belief that should they ever try to improve their lot again via a strike, they would simply lose their jobs forever.

The greatest fear of the corporatocracy is working people uniting to overthrow them, and so the corporatocracy has always waged a battle against unions on every front. In the last three decades, the corporatocracy has been able to successfully destroy much of the collective power that working people gained in previous generations. The corporatocracy has controlled politicians to create favorable legislation for them, moved production outside the United States to exploit inexpensive labor overseas, successfully waged anti-union publicity campaigns, and corrupted and weakened unions.

Just as the corporatocracy has been able to find foreign leaders it can corrupt and control, so too has it been able to find leaders in large unions that it can control. While some of these labor leaders compromised core worker values not for the sake of personal greed but in the belief that they were preserving their union institutions, the results were still often harmful. By compromising on democratic values, these union leaders have compromised away the energy and vitality of the union movement.

There are many things that one can compromise on in life, but when one compromises one's fundamental values, one loses integrity and strength. What most working people truly want is greater fairness and greater control over their lives, which means that managers, CEOs, and corporate boards would have less power. The hearts and souls of most working people reject the notion that bottom-line stock price should be the sole determinant of workplace decision making. Once working people resign themselves to the "reality" that company profits are the paramount value, they compromise their very hearts and souls. If working people are not inching closer to genuine democracy in their workplace—for example, gaining increasingly more representation and power on a corporate board of directors—but are instead accepting the hierarchical top-down control as a permanent reality, then they are losing individual self-respect and collective self-confidence.

There are owners of small and medium-size businesses who do care about being financially fair to their workers, and there are rare owners who are willing to share some power. But corporations, by legal design, are about increased profits and control. And so the corporatocracy, like the devil itself, may at times reward with a wage increase—at least temporarily—so long as those rewards come with an insidious abdication of power and a retreat from the fundamental value of genuine democracy in the workplace. Thus, even if a union gains higher wages, if that money comes with a loss of power, workers grow weaker. Once broken, workers can have small rewards taken away—this is called *give-backs*—and be completely shafted. That today is exactly what has happened.

Moneyism, Money-Centric Culture, and Weakness

> "In a society in which the money-maker has had no serious rival for repute and honor, the word 'practical' comes to mean useful for private gain, and 'common sense,' the sense to get ahead financially. The pursuit of the moneyed life is the commanding value, in relation to which the influence of other values has declined, so men easily become morally ruthless in the pursuit of easy money and fast estate-building."
>
> —C. Wright Mills, *The Power Elite*, 1956

> "Why don't Americans fight, protest, organize and in general raise hell when injustices are committed? The short answer is fear. But I think part of the answer is the relentless promotion of selfish values . . . In other societies where I have lived, people

feel a bit ashamed of selfish behaviors, it's not so accepted to be selfish. If you accept that being selfish and individualistic 100% of the time is a good value, then a corollary to this is that when shit happens, people tend to suffer alone because there is no solidarity anyway. "

—Adriana Heguy, *Atheistnexus*, December 14, 2009

To be *money-centric* means that money is the focal point and center of thought and activities, and the worship of money at the expense of all else is what I call *moneyism*. While greedy people have always been money-centric, a money-centric society can coerce everybody to be preoccupied with money. One may actually hate money but feel compelled to focus on it at the expense of everything else in order to survive. One may not be greedy and still be pained by money-centrism.

How do moneyism and money-centrism destroy individual self-respect and collective confidence? When one cares only about money, one neglects everything else necessary to build and maintain self-respect. One destroys integrity, and integrity is necessary for strength. When one is willing to do whatever it takes to make money, one assumes others are acting similarly, which destroys trust and makes it impossible to create the solidarity necessary to successfully challenge authority.

Moneyism has always been practiced. However, through much of human history, such greed has not had the "respectability" that it has recently gained. For the non-elite, financial greed was seen as the practice of villains such as Charles Dickens's Scrooge, a psychologically and spiritually sick man in need of conversion. As late as 1936, a sitting president of the United States running for reelection was unconcerned about being smeared as an extremist for blasting the greedy, selfish elite:

We know now that Government by organized money is just as dangerous as Government by organized mob. Never before in all our history have these forces been so united against one candidate as they stand today. They are unanimous in their hate for me—and I welcome their hatred. I should like to have

it said of my first Administration that in it the forces of selfishness and of lust for power met their match. I should like
to have it said of my second Administration that in it these
forces met their master.

That was Franklin D. Roosevelt on October 31, 1936. Contrast FDR's
speech with President Barack Obama's response in an interview with
Bloomberg Businessweek, published in February 2010. When asked about
Goldman Sachs CEO Lloyd Blankfein's $9 million bonus and JPMorgan
Chase CEO Jamie Dimon's $17 million bonus, Obama responded:

First of all, I know both those guys. They're very savvy busi-
nessmen. And I, like most of the American people, don't
begrudge people success or wealth. That's part of the free
market system. I do think that the compensation packages
that we've seen over the last decade at least have not matched
up always to performance . . . Listen, $17 million is an extraor-
dinary amount of money. Of course, there are some baseball
players who are making more than that who don't get to the
World Series either.

In one study, when Americans were asked in 1975 to define the
elements of the "good life," only 38 percent said "lots of money," but by
1996, 63 percent said "lots of money." Even more important than their
stated beliefs is how money-centric Americans' lives actually are.

Early in his administration, Obama told the American people that
with the stock market so low, it was a good time to invest in it. That kind
of presidential advice would have been unheard of in the United States
a century ago. In 1900, only 1 percent of Americans were in the stock
market; by 1950, this increased to only 4 percent; but by 2000, more than
50 percent of Americans were in the stock market. While some of these
people merely have pensions that own shares on their behalf and aren't
evidence of moneyism, many Americans have in fact chosen to invest in
the stock market. How many of those people are investing their money in

companies whose products they believe in? Almost none. The reality is that almost all stock investors are strictly looking at the potential return on their investment. The stock market is all about moneymaking, and the only real difference among investors is those who are risk takers versus those who play it a little more safely.

For those Americans not in the stock market and who are living from paycheck to paycheck or on public assistance, they also are assured by the state that it is quite okay to be money-centric and greedy. Many state governments not only offer lotteries but advertise them heavily on television, radio, and billboards. Lotteries offered by most state governments actually have worse odds of winning than many of the "numbers rackets" once offered by the mob.

Is anything even a close second to money in determining what controls decisions in the United States? Does anybody *not* believe that multibillionaires and corporations rule the world? Can a society in which money is central and routinely worshipped ever be a society that doesn't break people from caring about humanity and all of life? How did money-ism come to be so "respectable"?

What Paul of Tarsus (in the first century after the death of Jesus) was to the dissemination and legitimization of Christianity, Ayn Rand (in the last half of the twentieth century) was to the dissemination and legitimization of moneyism and selfishness. Rand authored *The Virtue of Selfishness* and other best sellers, and her disciples include former chairman of the Federal Reserve Alan Greenspan. Greenspan in the 1950s literally sat at Rand's feet in her "Collective" (her ironic name for her inner circle of self-identified radically selfish individualists). Other admirers of Rand's philosophy include Christopher Cox, chairman of the Securities and Exchange Commission in George W. Bush's second administration; Supreme Court Justice Clarence Thomas; talk-show host Rush Limbaugh; former South Carolina governor Mark Sanford; and millions of others who long to be part of the selfish elite.

Despite Rand's professed contempt for faith, God, and religion, both her work and her life reveal that she clearly had a faith, a God, and a religion. Rand ends *Atlas Shrugged*, her tour de force novel, with this image of its hero John Galt: "He raised his hand and over the desolate earth he traced in space the sign of the dollar." At Rand's funeral, in accordance with her specified arrangements, a six-foot floral arrangement in the shape of a dollar sign was placed near her casket. Her faith was in selfishness, her God was money, and her religion a fundamentalist capitalism.

Since Ronald Reagan, moneyists in the United States have been increasingly freed up to practice what they preach—and to call it integrity rather than sociopathy. Unlike the rest of the industrialized world and much of the developing world, it is "reasonable political discourse" in the United States to question whether people who lack money actually deserve health care.

When people allow for blatant injustices brought upon by greed, they must justify their lack of fight. To say that one is greedy or to say that one has stopped fighting against corruption because one is broken causes an unpleasant dissonance. For those too weak to rebel, one way to resolve this dissonance is by accepting the idea that unbridled selfishness is reasonable.

American society may profess that there are more important variables than the financial bottom line, but Americans are acting less and less in accordance with that belief. A lack of correspondence between beliefs and actions—that is, *hypocrisy*—renders human beings weaker. In a psychological sense, believing one thing and acting another way is called *incongruence* (regardless what level of dissonance this hypocrisy produces). An incongruence between our beliefs and our actions means we are not whole. When we lose our wholeness, our integrity, our congruence, we become weaker. The weaker we get, the less strength we have to resist pressure. It is a vicious cycle, and at some point we can completely spiral into abject brokenness.

Moneyism is especially malevolent when it attacks societal forces that have potential to be liberating. Much has been written about how liberating spiritual revolts begun by Jesus and other rebels eventually morph into organized religion, which then is driven by money and used by the elite as an "opiate of the masses." The elite in religious hierarchies have routinely commercialized faith and God, and by so doing reduced the power of faith and God as potent forces to take down the ruling elite.

But spirituality is not the only potentially rebellious force that has been destroyed by greed. Commercializing any powerful idea, belief, or emotion deadens its power. Even the rebellion of folk/protest music and rock-and-roll has been commercialized, resulting in a dissipation of actual rebellious energy.

In 1998, Bob Dylan and his son Jakob were paid $1 million to play for fifteen thousand employees of the Silicon Valley semiconductor company Applied Materials, and that's not the only "corporate gig" on Dylan's résumé. Next time you hear Dylan's "Blowin' in the Wind," how energizing will that be for you? The aim of many rock-and-roll bands is to exploit and commercialize the *idea* of rebellion, and so it should surprise no one that the Rolling Stones do corporate gigs, including one a decade ago in which they took in $2 million to entertain Pepsi bottlers in Hawaii. Equally widespread and probably even more responsible for dissipating rebellious energy is when songs of perceived rebellious artists are utilized as background music in commercials used to propagandize listeners into associating their rebellious urges with consumer products. Dylan's "The Times They Are A-Changin'" has been used by accounting firm Coopers & Lybrand and by the Bank of Montreal; and the Rolling Stones' "Start Me Up" has been used by Microsoft. Of course it is unfair to pick only on Dylan and the Rolling Stones, but it's simply too depressing for me to go through the entire list.

To defeat the elite, the rest of us need energy. Morality and rebellion are powerful ideas that can create such energy. When a powerful idea is used merely to attract an audience for financial profit, the idea itself becomes less powerful. So whether it is spirituality or rock-and-roll, when rebellious energy is commercialized, that energy dissipates.

Spirituality, music, theater, cinema, and other arts can be revolutionary forces, but the gross commercialization of these has deadened their capacity to energize rebellion. So now damn near everything—not just organized religion—has become an "opiate of the masses."

How Schools Teach Powerlessness

66 The highest percentage increase in our budget should go to our children's education . . . Measuring is the only way to know whether all our children are learning. And I want to know, because I refuse to leave any child behind in America. 99
　　—George W. Bush, address to Congress, February 27, 2001

66 We'll invest in innovative programs that are already helping schools meet high standards and close achievement gaps . . . And dropping out of high school is no longer an option. It's not just quitting on yourself, it's quitting on your country. 99
　　—Barack Obama, address to Congress, February 24, 2009

66 The truth is that schools don't really teach anything except how to obey orders. This is a great mystery to me because thousands of humane, caring people work in schools as teachers and aides and administrators, but the abstract logic of the institution overwhelms their individual contributions. 99
　　—John Taylor Gatto, accepting the New York City Teacher of the
Year Award, January 31, 1990

I am in my fifties, and I still have nightmares about school. When I go into a school to vote, to see a play, or for some other innocuous reason, I still get anxious, my stomach gets upset, and I just want to run from the building. I used to joke that school gave me post-traumatic stress disorder. But maybe it's no joke. A great pain reduction in my young life came when the New York City teachers went out on strike in the fall of 1968, my first year of junior high school. But then the strike ended, and the authorities decided to extend class periods to make up for "lost learning," and the ordinary torture of a school day became extraordinarily torturous. I have worked with children and adolescents for more than twenty-five years, and it still upsets me to see the joy on these kids' faces disappear in response to returning to school after a vacation.

Teachers in the classroom are stuck between a rock and a hard place. They have no authority to transform schools as a whole. And they need to maintain control in their classrooms, not simply for fear of losing their jobs if they don't, but also because it's even less enjoyable for teachers and students if there are no authoritarian controls functioning in a place designed for authoritarian control.

Teachers are increasingly pressured to raise students' test results or face firing. They are told that failure to raise test scores could result in their school being closed down. Teachers thus pressure parents to take their noncompliant and bored children for medical evaluations. It is not uncommon that students' failure to do their homework can ultimately result in a prescription for Ritalin, Adderall, Vyvanse, or some other such amphetamine.

While most of us have had a few teachers whom we liked and learned some useful things from, the reality is that most learning of real value takes place outside schooling, outside of programmed instruction. People learn informally. They learn by experience. They learn by what they are surrounded with. The books that I retained knowledge from were the books I chose to read, not the ones forced on to me. How many living skills did you learn in school versus outside of it? Did you learn to get along with other people in a classroom or outside of it? Did you learn to solve problems and think critically in school or outside of it?

William Bennett, former US secretary of education under Ronald Reagan, said, "The primordial task of the schools is transmission of the social and political values." Social critic H. L. Mencken, though in agreement, was not as thrilled about this as Bennett. Half a century before Bennett, Mencken wrote that

> The aim of public education is not to spread enlightenment at all; it is simply to reduce as many individuals as possible to the same safe level, to breed and train a standardized citizenry, to put down dissent and originality. That is its aim in the United States, whatever the pretensions of politicians, pedagogues, and other such mountebanks, and that is its aim everywhere else.

It certainly makes sense that the corporatocracy would try to use schools to transmit the corporatocracy's "social and political values," as Bennett says, and "breed and train a standardized citizenry" in the words of Mencken. Members of the elite would rather a student learn in school that elections mean that a society is a democracy, but they can tolerate students learning some radical content, such as Howard Zinn's *A People's History of the United States*. The elite know that far more important than the subject matter is the actual nature of school life.

I must confess that when I taught class part-time at a private high school, the same kiss-ass kids whom I would have disliked as a student were much more likable to me as a teacher. While this was a relatively progressive school, like almost all schools it still required compliance and order, and compliant students make teachers' lives easier while noncompliant students can create stress. Noncompliant kids would become much more likable for teachers if schools could be organized differently so that compliance wasn't so important and so that kids could learn in ways that don't require them to be constantly subject to imposed authorities.

Instead, standard school teaches compliance with hierarchy, including compliance with authorities whom one does not necessarily respect. Standard schools teach passivity, as one learns that authorities get very upset by unmanageable students and will punish them. The corporatocracy desperately wants its employees to comply with their hierarchy, to passively submit to authorities regardless of respect for them, and to perform meaningless activities for a paycheck.

The vast majority of class time in most schools is spent on lectures and workbooks, both of which are turnoffs for many kids, deadening their curiosity. When people focus on what they need to memorize in order to get a good grade, they stop asking their own questions and stop pursuing their own answers. Without such curiosity, acquiring and retaining knowledge become less joyful and more painful. As school critic John Holt noted, "To a very great degree, school is a place where children learn to be stupid . . . Children come to school *curious*; within a few years most of that curiosity is dead, or at least silent."

The nature of most classrooms, regardless of the subject matter, social-izes students to be passive and directed by others, to follow orders, to take seriously the rewards and punishments of authorities, to pretend to care about things they don't care about, and that they are impotent to affect their situation.

> 66 Growing up, I was part of a program known as GT or Gifted and Talented. I was selected for advanced learning courses, and accelerated pace in addition to tons of extra-curricular activities meant to shape me into a 'Future Leader.' I ate this up and felt special. This continued for years until I began arriv-ing at answers on my own, and not using pre-scripted regurgi-tated responses . . . receiving half off on grades due to having the correct conclusion, but the wrong system for arriving at the answer. My response was always to ask if we were being taught critical thinking. Normally this would result in my being removed from a unit and placed in suspension . . . [Eventually] I became disillusioned and 'Dropped out.' 99
>
> —Dropouts, *Prison Planet*, December 17, 2009

> 66 Once a man or woman has accepted the need for school, he or she is easy prey for other institutions. Once young people have allowed their imaginations to be formed by curricular instruction, they are conditioned to institutional planning of every sort. 99
>
> —Ivan Illich, *Deschooling Society* (1970)

Nowadays, far more than when I was a kid, young people are continu-ously occupied by the demands of authorities, and they are increasingly losing their free time. A key way to break people is to deprive them of free and private time to reflect on who they are and what they truly care about. For young people today, there is often required summer reading and increasingly more homework during the school year, so students are deprived of even more time in which they could think about or read about what they choose. Some teachers require that in addition to attendance, homework, and tests, students must submit class notes, without which they risk failure. And as previously noted, teachers post students' compliance and noncompliance on Web sites for parents to see, so kids are increasingly scolded and grounded throughout the school year by terrified parents who have been told that they are bad parents if they do not do this.

American society appears willing today to do whatever it takes—more tests, more homework, more fear—to have kids succeed at school. Key ways of breaking a person include creating fear, utilizing fear to make a person more dependent on those in power, and making a person feel powerless to extricate from that which is noxious or painful. School has always done a pretty good job in these areas, but it has gotten even better at it.

> **"**I look back on my time in high school and I shudder at how much I hated it. I even loved learning, but high school DID NOT help me learn much of anything and did not help me to become a competent individual . . . School is NOT education in any real way. It does not teach one to learn on one's own. It teaches one to follow orders and to respect authority so that we can all be good citizens and good employees not by being intelligent and educated individuals who are competent to think for themselves and make decisions, but to be docile and follow orders without asking for change.**"**
>
> —JoshuaLudd, *AlterNet*, January 28, 2008

A teacher can lecture about democracy, but schools are essentially undemocratic places, and so democracy is not what is instilled in students. Schools, for example, do not teach young people to assert their rights in any way that authorities will take seriously. School critic and author Jonathan Kozol was a student at an elite prep school and at Harvard, where he came to conclude, "Children come to realize, early in their school careers, the terrible danger to their own success in statements that give voice to strong intensities . . . Above all, they learn how to tone down, cushion and absorb each serious form of realistic confrontation." In his book *The Night Is Dark and I Am Far from Home*, Kozol focuses on how school breaks us from courageous actions through a series of disconnections. He observes that teachers inform us that "it is our obligation to obey our orders and to channel our dissent into innocuous patterns of polite 'discussion and investigation.'" Instead of direct action, Kozol explains how our schools, especially elitist institutions, teach us a kind of "inert concern" in which "caring"—in and of itself and without risking the consequences of actual action—is "ethical." School teaches us that we are "moral and mature" if we politely assert our concerns, but the essence of school—its demand for compliance—teaches us not to act in a friction-causing manner.

Colleges and universities? For most young people, these institutions are a major upgrade over high school in the sense of less class time, more freedom from parents, and easy partying. But with college classes of five hundred or more students, and many professors who never know their students' names, colleges are also introducing young people to the impersonal bureaucracy of modern life. And today, US colleges and universities have increasingly become places where young people are acquiring degree credentials that are badges of compliance for corporate employers in exchange for learning to accept bureaucratic domination and crushing debt.

Noncompliance as a Mental Illness

> **"**I was a teenager back in the early 80s. I spent a couple weeks in a mental hospital then. (I had punched the window in my bedroom.) Funny thing. Almost none of the other kids there had typical mental disorders such as schizophrenia or depression. Almost all the teens had been locked up (we were not free to leave the institution) basically because they had rebelled against their parents. We were all treated as if we were 'bad' kids. And, yes, most of these kids were given meds for what 'diseases' inflicted them.**"**
>
> –QQOblivion, *AlterNet*, January 28, 2008

66I rue the day when I went to a psychiatrist and thus began the guessing game and experimentation that is psychiatry . . . You can get labeled something different every time depending on the practitioner and the time of day and have a fist full of the corresponding drugs thrown at you. Now since you've been labeled you don't have the luxury of refusing or you're 'non-compliant.' And if you don't want to walk 'lock step' with this theory you get relegated to the periphery of society. It's the equivalent of being labeled a witch . . . only they don't take your life, they take everything else.99

—Marsha36, *AlterNet*, January 28, 2008

66Today the function of psychiatry, psychology and psychoanalysis threatens to become the tool in the manipulation of man. The specialists in this field tell you what the 'normal' person is, and, correspondingly, what is wrong with you; they devise the methods to help you adjust, be happy, be normal.99

—Erich Fromm, *The Sane Society* (1955)

Psychiatrists, psychologists, social workers, and other mental health professionals are trained to help people adjust to their environment—not to help people rebel against it. Prior to the 1980s, well-known and highly respected mental health professionals such as Erich Fromm (1900–1980) were concerned about this focus on "adjustment" with no focus on exactly what people were adjusting to.

Today, some mental health professionals view themselves as "rebellious" for questioning the proliferation of drug treatments. However, the essential confrontation for Fromm was not about psychiatric drugs per se (though he would certainly be sad that so many Americans, especially children, are prescribed psychotropic drugs in order to fit into inhospitable environments). Fromm's essential confrontation was directed at *all* mental health professionals—including nonprescribers such as psychologists, social workers, and counselors—who merely assist patients in adjusting to society and fail to validate their patients' alienation from society. Fromm observed, "Yet many psychiatrists and psychologists refuse to entertain the idea that society as a whole may be lacking in sanity."

In the "adjust and be happy" sense, there is commonality among all mainstream mental health professionals, whether they are drug prescribers, behavior-modification advocates, or even some "alternative" proponents. Though their competing programs may vary, they are often similar in that they instruct people on how to adjust, be happy, and be normal within our social and economic system.

From my experience, Fromm's observation that many Americans with emotional difficulties are simply alienated from their surroundings continues to be accurate. For Fromm, "An unhealthy society is one which creates mutual hostility [and] distrust, which transforms man into an instrument of use and exploitation for others, which deprives him of a sense of self, except inasmuch as he submits to others or becomes an automaton." Fromm viewed American society as an increasingly unhealthy one in which people routinely experience painful alienation that fuels emotional and behavioral difficulties.

Those comfortably atop societal hierarchies have difficulty recognizing that many American institutions promote helplessness, passivity, boredom, fear, isolation, and dehumanization for those who are not at the top. Those who benefit from the status quo have difficulty recognizing that many human beings feel alienated from one-size-fits-all schools, monotonous workplaces, and giant bureaucracies. Many people feel alienated from impersonal institutions that promote manipulative relationships rather than respectful ones, machine efficiency rather than human dignity, authoritarian hierarchies rather than participatory democracy, disconnectedness rather than community, and helplessness rather than empowerment.

It has been my experience that mental health professionals are schooled to equate a lack of adjustment with mental illness, and not to question the wisdom of fostering compliance with the status quo. This became especially clear in 1980 when the American Psychiatric Association created and installed in its diagnostic bible (the DSM) a new official mental disorder called oppositional defiant disorder (ODD).

ODD is not as widely known as other psychiatric disorders, and so when I mention it to people outside the mental health profession, they sometimes think I'm being sarcastic. ODD is in fact an official—and increasingly popular—diagnosis for children and teenagers. Young people diagnosed with ODD are often not doing anything illegal (illegal behaviors are a symptom of another listed disorder called conduct disorder). ODD is defined as "a pattern of negativistic, hostile, and defiant behavior." Some of the official symptoms of ODD are: "often actively defies or refuses to comply with adult requests or rules," "often argues with adults," "often touchy or easily annoyed by others," "often angry and resentful," and "often deliberately does things to annoy other people."

A 2009 *Psychiatric Times* article titled "ADHD & ODD: Confronting the Challenges of Disruptive Behavior" states: "Disruptive behavior is the most common mental health problem seen by pediatricians." *Disruptive Disorders*—that's the title on brochures I often receive that are advertising continuing education seminars. In mainstream mental health, opposition defiant disorder, conduct disorder, and attention deficit hyperactivity disorder are all viewed as "disruptive disorders."

By today's standards, Saul Alinsky (1909–1972), the legendary organizer and author of *Reveille for Radicals* and *Rules for Radicals*, would have been diagnosed with one or more disruptive disorders. Recalling his childhood, Alinsky said, "I never thought of walking on the grass until I saw a sign saying 'Keep off the grass.' Then I would stomp all over it." Alinsky also recalls a time when he was ten or eleven and his rabbi was tutoring him in Hebrew:

> One particular day I read three pages in a row without any errors in pronunciation, and suddenly a penny fell onto the Bible . . . Then the next day the rabbi turned up and he told me to start reading. And I wouldn't; I just sat there in silence, refusing to read. He asked me why I was so quiet, and I said, "This time it's a nickel or nothing." He threw back his arm and slammed me across the room . . . It wasn't defiance so much as curiosity in action, which seems to others to be defiance.

For more than twenty-five years, I have spent time with children and teenagers previously labeled with disruptive disorders, especially ODD. My experience has been that ODD-diagnosed young people can be obnoxious with adults whom they do not respect or whom they feel do not like them. In every case that I have seen in which parents, teachers, or other authorities have lost the respect or affection of these kids, there is a reason, often obvious ones such as these adults' dishonesty, lack of authenticity, hypocrisy, cowardice, selfishness, tantrums, and other childish behavior. Young people are always judging whether an adult should be taken seriously or not, and these ODD kids don't take many adults in their lives seriously because they judge few adults to be honest, authentic, unselfish, sensible, and capable of dealing with their emotions maturely. However, it has also been my experience that almost all of these ODD-labeled young people can be a delight with adults whom they do respect and whom they feel like them.

There are commonsense ways to transform disrespectful relationships, but many standard treatments used on ODD kids focus only on creating greater compliance, and most of these treatments are experienced by kids as quite coercive. What happens to human beings when they are coerced into complying with an authority whom they don't respect? Depending on temperament, there are different reactions. Some people actively rebel. Even more common is some type of passive defiance, and so there are several diagnoses in the DSM that I would consider passive rebellions.

Passive aggression is one of many nondisease explanations for attention deficit hyperactivity disorder (ADHD). What better way to get back at an adult who is perceived as always critical and never enthusiastic than to exasperate that adult by not paying attention? Studies show that most ADHD-diagnosed children will pay attention to activities that they enjoy or that they have chosen. In other words, when ADHD-labeled kids are having a good time and in control, the "disease" routinely goes away.

The assumption by mainstream professionals is that children have a disorder if they only pay attention to what they like and if they are only manageable in environments that they find enjoyable. Is *mental health* really tantamount to a capacity to pay attention and be manageable in undesirable environments?

There are other passive rebellions against authority that have been psychopathologized. I have talked to many people who earlier in their lives had been diagnosed with substance abuse and depression who in fact had been reacting with a kind of disorganized resistance to the demands of an oppressive environment.

Disruptive young people labeled with ADHD who are medicated with Ritalin, Adderall, and other amphetamines often report that these drugs make them "care less" about their boredom, resentments, and other negative emotions, thus making them more compliant and manageable. An April 2008 report from the market research firm Datamonitor on ADHD drugs stated: "US dominates the ADHD market with a 94 percent market share."

So-called atypical antipsychotics such as Zyprexa and Risperdal— powerful tranquilizing drugs—are increasingly prescribed to disruptive young Americans. A generation ago, antipsychotics were used only for those very few extremely disturbed people, and the antipsychotic industry was a tiny one. But today, thanks in large part to the expanding use of these drugs to control disruptive children, *Pharmacy Times* reported that in the United States in 2009, "Antipsychotics were the highest grossing class of medications, with sales of $14.6 billion." Among children receiving antipsychotic drugs, according to the *Journal of the American Medical Association* in 2010, many have nonpsychotic diagnoses of ADHD, ODD, or some other disruptive behavior disorder (this is especially true of Medicaid-covered pediatric patients).

> 66 Drugging our children into conformity in order to train them to acquiesce to the institutional management system is an important strategy in 'breaking' the wild out of the people. 99
> —Ren H, *thomhartmann.com*, December 14, 2009

> 66 Semi-coma, anyone? Used to be in the 'Old Days,' children were dropped in front of the television set, soon developing

> a life-long process of dumbing down and tuning out; a form
> of social control and parental sloth and irresponsibility. Now
> today, with the ever increasing authoritarian emphasis in our
> culture and thanks to Big Pharma, we have the neuro-chemical
> resources at hand, to put children and teens into semi-comas. **"**
>
> —wilty, *AlterNet*, January 29, 2008

Some people are so uncomfortable with any tension produced by conflict that they comply with any authority. Such children are unlikely to get into trouble with teachers. These are *not* the kids whom teachers "suggest" need to be taken for a medical evaluation. Actually, because they are more comfortable in standardized institutions, these are the children who are more likely to become teachers, psychiatrists, or psychologists.

One of the lessons I did learn in my professional training was just how extraordinarily compliant the majority of mental health professionals are. Moreover, they are often unaware of how extremely obedient they are. Gaining acceptance into graduate school or medical school and achieving a PhD or MD means jumping through many meaningless hoops, all of which require much behavioral, attentional, and emotional compliance to authorities, even those authorities that one lacks respect for.

On more than one occasion in my training to be a psychologist I was informed that I had "issues with authorities," and I had mixed feelings about being so labeled. On the one hand, I found it quite flattering. I had in my youth considered myself, at least compared with many other kids in my neighborhood, relatively compliant. After all, I had done my homework, studied, received good grades, and never had any legal problems. However, while this "issues with authorities" label made me grin because I was now being seen as a "bad boy," it also very much concerned me. Specifically, if they were labeling someone such as myself with "authority issues," what were they calling the kids I grew up with who were far more noncompliant with disrespected authorities but quite enjoyable with everyone else?

Roland Chrisjohn is a psychologist and a professor in the Native Studies Department at St. Thomas University, and he is also an Oneida of the Iroquois Nation. He says, "Protect me from my 'friends.'" What does he mean? He explains that while his enemies on the right murdered indigenous Americans to steal their land, Indians' so-called liberal friends forced assimilation through boarding schools that prohibited the use of tribal languages and customs, which made it easier to divide and conquer—and then "legally" rip them off. While the right favored massacres and were fond of saying, "The only good Indian is a dead Indian," the liberals preferred "curing" indigenous Americans and came up with sayings like, "Kill the Indian to save the child."

When I publicly question the wisdom of prescribing drugs to kids in order to get them to be manageable in a classroom, I get superficially different but essentially the same reactions from self-identified conservatives and liberals.

The conservative reacts, "Yeah, these kids don't need medication. They need their parents to get tough with them and show them who's boss. These teachers have their hands tied by liberals. Too much coddling has ruined America."

The liberal reacts, "While I agree that some children are incorrectly diagnosed and improperly medicated, my son was getting F's in school until he was prescribed Ritalin, and now he is headed for college."

No doubt both whippings and drugs can be effective in inducing compliance. However, similar to America's liberal-conservative "Indian problem" debate, something is missing from the liberal-conservative "problem child" debate. What's missing is the possibility that nothing is essentially wrong with these kids. What's missing is the possibility that they simply don't fit into the dominant culture. What's missing is the possibility that perhaps there is something admirable about these young people's rebellion against authoritarian hierarchies and manipulative relationships. The good news is that some parents do "get it" and are able to have happier families.

    "daughter labeled with ODD, ADD, Conduct Disorder . . . refused to ever medicate her . . . kicked out of high school for all 3 at 16 . . . now = incredible mom of 3 boys, dream husband,

own nice home . . . is an RN and going to grad school . . . she still
does have tongue piercing and tattoos but her husband does
too . . . what the schools wanted to do to her when she was
younger would have killed her spirit and made her a zombie
for life . . . now those 'labels' are a family badge of honor!!!"

—ellie, *AlterNet*, January 28, 2008

Two ways of subduing defiance are to criminalize it and to pathologize it, and US history is replete with examples of both. In the same era
that John Adams's Sedition Act criminalized criticism of US governmental policy, Dr. Benjamin Rush, the father of American psychiatry
(his image adorns the American Psychiatric Association seal), pathologized anti-authoritarianism. Dr. Rush diagnosed those rebelling against
a centralized federal authority as having an "excess of the passion for
liberty" that "constituted a form of insanity," and he labeled this illness
"anarchia." Throughout American history, both direct and indirect
resistance to authority has been pathologized. In an 1851 article in the
New Orleans Medical and Surgical Journal, Louisiana physician Samuel
Cartwright reported his discovery of "drapetomania," the disease that
caused slaves to flee captivity. Dr. Cartwright also reported his discovery of "dysaesthesia aethiopis," a disease that caused slaves to break,
waste, and destroy property and generally pay insufficient attention to
the master's needs.

In every generation there will be elitists and authoritarians, and there
will also be genuine anti-authoritarians who are so pained by exploitative
hierarchies that they take action. While it is unusual in American history
for these anti-authoritarians to take the kind of effective direct action
that inspires others to successfully revolt, every once in a while a Tom
Paine or Saul Alinsky comes along. So authoritarians take no chances.
They criminalize anti-authoritarianism, pathologize it, market drugs to
"cure" it, and financially intimidate those who might buck the system.

An anti-authoritarian nightmare is that every would-be Tom Paine
and Saul Alinsky gets diagnosed as a youngster with mental illness and is
quieted with a lifelong regimen of chill pills. Preventing that nightmare

from coming true is a major reason for my involvement in mental health treatment reform.

Elitism Training

The assumption of many afflicted Americans that a PhD psychologist is an elitist is not without merit. I may have grown up in a working-class neighborhood, but I was certainly trained as a professional to be an elitist. I was socialized to view people with little formal schooling as being "uneducated" rather than simply "unschooled." And I was socialized to believe that learning in a classroom via a textbook and a professor is superior to more informal experiences. My great luck was that I quickly discovered that the information I was receiving from authorities in my training was of dubious value, and that made it especially easy to question the entire elitist socialization process.

In graduate school, for instance, I received training in administering, scoring, and evaluating intelligence tests, and I immediately noticed that these IQ tests excluded a good part of what I considered intelligence. On the most respected IQ tests, there were no tasks that assessed someone's ability to read between the lines, see truth beyond obfuscation, and detect bullshit. I also noticed that a quick wit and a sense of humor—which I had always associated with intelligence—were in no way measured by IQ tests. And interpersonal intelligence (for example, one's capacity to perceive and use nonverbal forms of communication) was also not measured on these IQ tests. It was clear to me that the status of a high IQ was granted for the kinds of mental abilities that more measured one's ability to adapt to the status quo rather than to challenge it.

Similarly, I noticed in my training that people who were stubborn, shy, or more pained by life's realities were far more likely to get a mental illness diagnosis than those who were compliant, extroverted, or Pollyannaish. The status of "mental health" was more often awarded to those who caused the fewest problems for the societal status quo, and the labels of "disorder" or "mental illness" were more often assigned to those whose personality traits created problems for the status quo.

I am not the only former psychology major who had some doubts about the value of academic psychology. Jon Stewart in a 2007 *Daily Show* interview was rough on Tal Ben-Shahar, who teaches positive psychology at Harvard and had written a self-help book. Stewart told him, "I am a psychology major, so I know a lot of it is bullshit." Stewart, no anti-intellectual, is clearly an anti-pseudointellectual, and he mocked the scientific-sounding jargon so often used by psychologists to create the illusion that psychologists have something special to offer. This use of insider jargon makes psychologists no different from many other professionals who also need to justify their paycheck.

When I attended graduate school in clinical psychology, the now quite conventional common sense of *cognitive psychology* was considered a radical shift from *behaviorism*, which had dogmatically focused only on *observable events*. The cognitive "revolution" was that although you cannot see people's thoughts, people actually do think, and those thoughts affect our emotions. Was this a new discovery or simply a rediscovery of basic common sense? Another hot field for a time was *interpersonal psychotherapy*, which declared that how people act toward other people creates reactions in other people, which in turn will affect them. I recall one professor trying to make this stuff into a big deal. He wrote on the blackboard the word *friendly* next to an arrow pointed to another *friendly*, and then he wrote the word *hostile* next to an arrow pointed at another *hostile*. I raised my hand and stated that this reminded me of an episode of *Laverne & Shirley* in which Laverne was being mean and Shirley told her, "Laverne, remember nice gets nice." Again, obvious truisms were being elevated by jargon or abstruse presentation.

It seemed to me that many "discoveries" by psychologists were really common sense buried by previous generations of psychologists. So if Jon Stewart meant by *bullshit* the substitution of jargon for basic common sense in order to provide the illusion of special expertise, then I'd have to agree with him.

Transforming knowledge that could be shared easily through simple language into something esoteric accessible only by the elite is antidemocratic in its nature. This kind of elitism, like any elitism, creates a hostile backlash, and so there are many people who reflexively mock any psychologist's explanations as "psychobabble." A contempt for pseudo-intellectual elitism can also lead some people to distrust those who possess advanced degrees out of hand even when such people are saying something worth hearing—this is one of the many reasons that an extraordinary number of Americans reject real scientific knowledge.

People with expertise in a specific area who don't see themselves as entitled to any special prestige and who help others in their community gain greater expertise, self-respect, and self-confidence are good for democracy. They are quite different from elitists who are granted authority and prestige based on certain credentials and not on any real expertise or wisdom and who actually undermine self-respect, self-confidence, and community.

Becoming an elitist encourages identification and loyalty toward a system of hierarchy and elitism as the natural way of life, a system that claims it is reasonable for people to be dependent on experts and not themselves to solve problems in their community.

There is an understandable resentment for elitists who undermine rather than assist people's own capacity to solve problems and who insidiously subvert community. Community activist John McKnight points out in his book *The Careless Society* that for there to be genuine democracy, there must be genuine community in which citizens themselves—and not elitist authorities—claim the power to decide what is actually a problem and how to solve it, and who then themselves implement solutions.

The low regard that many Americans have for mental health professionals is caused, I believe, only in part by ill-mannered, know-it-all, exploitative television psychiatrists and psychologists. At a deeper level, there is distrust for professionals who claim to promote mental health but in practice attempt to modify, manipulate, and medicate people to adjust to institutions regardless of how dehumanizing and undemocratic these environments are.

What then should a psychologist who actually wants to contribute to a truly democratic movement do? Populist historian Lawrence Goodwyn tells us the following about individual self-respect and collective self-confidence: "Their development permits people to conceive of the idea of acting in self-generated democratic ways—as distinct from passively participating in various hierarchical modes bequeathed by the received culture." So psychologists—as well as teachers, clergy, journalists, parents, and others who care about a genuinely democratic movement—should be searching for answers to the following questions: *What can I do to increase my own self-respect and that of people whom I have contact with? What can I do to increase collective confidence that it is possible to attain power and create genuine democracy?* Those are the questions that I will attempt to answer in chapter 4.

Liars, Hypocrites, Egomaniacs, and the Corporate Media

This is a book about unifying Americans who genuinely want democracy. That means overcoming conflicts among a very large and diverse group. But it also means not getting distracted, divided, and defeated by liars, egomaniacs, and hypocrites.

When I was fourteen years old in 1970, the Vietnam War continued to rage, and I began to worry about the draft. I felt the fears of the older guys in my neighborhood, and I began worrying about what my lottery number would be when I became eligible. It did not seem to me that the war would end anytime soon, and that turned out to be correct. It was obvious to me that there were distant authorities who didn't care about me. They didn't care if I lost my legs or got killed, and maybe they would even be happy if I became a prisoner of war because then I would be one more excuse to stay in the war. That's what I thought at the time, and that reality frightened and enraged me. It told me how little power I had over what could happen to me.

I remember thinking that it wasn't just Richard Nixon, Spiro Agnew, the Republicans, and the conservatives who didn't care about me. It was also the Democrats, elitist intellectuals, and even some of the so-called radicals, at least the clownish and violent ones who were on television.

Even fourteen-year-old kids knew it was the Democrats who had gotten us into the Vietnam War. Before Nixon, it was Democratic president

Lyndon Baines Johnson—"Hey, hey, LBJ, how many kids did you kill today?"—who had escalated the war. When I was sixteen, I read David Halberstam's *The Best and the Brightest* about Ivy League elitist Democrat and Republican advisers who thought they were the "best and the brightest" but who were arrogant liars, especially Defense Secretary Robert McNamara, whom I began to despise as much as I despised Richard Nixon and Henry Kissinger.

I remember thinking that many Democratic and Republican politicians and their elitist advisers were liars. Nixon lied about a secret plan to end the Vietnam War, then he lied about bombing Cambodia, and he had a face that looked like it lied far more than it told the truth. Johnson lied about the Gulf of Tonkin, a major reason that the Vietnam War expanded, and he also had a liar's face. But American adults had elected them both to be president, and this made me afraid that becoming an adult meant that one lost the ability to see and smell out liars.

I also remember seeing on television the Yippies, who seemed to enjoy their clownish radical identity. These Yippies did tell some truths; however, what my young eyes saw in them was thirty-year-old men creating havoc to gain attention for themselves. I remember thinking that the Yippies weren't stupid, and anybody knew that the way they got attention frightened many Americans so much that they wanted only "law and order." One of the Yippie founders later became a Yuppie businessman. The other Yippie founder later seemed to actually care more about justice than getting attention, became quite pained, and committed suicide.

Even worse than the clownish attention-seeking radicals were the violent ego trippers such as the Weathermen. It was clear to me as a kid that the Weathermen didn't care about the fact that they were destroying unity among those resisting the war in particular and the corporatocracy in general, most directly by destroying Students for a Democratic Society, the largest and most powerful student organization in American history genuinely committed to democracy. Even as a teenager I could see that the Weathermen's violent tactics were exactly what the corporatocracy could exploit to terrorize Americans and push them toward authoritarianism. The Weathermen were not nineteen-year-olds who could be excused for fantasizing about being the next Che Guevara. They were over thirty, and if I as a teenager knew the outcome of their tactics in the United States, they had to know and not care.

Today Americans utilizing violent tactics against the US government are more likely to be right-wing militia groups rather than leftist groups. Whether left, right, domestic, or foreign, such violent tactics are welcome news for the corporatocracy. The corporatocracy knows that these small groups are no real threat to its power but provide justification for more money for security and military industries and greater authoritarian controls.

For at least two reasons, the corporate media routinely covers anti-corporate activists who are more egotistically attached to their own name-recognition advancement than they are to meaningfully promoting genuine democracy. First, egomaniacs tend to be more colorful, bizarre, and possibly even violent—and those characteristics get good ratings. Second, the corporate elite know that egomaniacs will use reckless tactics designed more to receive attention than to achieve actual victory; the resulting failures and negative public reaction are victories for the corpo-ratocracy that diminish the collective self-confidence of the rest of us.

There are, across the liberal-conservative political spectrum, hypo-critical elitists who do not practice what they preach. I grew up in a Queens, New York City, neighborhood called Arverne in the Rockaways. The neighborhood was composed mostly of Italian Americans, Irish Americans, Greek Americans, Puerto Rican Americans, African Americans, and Jewish Americans. Nobody in Arverne and its adjacent communities of Edgemere and Hammels was rich or even upper middle class. Most were working class; some were financially impoverished. Poor people lived in what we called the "projects," and there were a few large ones. The limousine liberals, living in wealthy neighborhoods without any projects, decided that since my neighborhood already had a few large low-income projects, then it would be a fine place to build more. There were no wealthy people in our neighborhoods with the power to stop it, and so more projects were built. This tipped the balance, and these limousine liberal elitists turned my neighborhood into a slum. The liberal elite preached that opposition to these projects was racism. There were some racists in my neighborhood, as there are in every neighborhood, but I remember that the opposition to building more projects came from *all* racial and ethnic groups. No racial or ethnic group wanted our neighborhood turned into a slum, as had happened to so many other neighborhoods in New York City. So I learned early in life that there are all kinds of elitists who could cause me all kinds of grief.

On the right, hypocritical elitists include *chickenhawks*, politicians, and pundits who support wars and military interventions but who actively avoided military service when of age, and *neocon con men*, who exploit the ideas of liberty and patriotism to justify wars that benefit elite interests. Across the political spectrum, there are elitists who see themselves as superior to the masses and use appealing ideas to advance their own ends.

The corporate media paints political engagement as a battle of Democrats versus Republicans, liberals versus conservatives, natives versus immigrants, whites versus blacks, extremists versus moderates, and so forth. The net effect of the corporate media's depiction of political activism is to (1) divide powerless people into teams that are frightened of or enraged by one another; (2) create cynicism that all activists are liars, egomaniacs, and hypocrites; (3) make people apathetic about political engagement; and (4) create helplessness, defeatism, and fatalism.

Though the corporate media will always give liars, egomaniacs, and hypocrites a great deal of attention, the rest of us shouldn't bother. The good news is that most people—unlike these liars, egomaniacs, and hypocrites—do care about frightened fourteen-year-olds.

The US Electoral System and Learned Helplessness

> "The Obama presidency has, for me, created the ultimate state of learned helplessness . . . In reality, the Dem party gave us two choices at the outset: Hillary and Barack. Hillary ran around campaigning about obliterating Iran and forcing people to buy health insurance and about a dozen other things that made her unacceptable. Obama made it through

the primaries, won the election and continued Bush's legacy on just about every front. We really are helpless. We have no representation."

—FiveGoodMen, *Democratic Underground*, December 14, 2009

"The problem is that progressives have been suckered, and suckered again, just like Lucy always suckers Charlie Brown. She promises to let him kick the football. Then she yanks it away just as he's swinging his foot. Why do the so-called 'progressive' politicians do that to us? They're corrupt. They say the progressive words. But they vote for special interests . . . Just about everything the Democrats do is aimed at talking a moderate progressive talk, but walking a corrupt special-interest-serving walk . . . Yes, We Can . . . be fooled, over and over."

—Urgelt, *AlterNet*, January 7, 2010

Do US national elections promote learned helplessness? Polls show that the majority of Americans reject corporate control and unnecessary wars, but do Americans really have any influence over this at the voting booth?

When the Republicans win, Americans get senseless wars and corporate control. When the Democrats win, Americans get senseless wars and corporate control. When Americans vote for an independent party such as the Green Party, which opposes unnecessary wars and corporate control, either the Democrats or the Republicans still win, and Americans get senseless wars and corporate control.

There is of course a fourth choice—not voting at all. That's the choice for 40 to 50 percent of Americans in presidential elections (and even more in off-years when the presidency is not contested). Not voting doesn't change the fact that the Democrats or Republicans still win, resulting in senseless wars and corporate control.

The bottom line—and many Americans get this—is that regardless of what we do or don't do in the election booth, we continue to get senseless wars and corporate control. So US presidential and congressional elections are, in effect, an experiment of sorts in learned helplessness. Learned helplessness means believing that no matter what one does or does not do, one cannot decrease one's level of pain.

An abused child thinks, *Stay at home and get beaten, or run away and be out in the cold and die.* An abused prostitute/sex worker may believe, *Stay and my pimp beats me, or leave and he will find me and beat me even worse.* Critically thinking progressives think, *Vote for the Democrats and I get empty talk, senseless wars, corporate control, and pain. Vote for the Greens, and I may help put a Republican in office and get all the pain of the Democrats plus some extra pain.* Critically thinking libertarians think, *Vote for the libertarians, and I will put a Democrat in office and get all the pain of Republicans plus some extra pain.* Or we all may think, *Don't vote at all, and get the pain of a Republican or a Democrat, plus the pain of self-righteous voters trying to shame me and tell me I have no right to complain.*

> 66 Nothing new: By design, we've always been broken. Without direct democracy (and its own flaws), the people can never directly control their country's destiny, and therefore, we've always been mostly helpless, except for the very few mass movements that effected some real change in our history. 99
> —Stevietheman, *AlterNet*, December 13, 2009

For many Americans, the Democratic-Republican contest is analogous to World Wrestling Federation matches, with fake public posturing of animosity between opponents who really care only about money continuing to flow into their industry. That's the view of former professional wrestler and Minnesota governor Jesse Ventura. Are elections in the United States and other elitist societies contests that create the illusion of democracy but are in reality completely meaningless?

The problem for people's psyches is that US national elections are not *completely* meaningless. While the corporate elite can financially control national elections with respect to any issue that the corporatocracy truly cares about—such as maintaining high corporate profits and a long-term ability to manage the system—there are issues that the corporatocracy doesn't care about that are important to people's lives. Issues that don't involve corporate moneymaking and power are issues that the corporatocracy is quite happy to hand over to the public, which then breaks out into divided camps of mutual distrust. These issues include abortion, same-sex marriage, and other civil rights concerns.

There are also differences between the Democrats and Republicans in regard to the alleviation of some suffering—for example, the extension of unemployment benefits—and this too makes it difficult for people to walk away from elections. If it was true that there were absolutely no differences between what the Democratic and Republican Parties stand for, the issue of participation in elections would be a far easier one. Instead, election participation has some similarities (though it is clearly not the same) to the plight of people stuck in abusive relationships in which there is usually some understandable reason—often a financial one—to remain in it despite the fact that one is losing self-respect in the process.

It's easy for an outsider to tell an abused wife with small children and no immediate means of economic support to walk away from her marriage; and it's easy for people whose suffering is unaffected by an issue that an election can actually decide to urge others not to vote because participating in national elections maintains the illusion of real democracy. In both cases, compassion and wisdom don't always come easily. In chapter 5, I will offer some solutions to this complex conundrum surrounding voting.

While the people of the United States have always recognized it was an uphill fight to defeat the elite, they have not always felt it was hopeless. And it hasn't always felt to so many people that there is so little difference between the Democratic and Republican Parties in terms of corporate control and unnecessary wars.

> Who demands a standing army? Is it the poor man as he goes
> about his work, or is it the capitalist who wants that army to
> supplement the local government in protecting his property
> when he enters into a contest with employes? [sic]

Was that Karl Marx? Anarchist Emma Goldman? Socialist Eugene Debs? No, these are the words of William Jennings Bryan (in 1894), who was the Democratic Party presidential candidate in 1896, then again in 1900 and 1908. Each time Bryan was hugely outspent and defeated by a Republican candidate. This was an era when the corporatocracy owned only one of the two major political parties.

In his biography of William Jennings Bryan, *A Godly Hero*, Michael Kazin reports that in 1896, Bryan urged wage earners not simply to look at the size of their paycheck but to understand that the real evil was a corporate system that was, as he put it, "condemning the boys of this country to perpetual clerkship." A month before the 1896 election, Bryan's message of hope was, "The day will come when corporations will cease to consider themselves greater than the Government which created them."

In that 1896 presidential election, 79 percent of all those eligible to vote actually voted, with a 90 percent turnout in the most contested regions. Following Bryan's second presidential bid defeat, Kazin notes that despair among his supporters set in: "The frustrating campaign of 1900 and its demoralizing conclusion struck loyal Bryanites as a sign that the republic was in deeper trouble than they had realized. A majority of Americans seemed content to live in an imperial nation dominated by trusts, whether or not they actively supported Republican politics."

William Jennings Bryan and his Democratic Party had deep flaws, especially with respect to civil rights, but they did stand for something very different from corporate control and unnecessary wars. When the Republican-corporate partnership narrowly defeated Bryan in 1896— twice again more convincingly—this sucked the life out of the movement that had backed him. From that point forward, for huge numbers of people committed to genuine democracy, it appeared that they may never again have a candidate who opposed corporate control and unnecessary wars—and who also had a chance to win. At best, a candidate might come along who would mitigate some of the suffering caused by the corporatocracy, but the idea of acquiring real power began to die. One can certainly debate whether or not Bryan would have sold out to corporate control had he won, but there is no debate that back in 1896 anti-elitists were not at all hopeless—they believed that they could vote in a genuine democracy.

I have attempted to describe those institutions and those aspects of our culture that are especially striking to me in creating a passive, unengaged, and demoralized US population and that have subverted the individual self-respect and collective self-confidence necessary for a genuinely democratic mass movement. There are, however, other forces contributing to this quandary. To repeat Ralph Waldo Emerson's astute observation: "All our things are right and wrong together. The wave of evil washes all our institutions alike."

Energy to Do Battle

Liberation Psychology, Individual Self-Respect,
and Collective Self-Confidence

Genuine democracy can happen only if enough people believe in it, are capable of fighting for it, and are willing to fight for it. These people must believe that they are worthy of power. The belief in their worthiness comes when, at an individual level, there is genuine self-respect.

There are many battlefields on which individual self-respect can be either be won or lost, and it is in the interest of the elite to make sure that their opponents lose sight of these multiple battlefields. The family, the classroom, and many of the ordinary events of our day are battlefields of self-respect. If we don't know that we're on a battlefield, there is little chance of winning the battle, and we can lose multiple opportunities to be activists for democracy.

People seeking democracy, in addition to having individual self-respect, must also have collective self-confidence—the belief that they can succeed as a group—if their goal is to be achieved and sustained. They must have faith that, though imperfect in their decision making, they are capable of creating a freer and more just society than one organized and controlled by the elite.

Thus, in this war, human relationships are vitally important. It is in the interest of the elite to keep people divided and to keep them distrusting one another. It is in the interest of people working toward democracy to build respectful and cooperative human relationships across all levels of society.

When one understands that the battle for democracy begins with the battle to restore individual self-respect and collective self-confidence, one then sees the entire society and culture replete with battlefields in which such self-respect and collective confidence can be won or lost.

Some people, including many progressives, are uncomfortable with the term *battlefield*, as they are much more comfortable with the language of cooperation and harmony than with that of competition and friction. However, if there is an adversary aimed at subduing us, we are de-skilling and disempowering ourselves if we do not become more comfortable with this other language. Some of us have gotten this:

Change means movement. Movement means friction. Only in the frictionless vacuum of a nonexistent abstract world can movement or change occur without that abrasive friction of conflict. —*Saul Alinsky*

Those who profess to freedom and yet deprecate agitation are men who want crops without plowing. They want rain without thunder and lightning. They want the ocean without the awful roar of its many waters. This struggle may be a moral one, or it may be physical, but it must be a struggle. Power concedes nothing without a demand. It never did and it never will. —*Frederick Douglass*

Nobody can give you freedom. Nobody can give you equality or justice or anything. If you're a man, you take it. —*Malcolm X*

Take it easy, but take it. —*Woody Guthrie (and Studs Terkel sign-off)*

Critical Thinking and Morale

Strategies, tactics, and an understanding of your enemy, your allies, and the terrain are important, but without morale it is difficult to win any war. With morale, people can take actions that restore individual self-respect, and they can start the road back to regain collective self-confidence.

What exactly is morale? General George C. Marshall stated, "Morale is the state of mind. It is steadfastness and courage and hope. It is confidence and zeal and loyalty. It is élan, esprit de corps and determination." How important is morale? General (and then President) Dwight D. Eisenhower believed, "Morale is the greatest single factor in successful wars."

In war, morale is a huge issue, but of course it's not the only one. The elite's money—and the influence that it buys—is an extremely powerful weapon. So it's understandable that so many people who are defeated and demoralized focus on their lack of money rather than on their lack of morale. However, we must keep in mind that in war, *especially* when one's side lacks financial resources, morale becomes even more crucial.

In athletics, most coaches and their players know that morale can trump superior skills. They know that while overconfidence can cost a team humility, discipline, and victory, underconfidence can lead to demoralization and avoidable defeat. Coaches and players are constantly focusing on morale, telling themselves and one another everything possible to maintain and regain energizing confidence.

Similar to people in the military and athletics, there are many business-people who value morale. I have known many business managers who obsess on how to maintain their own morale and that of their employees. These managers know that to maintain morale, employees must believe that their contributions, their ideas, and they themselves are valued. For morale, employees must perceive that they have a certain status within an organization, and that their organization has a certain status in society. And so high-level managers try to create these perceptions—whether or not they are actually true.

Some people cringe when I bring up the issue of morale. They equate the term *morale* with being Pollyannaish and the absence of critical thinking. After he read an article of mine, Gerald Iversen e-mailed me with some advice:

> As one involved in progressive social change for 35 years, I find your solution of "morale" too smiley-faced . . . I urge you to read *Bright-Sided* by Barbara Ehrenreich.

I am a fan of Barbara Ehrenreich, and I agree with what she says in *Bright-Sided*. Blaming *all* misery on a lack of a positive attitude is wrong and often heartless. Ehrenreich is absolutely right that it is cruel, and plainly false, to tell people that they got cancer—or didn't go into remission—because they weren't positive enough. And it is similarly untrue and damaging to tell people that they are not wealthy because they weren't positive enough. However, such silly, smiley-faced positive thinking is not the same as morale. With Ehrenreich's roots in the working class and union organizing, she would know that morale can mean the difference in organizing a union and in winning a strike. She would know of Joe Hill, who wrote songs precisely to keep up the morale of working people as they attempted to organize and to win strikes.

Silly, smiley-faced positive thinking can be painfully counterproductive for those people who are *critical thinkers*. A major reason I wrote my previous book, *Surviving America's Depression Epidemic*, was to provide critically thinking depressed individuals with tools for building morale and a path out of their depression that doesn't insult their intelligence. Here I hope to provide critically thinking opponents of the corporatocracy with ideas about morale that do not insult their intelligence.

If you are critically thinking enough to see the reality of just how much influence the corporatocracy has on social policy and how little power you have, then you are going to experience more pain of injustice than those who do not see these truths. The price for seeing such truths is more pain, and overwhelming pain can fuel depression, apathy, and immobilization.

Research shows that a more accurate notion of how truly powerless one is can result in a greater feeling of helplessness and is associated with increased depression. Several classic studies show that moderately depressed people are more critically thinking than those who are not depressed. Depressed people are, on average, more accurate and less self-deceptive than nondepressed people in their judgment of how much control they have over events.

Before modern research had borne out the relationship between depression and critical thinking, the great American psychologist, philosopher, and occasional political activist William James (1842–1910) intuitively knew this. While most psychology majors have heard of James (and the James-Lange Theory of Emotions), few know that he was a member of the Anti-Imperialist League and during the Spanish-American War said, "God damn the US for its vile conduct in the Philippine Isles." James had a history of severe depression, which helped fuel some of his greatest wisdom as to how to overcome depression for himself and others. In *The Thought and Character of William James*, Ralph Barton Perry's classic biography of his teacher, we learn that James at age twenty-seven described himself as going through a period of a "disgust for life," which Perry describes as an "ebbing of the will to live . . . a personal crisis that could only be relieved by philosophical insight." What was James's transformative insight?

James was a critical thinker and had little stomach for silly, smiley-faced positive thinking. He knew that such optimism was impossible for him, but he also concluded that his pessimism might just destroy him. So while James continued to pursue and embrace scientifically proven facts, he also came to accept that certain realities (such as whether life was or was not worth living) are beyond the realm of empirical proof. With his critical thinking, he came quite pragmatically to "believe in belief," but he recognized that one could not maintain self-respect by choosing to believe in *whatever* one wanted. He knew that a critical thinker such as himself would lose self-respect if he attempted to believe in things that critical thinking told him were untrue. So for James, one cannot choose to believe that 2 + 2 = 5. However, there is a wide range of human experience from which one can choose beliefs, and James came to understand that, "Faith in a fact can help create the fact." For example, a *belief* that one has a significant contribution to make to the world can keep one from committing suicide during a time of deep despair, and remaining alive makes it possible to *in fact* make a significant contribution. Belief in a possibility does not guarantee that it will happen, but loss of belief in a possibility can guarantee that it will not happen.

Antonio Gramsci (1891–1937), an Italian political theorist and Marxist activist who was imprisoned by Mussolini, came to the same conclusions as James. Gramsci's phrase *pessimism of the intellect, optimism of the will* has inspired many critical thinkers since to maintain their efforts in the face of difficult challenges.

The battle against the corporatocracy consists of critical thinking, which results in seeing some ugly truths about reality. This critical thinking is absolutely necessary. Without it, one is more likely to engage in tactics that can make matters worse. But critical thinking also means the ability to think critically about one's pessimism—realizing that pessimism can cripple the will and destroy motivation. A critical thinker recognizes how negativism can cause inaction, which results in maintaining the status quo.

As previously noted, there are many parallels between personal depression and political passivity. Whether one is abused by a spouse or by the corporatocracy, the pain of that humiliation can be anesthetized by drugs, depression, apathy, and a wide range of other diversions. And all anesthetizations and diversions can be addictive, which means people get into the habit of using them to shut down pain. This is the vicious cycle of depression and apathy. Human beings use depression and apathy as strategies to dull their pain; but these strategies weaken them and create passivity and immobilization, which can be humiliatingly painful; and in a vicious cycle, human beings use even more shutdown strategies to dull this increasing pain.

When one is in such a debilitating vicious cycle, painful truths about the cause of one's malaise may well not be energizing. Instead, one may take such truths as confirmation that pessimism and hopelessness are warranted. The vicious cycle continues.

People who have never been overwhelmed by pain may not comprehend how human beings can feel such despair that they need to shut down facets of their being so as to be able to function at all. People who have never been overwhelmed by pain often fail to understand how attempts to shut down pain can lead to more immobilization, depression, apathy, or flailing out in desperation.

Depressed people need helpers skilled at the craft of morale building, which involves talents and skills that mental health professionals routinely are not selected for or trained in. Similarly, activists schooled only in academia may not have learned about demoralization and morale building. In previous eras, when political activists were schooled on the streets rather than in the classroom, they have been more skilled in the craft of morale building.

Great morale builders are often risk takers. They themselves are energized by challenging authority and speaking truth to power. They have faith that the current reality is not permanent. They are often mischievous, humorous, irreverent, outrageous, imaginative, unpredictable, and capable of creating energizing drama. With these talents, they are able to distract people from their debilitating pain and thus break up the vicious cycle of pain and immobilization. The craft of morale building is subjective and difficult to quantify—and thus, from my experience, often ignored in academia.

Whether great morale builders are poets, musicians, songwriters, philosophers, union leaders, clergy, or neighbors, they are able to grasp that painful truths are fuel that can either demoralize people or be transformed into powerful constructive energy. In the hands of great morale builders, even periods of great despair can be fuels for energy. Rabbi Tarfon, during the era of domination by the Roman Empire, transformed many of his people's pain into energy with words such as these: "It was not granted you to complete the task, and yet you may not give it up."

Energizing People: Morality and Other Fuels

> **"**In order for somebody to win an important, major fight 100 years hence, a lot of other people have got to be willing—for the sheer fun and joy of it—to go right ahead and fight, knowing you're going to lose. You mustn't feel like a martyr. You've got to enjoy it.**"**
>
> —I. F. Stone

What energizes people?

Activists, organizers, and other "helpers," such as parents, teachers, and mental health professionals, can become frustrated with a "helpee's" passivity, and these helpers themselves can then become demoralized. Often "helper frustration" is caused by a rigid attachment to a single way of gaining energy. High-level activism and organizing mean understanding and respecting that while many people may share concerns about achieving genuine democracy, human beings do not all have the same temperaments—and are energized differently. Thus, another unnecessary divide among people committed to a more democratic society is on how to create energy and morale.

In my initial article, "Are Americans a Broken People?," I stated— I thought uncontroversially—that for some demoralized people "small victories" can be a morale boost. For a good part of my life, all my victories were small, specifically at the individual and family level, and I still get inspired by modest victories that I see people pull off. However, a couple of progressives took issue with this "small victories" point. David Swanson, who served as press secretary for Dennis Kucinich's 2004 presidential campaign, wrote:

> Levine finds solutions in "encouragement, small victories, models of courageous behaviors" . . . I find myself motivated primarily by the moral need to press for change, regardless of whether the wisest spectators predict success next week or next decade . . . So, I'm reluctant to endorse small victories, and even more so the expectation of early victories, as a necessary ingredient in civic engagement.

Swanson's "moral need" can be a powerful energizer, and a movement can so compromise its fundamental integrity in search of easy victories that it becomes de-energized. However, success is also important in recruiting members and maintaining morale. Some people are energized by morality, and others by success. People are also energized by fraternity, by challenge, and—as was the case for investigative journalist I. F. Stone—"the sheer fun and joy of it." Moreover, any one person may depend on different sources of energy at different times—morality might bring them to a movement, fraternity keeps them there, and occasional successes seal the deal.

City Life/Vida Urbana has won victories over some of America's largest banks and has kept people from being evicted from their homes. City Life organizer Steve Meacham believes that a vital ingredient in organizing is focusing on morality—and being energized by the immorality of the opposition. People have been led to believe that their oppression is "normal"; they are told, "Nothing personal, it's just the market." Meacham believes that organizing is about changing this framing. Specifically, it means applying a moral lens to an aspect of life that people have become accustomed to thinking lies outside the realm of morality, and instead have accepted as the "natural" way of life. For Meacham, a bank's decision to foreclose on a house and evict the residents rather than allow them to remain as renters is not inevitable, the way that it's inevitable for water to flow downhill. And because the bank has a choice, it's simply immoral for a bank to evict people and cause untold suffering because that bank doesn't want to temporarily be a landlord. He believes that individuals involved in this immorality cannot hide behind claims of "It's just business," but instead must be morally condemned. Meacham concludes, "Bringing the moral lens to that stuff really helps our people and helps us organize the resistance." For City Life, morality is both the argument they make publicly to shame banks into behaving differently, and the call to arms they use to maintain morale among supporters and to attract new supporters.

However, morality is not City Life's only energizer. When people come to City Life, they also gain support, solidarity, examples of success, and confidence that they can gain power. They go through a psychological transformation from feeling like victims to becoming activists—not simply for themselves but on behalf of others as well. Melonie Griffiths got involved in City Life and said:

> Foreclosure was kind of like one of the best things that happened to me . . . so much good came from it. I was able to help so many other people. I learned so much good information . . . I can just turn it onto other people and help them not make the same mistake. And I kind of feel like it gave me my calling.

Meacham observes that most people threatened by eviction prior to contact with City Life believe that they don't have the right to resist, and that there's nothing that they can do to resist. People lack confidence that their efforts will succeed, and they feel powerless. Quickly though, people learn that there is power in the City Life community, and that they can contribute to that power. First they become activists on their own behalf, then they go beyond that and become activists on behalf of others. And then, as Meacham describes:

> They become activists on other issues besides housing. And pretty soon they're trying to change the system. And the process by which people go through all those stages is a vital part of community organizing. It's not only a "community organizing" way of being, and not only builds organization, that it does. But if empathy is somehow the quintessential human emotion, the quintessential thing that makes us human, then solidarity is its expression . . . And I think that experience of solidarity is something that feels so good that people come back just for that.

So morality and altruism certainly energize people. But so do truth, solidarity, fraternity, loyalty, and success. People are also motivated by experiences of joy. And they can be drawn to what they feel is unique and novel. Given a person's particular temperament, each of these will be more or less energizing. Some people need face-to-face attention to be energized, while others might become energized by a book. Some people are energized by seeing an immediate impact of their actions; others by the idea itself of change for the better.

I have learned by successes and failures in more than twenty-five years of work with extremely depressed people that we all, given the nature of our temperaments, have comfort zones in which we get our energy. I have also learned that one of the ways in which people get immobilized and stuck in life is by becoming rigidly attached to their comfort zone. So those attached to morality as an energizer might want see the value of fun; those attached to the attention of others as an energizer might want to try getting energized by ideas; and those who are most comfortable getting energized by ideas might want to try helping others.

Healing from "Battered People's Syndrome" and "Corporatocracy Abuse"

Whether one's abuser is a spouse, a parent, or the corporatocracy, there are parallels when it comes to how one can maintain enough strength to be able to free oneself when the opportunity presents itself, and then heal and attain even greater strength. This difficult process requires:

- Honesty that one is in an abusive relationship.
- Self-forgiveness that one is in an abusive relationship.
- A sense of humor about one's predicament.
- The good luck of support, and the wisdom to utilize this good luck.

One abusive situation of sorts that I found myself in was in my professional training. I had studied hard in college to achieve the grades and test scores required for entrance into an American Psychological Association–approved PhD clinical psychology graduate program, and I looked forward to my graduate training. But then I met my professors and became deflated. These professors, for the most part, focused on their own self-importance and taught little that would make me more effective as a psychologist. There was little respect for students' needs, and many students felt completely powerless when it came to their master's theses, doctoral dissertations, and other academic requirements. A single negligent or ego-tripping professor could, and routinely would, ruin a student's life for a couple of years.

I considered leaving graduate school almost every day. Transferring made no sense, because I discovered from several students who experienced other clinical psychology PhD programs that my program wasn't unusual; it was actually somewhat better than most in that it offered far more clinical experience. Among my peers, the ones with the most talent for actually helping people were the ones who had the least stomach for the degree/licensing, hoop-jumping process. So most of the best therapists whom I knew never acquired their PhDs, some quitting the mental health profession altogether. However, I remained. It was the late 1970s and early 1980s; the economy was stagnant, and a decent-paying job was hard to find. At least that's what I told myself. I felt locked in. I had no viable financial backup plan. Without that PhD, I could not become a licensed psychologist, and I told myself that I needed the PhD to make a living. Like any abuse victim, whether it was true or not, I felt dependent on my abuser.

I did not have enough money in graduate school to regularly hit the bars to dull my pain, but occasionally I would hang out at a bar with another graduate student who was a couple of years ahead of me and who had even more contempt for the program than I did. We would drink cheap beer, play Pac-Man for 25 cents a game, and try to maintain some self-respect by at least being honest enough to admit that our "training" was mostly about eating shit. We traded comical stories of our pathetic attempts to evade humiliating compliance. And we joked that while we may not have the balls we started out with, at least we still had Wiffle balls, which was a hell of a lot more than most of our peers, who appeared to have an extraordinary talent for unquestioning compliance.

I was lucky. I also had a colleague who was in all my classes and felt the same way I did. Every day we hung out after classes and tried to keep each other sane. I appreciated my luck. Finally, I graduated, got licensed, and started to heal.

At some point, circumstances can change and make it easier to extricate from an abusive relationship, and one must keep the faith that this will happen. One may, for example, finally be able to financially support oneself and leave an abusive parent. And every day, people are extricating from abusive spouses, bosses, and disrespectful training programs.

Extricating from parental, spousal, or institutional abuse is difficult enough, but this is just the beginning of recovering wholeness and full strength. If one does not heal from abuse, one remains a victim—or one becomes an abuser. Most people incarcerated in prison for violent crimes were themselves abused. Unhealed from abusive relationships, people repeat abusive relationships.

An important aspect of healing and rejecting the acceptability of abusive relationships is seeing and accepting all truths surrounding abuse. Parental, spousal, and corporate abuse are replete with lies and propaganda. To heal, one needs to recognize lies. Though one may have fought off some of these, other lies may well have been implanted. There is a dignity, humility, and strength in facing the fact that while one may have once bought into some lies, one no longer does so. One should not be ashamed of having previously believed those lies, and it also helps to have compassion for those who continue to believe them—the liars we face are often quite good at lying.

Victims of spousal, child, and institutional abuse have experienced emotional trauma. Part of healing from emotional trauma means honestly confronting one's emotions, even if this is embarrassing. One may still have fear, terror, and rage. These emotions need to be accepted and respected so they are not controlling demons.

Often victims of abuse have shame about having allowed abuse to occur. Shame keeps us captive. Shame is painful and causes people to use shutdowns such as depression, alcohol, and drugs, and so shame ultimately weakens people. Shame makes people feel unworthy, reducing their confidence that others will want to connect with them, and so shame increases social isolation. Part of healing from shame is learning self-compassion, which also results in more compassion for others caught up in the abuse cycle.

Self-forgiveness is a large part of healing from trauma. One may need to forgive oneself for accepting the abuser's lies; submitting to the abuser; accepting that those with power have the right to abuse; being abusive to others; or not supporting others' rebellions against abuse. One may need to forgive oneself for supporting a war and then discovering its rationale was based on lies; voting for politicians who couldn't care less; or making a living that in some way maintains the corporatocracy.

People who are abused learn helplessness about relationships. They may learn to have no *relationship boundaries*. Such boundaries mean that there are certain things people cannot do because they are personal violations. Abusers act with no regard for their victims, and victims do not assert boundaries. Victims who heal learn to choose relationships in which it is taboo to violate boundaries; have control over the terms of their relationships; enforce the boundaries they set; and minimize contact with abusers if it is not possible to completely extricate from them.

It is common for unhealed abuse victims to feel as if there are only two paths in life, victimizer or victim; many choose the latter and have a "victim mentality." The victim mentality instructs people that they are helpless to succeed so they don't try. Part of healing means believing that one is not helpless. It means having faith that one can actually make changes that improve one's life as well as the lives of those whom one cares about.

Critical to healing and gaining strength is a liberation from one's fatalism, which has become an internal oppression. External oppression left unchallenged results ultimately in fatalism, which makes it less likely one will challenge oppression and abuse.

One way of extricating from this fatalistic vicious cycle is the development of a certain kind of "critical consciousness," called *conscientizacao* by Paulo Freire, the Brazilian educator and author of *Pedagogy of the Oppressed*. With critical consciousness, individuals can identify both external oppression and self-imposed internal oppression. Critical consciousness is aimed at ending fatalism so that one can free oneself from self-imposed powerlessness. It is a process in which changes in one's internal world result in taking actions to change one's external world, and taking actions changes one's internal world. Critical consciousness cannot be learned in a top-down manner. It is essentially a self-education process among equals. Liberation from fatalism and powerlessness is a process in which participants are not mere objects of instruction or of treatment. Instead of being acted upon, they are taking actions, learning, and then taking even more powerful actions.

People who have begun healing grasp that even when their efforts fail, they will learn something by their failure and feel stronger for making the effort. Abusive people and institutions often shame people for making mistakes, and this keeps people from trying. The truth is that failures and mistakes are necessary to learn and are nothing to be ashamed of. Healing means forgiving ourselves for past failures and mistakes, and giving ourselves permission to take risks that will sometimes incur failure and mistakes. The more one gets into the habit of making an effort, the more one feels empowered.

Identifying an Abusive Institution or Individual

1. Does it routinely lie to get its needs met?
2. Do relatively small frustrations trigger violent retributions?
3. Does it not admit its violence? Get defensive? Claim that its aggressive violent acts were in self-defense or for the good of the victim? Refuse to discuss problems?
4. Does it degrade, punish, drug, or bribe to force compliance?
5. Does it deprive others of privacy and monitor their behavior?
6. Does it ensure that others become impotent to stop their pain?
7. Does it discount others' basic needs, dignity, and essential humanity?
8. Does it isolate people and make it difficult to meet others and maintain relationships?
9. Does it have a criminal record of abuse? Police reports? Historical evidence of slavery, stolen lands, genocide, illegal wars launched under false pretenses, illegal surveillance?

Recommendations for Healing from Corporatocracy Abuse

1. Forgive yourself for believing the lies of the corporatocracy.
2. Stop allowing the abuser's definition of you to shape your life. The corporatocracy tried to convince you that you can be completely manipulated through your fear and greed. This is not true. Your beliefs and values are important to you.
3. Discover other survivors. Get energized by stories of survival. Form relationships in which there is mutual respect and affection.

4. Wherever possible, set boundaries with the corporatocracy and eliminate or limit relationships with corporatocracy apologists.

5. Stop beating yourself up for having been in an abusive relationship. It is a waste of energy. Energy is better spent on forgiving yourself and healing, and then working to change the abusive system.

6. Use your energy to redefine yourself as a valuable and strong human being who is worthy of respect and can effect change. Use your energy to provide respect and confidence for others. Increased self-respect and mutual confidence in others provides energy.

Combating Social Isolation and Building Community

Americans have become increasingly separated from one another, and isolated people are far easier to control. Social isolation weakens people, sapping them of the strength necessary to resist. Social isolation is depressing, and the more depressed one is, the less likely one will have the energy to seek or maintain relationships. It's another vicious cycle.

Social connectedness is an antidote for both depression and apathy. Social connectedness and genuine community strengthen people. People can share information and receive mutual validation that their misery is not necessarily the result of their own inadequacy. Fear weakens people, but with genuine community, people become less afraid of the consequences of their resistance. They have faith that others will support them should they be punished economically, legally, or otherwise. The end of social isolation is the beginning of those bonds that provide people with collective self-confidence that they can overcome the elite.

So how does one become less socially isolated and gain genuine community?

First, a confession. While I fought off a good deal of nonsense about psychiatric diagnoses, intelligence testing, and manipulative treatments while I was in my training, I actually did not fight off *enough* of what I was taught. One idea that seemed reasonable was that lonely people—who often seek out mental health practitioners—are socially isolated because they lack *social skills*, and so they need *social skills training* (SST).

SST consists of teaching people verbal and nonverbal behaviors that will make them more socially attractive and enjoyable to be with. SST includes listening skills (for example, paraphrasing what the other person has said and making eye contact), along with other communication skills so that people don't turn off others by being either too aggressive or too passive. It may also include helping people to pay more attention to social cues, such as whether another person does or does not want to engage with them. SST may include teaching people how to make "small talk" at a party or have better "interview skills." It utilizes modeling, role playing, and feedback from a therapist and/or a group. For socially isolated people, SST did seem to make sense. However, a series of events forced me to reconsider whether it was really the best antidote for most isolated people.

Even before reading books such as Robert Putnam's *Bowling Alone* that quantitatively detail the breakdown of community in the United States, it was clear to me that there were major forces operating in our society that were keeping people—even those who were socially capable—isolated. If one is alone, it can sometimes be helpful to know that perhaps the reason for one's loneliness is *not* social inadequacy, but that in fact a television-suburbanized-car-consumer culture is making many Americans more isolated.

After several years of practice, it became clear to me that while some of my lonely clients lacked significant social skills, most did not. Many were attractive and conversationally charming and engaging, but they were still isolated and alone. Sadly, many of these people were well schooled, and they had learned that their social isolation and loneliness were caused by their social incompetence and/or low self-esteem. So in addition to their problem of loneliness, they also believed that they were socially inadequate. However, after seeing so many people who were socially isolated despite having excellent social skills, I began to reconsider the antidote to social isolation.

Outside of my practice, I discovered that there are many people who may not have the greatest social skills but who do have genuine community. One group of people that truly informed me about the importance of something besides social skills is the "psychiatric survivor" community, which I discovered in 1994. That year I wrote a letter to the editor criticizing the validity of yet another newly minted mental illness, and the letter was spotted by a leading organizer and activist in the psychiatric survivor movement, David Oaks, who contacted me. Through him, I learned about this group.

Self-identified *psychiatric survivors* are people who believe that their psychiatric treatments have been unhelpful and dehumanizing; the goal of their movement is truly informed treatment choices and a wider range of treatment options. They fight to make it easier for the public to have treatment information beyond what's provided by pharmaceutical companies and by those mental health institutions that Big Pharma controls. They also fight for treatment options beyond medications. Some psychiatric survivors, such as MindFreedom director David Oaks, stopped taking psychiatric drugs decades ago and are functioning quite well. Others continue to take their drugs to help take the "edge off" but have no illusions that they are curing any kind of chemical brain imbalance. I have become friends with David Oaks and several other psychiatric survivors. While David (who had once been diagnosed with schizophrenia) and many like him are highly articulate and socially skilled, other survivors are not. Some survivors may have spent significant time in psychiatric hospitals and were forced to take antipsychotic drugs such as Thorazine, Haldol, Risperadal, and Zyprexa, which can produce severe and chronic adverse effects (such as the involuntary facial movements associated with tardive dyskinesia).

If those psychiatric survivors with excellent social skills didn't discuss their past, the world would never guess that they had been diagnosed as psychotic. Many others, however—because of the adverse affects of psychiatric drugs and years of extreme social isolation—would be identified as "lacking in social skills." Yet the self-identified psychiatric survivors I have come to know are no longer isolated. They have come to have *genu-*

ine community, not simply acquaintances. They have real friends within the psychiatric survivor community who provide mutual emotional and social support.

The irony for me is that in my practice I have worked with many people whom the world would judge as physically and intellectually attractive with high-level social skills but who are isolated and without community; and outside my practice, I have met people who were once diagnosed with severe mental disorders but who have genuine community. This compelled me to reconsider exactly what was the most important antidote to social isolation.

What I have come to believe is that social skills and a strong need for a social life do not necessarily create social connectedness. Instead, people succeed at creating and maintaining genuine community because they care about something else beyond their loneliness, and beyond their private world. This is how the psychiatric survivors I met formed community. They stopped focusing only on their private hurt and personal victimization. They realized that there must be others who have experienced what they did. And through organizations such as MindFreedom, they connected to help one another and to reform mental health treatment.

Ultimately, many psychiatric survivors who have formed community see the lack of democracy within mental health institutions as no anomaly, and they began connecting with others outside the survivor community who seek greater democracy in other aspects of life. These psychiatric survivors' pain over their own private victimization became energy to connect with an entire world seeking to rehumanize society.

People who have community care about something beside their own loneliness. They have not allowed school or mindless work to drum their cares and concerns out of them. And they use their cares and concerns to connect with others.

Passions and problems are the fuels that form friendship and community. Most people I have met who've created community see their problems differently from how they were socialized to think about them. They no longer are so terrified of problems that they immediately hand them over to a distant authority. They assess the problem's potential for creating human connectedness. For example, they may have an unattractive home or garden, but instead of paying a designer, they ask a neighbor whose home or garden they admire for advice, and the complimented neighbor becomes a friend.

Social connectedness strengthens people. When people build genuine bonds over concerns that they share, it provides genuine community. With genuine community, people build trust, and they discover they can function effectively as a group. This is the beginning of the path to gaining collective self-confidence that they can overcome the elite.

Individual Self-Respect and Empowerment

A population lacking what historian Lawrence Goodwyn calls *individual self-respect* does not initiate democratic movements. Individuals without self-respect are more likely to passively accept the "various hierarchical modes bequeathed by the received culture," to use Goodwyn's phrase. Such "hierarchical modes" include financial class and academic rank. Individuals lacking in self-respect believe that they are inferior if they are not at the top of such hierarchies, and that they *should* have less say over social policies. When one lacks self-respect, it is more difficult to distinguish between those experts who help us gain greater expertise, self-respect, and self-confidence and the elitists who lack any real expertise or wisdom and who reduce self-respect and self-confidence.

Individual self-respect means a regard for one's own worth regardless of one's rank in an imposed hierarchy. One can possess the best organizational strategies and tactics, but if the individuals one is trying to organize lack self-respect, they will neither believe they deserve genuine democracy nor fight for it. And so it is the job of *all* who genuinely care about democracy to retain their own self-respect and help others do the same. While each of us has a responsibility to promote self-respect, there is a special responsibility for parents, teachers, psychologists, and others who have direct influence over young people.

Integrity means taking actions in accordance with one's beliefs; one cannot have real self-respect without integrity. Life often presents scenarios that cause conflict among our beliefs (for example, a vegetarian, who also believes it is immoral to refuse food offered by a host, is served meat by a host), and integrity means distinguishing which of our beliefs are more important than others—and acting on our core values.

If one maintains abusive relationships, then by one's actions one is saying, *I am not worthy of respect*, and one's self-respect will diminish. One cannot maintain self-respect if one believes that one is incapable of acting on one's core beliefs. And if one believes one is powerless, one will not take actions congruent with one's core values and will then lose integrity and self-respect. So self-respect is maintained by refusing to accept abuse, and it is maintained by taking actions on one's core values and beliefs.

Self-respect is quite different from self-absorption, and too often parents, teachers, and even mental health professionals do not make this important distinction. Self-absorption is an incessant focus on one's own feelings, dissatisfactions, and image; this can ultimately diminish one's self-respect. People lacking self-respect are often self-absorbed, insecure, and so ego-attached to their opinions that they are incapable of listening to others and having respectful discussions. Thus, self-absorption contributes to social isolation and prevents respectful relationships.

It is my experience that children who grow up to be self-absorbed adults often have a history of either having no one caring about their feelings—and so they overcompensate—or having parents who were too easily manipulated by emotions. People who take their own feelings too seriously at the expense of everything else will both violate their own values and violate others for the sake of a temporary pleasurable feeling. Ironically, I have known many people whose previous mental health treatment resulted in more self-absorption and less self-respect; an incessant focus on feelings, needs, and symptoms resulted in a neglect of valued beliefs as well as an absence of actions that could create more integrity, self-respect, and satisfying relationships.

There are many areas of life in which one can take actions so as to achieve greater integrity and greater self-respect. And with each increase in integrity and self-respect, there is an increase in strength—and a greater capacity to achieve greater self-respect in other areas.

Human beings can achieve greater self-respect and strength by gaining skills that they value as well as by making personal transformations that they respect. Acquiring such skills and making such transformations require self-discipline. Self-discipline means overcoming one's mood so as to accomplish something that one is proud of. Disciplining one's moods means having power over them. Too often, authorities confuse children about discipline. When a child is coerced to comply via rewards and punishments, that child is not learning self-discipline. Just the opposite. A child who is coerced into compliance feels resentment. Resentment is a belief that one's being has been violated. Resentment breeds victimization and weakness.

School is a major battleground in which self-respect can be won or lost. Unfortunately, school is often a place in which people acquire resentment and lose self-discipline. Most young people feel coerced to learn things. Some may, because of fear, comply and regurgitate material that they don't care about, but they have not learned self-discipline. Other young people may rebel, but if they aren't transcending their mood to learn something they do care about, then they too are failing to learn self-discipline. Many young people are so fatigued from either complying with or resisting the demands of school that they use their free time for escapist diversions. While this is understandable, compliance, resentment, escapes, and a lack of discipline means an absence of strength.

Teaching young people in a manner that creates greater self-respect for them also creates greater respect for those teaching them. Teachers gain respect when they respect the intrinsic interests of their students and help them expand upon these interests. Teachers also gain respect when they themselves are excited by their own learning—the world needs more models and fewer critics. Promoting self-respect means welcoming honest mistakes rather than creating people terrified of failure.

Another major component of self-respect is *resiliency*—the ability to recover from life's misfortunes and maintain one's integrity. It is my experience that people who are highly resilient view setbacks as challenges rather than threats, take pride in their problem-solving ability, find humor in difficult situations, tolerate high levels of ambiguity, and see the potential for "bad events" to ultimately become "good events."

People also achieve self-respect through what they do for a livelihood. Not all jobs produce self-respect. If one does not believe in the value of what one is doing to make a living, then one is not acting in accordance with one's beliefs, and integrity and self-respect can decrease. We all have values. If we don't pay attention to our values and indiscriminately meet the demands of employers or customers, this can cause an absence of integrity and a lack of self-respect.

Most people want to have meaningful lives in which they learn new things and have the opportunity to be creative. If, at present, one has no employment opportunities that provide such meaning, one can achieve self-respect by maintaining resiliency—taking a job only for a paycheck but bouncing back to get work that meets more of what one believes in. Given the prospect of homelessness, landing any job that keeps a roof over one's family can help one's self-respect. Given certain life circumstances, there is certainly no shame in doing whatever it takes to put bread on the table, and there can be increased self-respect if one survives desperate times, maintains one's resiliency, and eventually gains a livelihood that is closer to one's beliefs.

Focus on the Non-Fascist Family: Creating Respectful Relationships

People who feel fragile can fear being overwhelmed by the tension of conflict, and they will often accept authoritarian societies—including fascist ones—to eliminate such tension. And in a vicious cycle, authoritarian societies breed child-like dependency, fragility, and a fear of being overwhelmed. This fear of being overwhelmed is, essentially, a belief in one's weakness—and such a belief can be source of shame. So in authoritarian societies, the tension produced by conflict is a malignancy that needs to be rooted out, imprisoned, or killed. Tensionlessness is the promise of authoritarianism. In the "fascist fantasy" of tensionlessness, there are no human differences and no disagreements.

In contrast, at the core of genuine democracy is strength and a fearless-ness around conflict. At the core of a democratic society are families that nurture the kind of citizens necessary for democracy. Whether the famil-ial relationship is between spouses, parent and child, or siblings, what is critical is having a certain comfort level with the tension produced by disruption and conflict. What is critical is being unafraid of tension. Disagreements are part of any relationship, and anytime people disagree with one another, there will be friction. When people are comfortable with tension, they do not overreact to it.

Authoritarians fear and resent tension, and they try to eliminate it as quickly as possible. However, with such fear and resentment, they cannot reflect on the source of the tension and how to resolve it in a way that promotes respectful relationships and a stronger family and society.

In families that care about nurturing self-respect, conflict and disrup-tion are not evils. Rather, there is enough time, strength, and concern to inspect these tensions and make judgments as to how to most respect-fully resolve them. Is the disruptiveness produced by self-absorption and unkindness, or is it a result of a reasonable effort to correct a perceived injustice?

For more than twenty-five years, I have watched a certain cascade of pressure and resentment destroy family relationships. The corporatocracy creates standards for schools, and it threatens school administrators with a loss of funds should they fail to meet those standards. School administra-tors, in turn, pressure teachers to ensure that students conform. Teachers then pressure parents of nonconforming students. Pressured parents then pressure their children to fit into their standard schools. Some of the pres-sured students comply with resentment, and others rebel with resentment. This resentment fuels behaviors that make family life decidedly unfun.

Intimidated parents buy into the idea that being a "good parent" means using every means possible—from behavior modification to psychiatric drugs—to get their child to fit into standard schools. Tragically, the effects of these frustrated parental attempts are often experienced by their child as a lack of caring. Often, parents believe that they are doing what's best for their child by trying to get them to conform. However, these parents are often perceived by their child as caring only about their own need to reduce tension in their lives. Whether people are being bribed, punished, or medicated into fitting in, they often feel resentment.

Parents, therapists, and teachers who genuinely care about democracy are not intimidated by friction. They are not worried about being temporarily disliked, and they are unafraid of *necessary* conflict. Necessary conflict means confronting behaviors that are truly self-destructive or destructive to others. However, to the extent that adults have themselves lost their integrity, they find it normal and reasonable to pressure compliance and conformity that is detrimental to a child's development. This creates rebellion and/or resentment.

Society rightfully condemns corporal punishment, sexual molestation, and physical neglect; however, there is another abuse that society considers quite normal. This is the abuse of coercing a child into being someone that he or she is not. My experience is that children don't resent parents who set limits on destructive or self-destructive behaviors, but they do resent parents who do not accept their basic being. Resentment of those whom one is dependent on weakens and breaks human beings, so young people who resent parents and other authorities but continue to maintain relationships out of fear lose integrity and self-respect. Much of what are labeled "mental disorders" are really the products of such resentment and loss of self-respect.

A population is far more likely to have individual self-respect if its young people are treated with respect. This means making wise judgments about confronting what is detrimental. But it also means refraining from trying to control actions and inactions that are not self-destructive or destructive to others and may well be necessary for learning and growth. This is essential for self-respect, and individual self-respect is an essential building block for a democratic movement.

Liberation Psychology

When I first heard the term *liberation theology* (in opposition to a theology that fosters compliance with the status quo), I thought there should also be a *liberation psychology*—a psychology that doesn't equate a lack of adjustment with mental illness, but instead promotes constructive rebellion against dehumanizing institutions, and which also provides strategies to build a genuinely democratic society.

It turned out that somebody else had thought of the same thing before I had. Ignacio Martín-Baró (1942–1989) was both a priest and a psychologist, and it is he who should be given credit for popularizing the term *liberation psychology*. Martín-Baró's liberation theology, liberation psychology, and activism for the people of El Salvador cost him his life. In the middle of the night on November 16, 1989, Martín-Baró, together with five colleagues, their housekeeper, and her teenage daughter, were forced out to a courtyard on the campus of Universidad Centroamericana José Simeón Cañas, where they were murdered by the US-trained troops of the Salvadoran government's elite Atlacatl Battalion.

As a Jesuit priest, Martín-Baró embraced liberation theology in opposition to a theology that oppressed the poor, and as a social psychologist, he believed that imported North American psychology also oppresses marginalized people.

Martín-Baró believed that the prevailing mainstream psychology had become infatuated with methods and measurements and thus was ignoring unquantifiable realities necessary for liberation. Such unquantifiable but powerful human dimensions include commitment, solidarity, hope, and courage. He saw a mainstream psychology that either ignored or only paid lip service to social and economic conditions that shape people's lives.

In *Writings for a Liberation Psychology*, a compilation of Martín-Baró's essays, editors Adrianne Aron and Shawn Corne point out that liberation psychology is about looking at the world from the point of view of the dominated instead of the dominators. Martín-Baró drew heavily on the work of Paulo Freire, who recognized a certain "psychology of oppression" in which the downtrodden become fatalistic, believing they are powerless to alter their circumstances, thus becoming resigned to their situation.

The prevailing organizational psychology that Martín-Baró criticizes is one that promotes an alienation of working people by serving the needs of industry. In his essay "Toward a Liberation Psychology," Martin-Baró points out:

> What has happened to Latin American psychology is similar to North American psychology at the beginning of the twentieth century, when it ran so fast after scientific recognition and social status that it stumbled . . . In order to get social position and rank, it negotiated how it would contribute to the needs of the established power structure.

Prevailing psychological theories are not politically neutral. Martin-Baró astutely observed that many mainstream psychological schools of thought—be they psychoanalytic, behavioral, or biochemical—accept the maximization of pleasure as the motivating force for human behavior, the same maximization of pleasure that is assumed by neoclassical economic theorists. This ignores the human need for fairness, social justice, freedom, and autonomy as well as other motivations that would transform society.

Martin-Baró pointed out that when knowledge is limited to verifiable facts and events, we "become blind to the most important meanings of human existence." Great scientists recognize this, as a sign hanging in Albert Einstein's office at Princeton stated: NOT EVERYTHING THAT CAN BE COUNTED COUNTS, AND NOT EVERYTHING THAT COUNTS CAN BE COUNTED. Much of what makes us fully human and capable of overcoming injustices—including our courage and solidarity—cannot be reduced to simplistic, verifiable, objective variables.

In American society, mental health treatment is a significant force that can work either for or against genuine democracy. There are approaching eight hundred thousand social workers, psychiatrists, and psychologists working in the United States today (though not all provide mental health services), as well as many mental health counselors and paraprofessionals. The US Surgeon General reported in 1999 that 15 percent of adults and 21 percent of children and adolescents in the United States utilize mental health services each year, and it is likely that these percentages have increased.

Whether they realize it or not, mental health professionals who narrowly treat their clients in a way that encourages compliance with the status quo are acting politically. Similarly, validating a client's challenging of these undemocratic hierarchical modes is also a political act. I believe that mental health professionals have an obligation to recognize the broader issues that form a context for their clients' mental well-being, and to be honest with their clientele about which side of this issue they are on.

Martin-Baró, tragically prescient, once quipped to a North American colleague, "In your country, it's publish or perish. In ours, it's publish *and* perish." In contrast with Martin-Baró, US intellectual activists have a considerable degree of free speech, and it requires no great heroism for US citizens to acquire their books or hear them speak and to discover truths.

Truths do sometimes set people free, especially when people have a basis of strength to start with. And truths can be especially energizing when, as was the case with Martin-Baró, proclaiming them takes courage. Similarly, Tom Paine's truths in *Common Sense* energized many colonials to take action against the British. Paine's readers had not lost their self-respect, community, and sense of power. Paine's audience also knew that Paine was risking his life to write and publish *Common Sense*. The power of truth to energize often lies in the risk that it takes to state it.

Generally in the United States, telling the truth about corporate-government tyranny and injustice requires little real risk, and so such truths provide little energy. It is not that there is no value in exposing more truths about the corporatocracy. However, many professional activists and educators have become lazy, pursing only easy, risk-free truths that are not energizing.

I wish my declaring the truth of people's personal abusive relationships or the truth of their systemic corporate-governmental abuse were enough to set them free. I wish that the people I know caught up in this state of helplessness could be spurred to action by lectures—that would be an easy fix. But more often, lectures are a turnoff. What these victims of abuse need is the strength to do something with the truth of their abuse—strength that comes from support, morale, healing, and self-respect, as well as practical strategies and tactics.

The oppression faced by the Salvadorans whom Martin-Baró worked with was different from the oppression we face in the United States today, yet oppression need not be physically brutalizing in order to damage the bonds of community and people's sense of self-worth. We would do well to reject a mainstream psychology that tacitly fosters compliance to the status quo. In contrast, we need a liberation psychology that promotes constructive rebellion against dehumanizing institutions and, at the same time, aims at building a genuinely democratic society. In the United States, liberation psychology needs to focus on the specific ways Americans have been pacified and demoralized. And it must focus on how we can be made whole again, so as to regain strength to fight for ourselves and our communities.

My form of practiced liberation psychology stems from my clinical experience. It is decidedly in opposition to resentment-producing coercions; it is about helping individuals and families build respectful relationships.

I have counseled hundreds of young people and adults who had been previously labeled with oppositional defiant disorder, attention deficit hyperactivity disorder, substance abuse, depression, schizophrenia, and other psychiatric diagnoses. What strikes me is how many of these people are essentially anti-authoritarians. A major problem for these young anti-authoritarians is that most mental health professionals who had previously diagnosed them have no familiarity with political ideologies that far better characterize these teenagers' thinking and behaviors than does any mental disorder.

The word *anarchism* is routinely used by today's mass media synonymously with *chaos*, but for philosophers and political scientists, anarchism means people organizing themselves without authoritarian hierarchies. *Practical anarchism* is not a dogmatic system and actually does not oppose all authority. So, for example, practical anarchist parents will use their authority to grab their child who has begun to run out in traffic. However, practical anarchists strongly believe that all authorities have the burden of proof to justify control, and that most authorities in modern society cannot bear that burden and are thus illegitimate—and should be eliminated and replaced by noncoercive, freely participating relationships.

A minority of the anti-authoritarian kids I have worked with are aware of anarchism and identify themselves as anarchists, perhaps having T-shirts with a circle drawn around an A. However, even among those adolescents who know nothing of the political significance of the term *anarchism*, I cannot remember one who didn't become excited to discover that there is an actual political ideology that encompasses their point of view. They immediately became more whole after they discovered that answering "yes" to the following questions does not mean that they suffer from a mental disorder but that they have a certain political philosophy:

- Do you hate coercion?
- Do you love freedom?
- Are you willing to risk punishments to gain freedom?
- Do you distrust large, impersonal, and distant authorities?
- Do you reject centralized authority and believe in participatory democracy?
- Do you hate powerful bigness of any kind?
- Do you hate laws and rules that benefit the people at the top and make life miserable for people at the bottom?

There are different varieties of anarchism and there are different varieties of disruptive people, and these varieties are worth examining. One group of freedom lovers hates money, inequality, and exploitation of any kind. They reject a capitalist economy and aim for a society based on cooperative, mutually owned enterprise. They are essentially leftist-anarchists—"anarcho-socialists," "anarcho-syndicalists," or "anarcho-communitarians." If they discover what Noam Chomsky, Peter Kropotkin, and Emma Goldman have to say, they identify with them. They have a strong moral streak of egalitarianism and a desire for social and economic justice.

Another group of freedom lovers also hates the coercion of parents, schools, and the state but, unlike these left-anarchists, they view capitalist markets as ideal for organizing virtually all aspects of society, and they lack an egalitarian moral streak. A political ideology that they can connect with is called "anarcho-capitalism," "libertarian anarchy," or "market anarchy," and some become fans of Murray Rothbard or Ayn Rand.

Anti-authoritarians also can be distinguished by their views on violence as a way of achieving their goals. While many freedom lovers adhere to nonviolence, others consider violence an acceptable tool and will physically or psychologically victimize others to get what they want. Historically, the question of violence has sharply divided anti-authoritarians in their battle to eliminate unjust and illegitimate authority.

If a nonviolent anarcho-communitarian is dragged by parents into my office for failing to take school seriously but is otherwise pleasant and industrious, I tell parents that I do not believe that there is anything essentially "disordered" with their child. This sometimes gets me fired, but not all that often. It is my experience that most parents may think that believing a society can function without coercion is naive but they agree that it's not a mental illness, and they're open to suggestions that will create greater harmony and joy within their family.

I work hard with parents to have them understand that their attempt to coerce their anti-authoritarian child not only has failed—that's why they're in my office—but will likely continue to fail. And increasingly, the pain of their failed coercion will be compounded by the pain of their child's resentment, which will destroy their relationship with their child and create even more family pain. Many parents acknowledge that this resentment has already begun to happen. I ask them if they would try to coerce their homosexual child into being heterosexual or vice versa, and most say, "Of course not!" And so they begin to see that temperamentally anti-authoritarian children cannot be similarly coerced without great resentment.

I work very differently with those anti-authoritarian kids who care only about freedom for themselves and have no problem victimizing others to get their way. These kids usually are initially receptive to me, especially when they hear my viewpoint on traditional schools. However, tension eventually enters our relationship when they hear my views on other matters, especially on the "soul."

I may, for example, tell them that while I believe that they have not lost their soul, eventually people do lose their souls to the extent that they lie to others and to themselves, or to the extent that they act in ways to get the best deal for themselves without caring about the impact on others. Often these kids will ask, "What happens if we lose our souls?" I tell them that in our current economy, it is quite possible to be financially successful without a soul; but they will never have a friend whom they really care about, and so eventually nobody will care about them because human beings eventually stop caring about those who don't care about them, and so they will have a friendless, loveless life. Sometimes this has an impact, sometimes not. Just like political activism, therapy may have an immediate effect, have a delayed one, or not work at all.

Activists and therapists need to have humility, especially with regard to their affection and respect—or lack of thereof—for those they are working with. If an activist or a therapist lacks such affection and respect, those whom they are working with will sense it and will likely be unreceptive. Humility also means accepting that one is not capable of being helpful to everyone, and having faith that somebody else, perhaps at some other point of time, may well be helpful.

Liberation psychology, in short, is about helping create self-respect, respectful relationships, and empowerment, and it is about helping people reject the role of either victim or victimizer.

Forging an Alliance among Populists

The corporatocracy uses its money and power to try to persuade Americans that it is "populist demagoguery" to even bring up the subject of a class war, and that populism means pandering to destructive prejudices. Fortunately, despite the corporatocracy's great efforts here, many don't buy it.

In March 2009, a Rasmussen Reports poll reported that "55% of Americans Are Populist." They defined *populist* as trusting the American people's judgment more than America's political leaders, as seeing government and big business as political allies working against the interest of most people, and as seeing the federal government as one more special-interest group that is primarily looking after its own needs. Specifically, they asked Americans three questions:

1. Generally speaking, when it comes to important national issues, whose judgment do you trust more—the American people or America's political leaders?
2. Do government and big business often work together in ways that hurt consumers and investors?
3. Some people believe that the federal government has become a special interest group that looks out primarily for its own interests. Has the federal government become a special interest group?

Each pro-populist response earned +1; not sure earned 0; and anti-populist earned a -1. Those who scored 2 or higher were considered populists. Those who scored -2 or lower were considered "aligned with the political class" with a more elitist view. With this scoring—as of March 2009—55 percent of Americans were populists, and only 7 percent trusted an elite ruling class. According to this measure, 52 percent of Democrats, 62 percent of Republicans, and 51 percent of those not affiliated with either major party were populists.

Today in the United States, unlike the end of the nineteenth century, there is confusion about populism. While all self-identified populists continue to reject control by the elite, there are different views of exactly who the elite are and what form of anti-elitism would be best. There are populists who most emphasize "liberty and freedom," and there are those who most emphasize "social and economic justice." And a major difference among many modern populists is their view of "government" and the "free market."

Today some self-identified populists—unlike nineteenth-century Populists—believe it is naive to trust *any* government, including one created in the name of the people, because such a government will be taken over by an elitist cadre. In contrast, other modern self-identified populists—similar to those nineteenth-century agrarian Populist rebels—

believe it is naive to trust the unbridled free market because concentrated economic power (inevitable in an unregulated market economy) can be just as dangerous as concentrated political power, in no small part because those holding concentrated economic power can too easily acquire undue political power for themselves; and therefore, the people must take control of government to counterbalance economic power run amok.

Populists also differ on what's most important to wrest away from the elite, and they can differ on their views of human nature. Some self-identified libertarians are more focused on liberty and autonomy and believe that people are essentially competitive and motivated by self-interest. Some self-identified leftist populists may also care deeply about liberty and autonomy but stress more the need for economic and social justice, and they believe that human beings are essentially cooperative and altruistic.

To make a case for the *true essence* of human beings, we can all pick out personal, historical, sociological, anthropological, and animal-kingdom examples, but no one can definitively prove their case. It comes down to beliefs. I believe that human beings can be both selfish and altruistic, and I believe that human beings are both competitive and cooperative. And I believe that the kind of family, culture, and society people live in will bring out more or less of these traits. Common sense and research show that selfishness and competition elicit selfishness and competition, which can create a more unfriendly, hostile, and even war-like family, culture, and society, which I believe is not a heck of a lot of fun to live in. Cooperation and altruism create a more cooperative, friendly, peaceful, and harmonious family, culture, and society, which I believe is more fun to live in. I also believe there exist healthy forms of competition and reasonable degrees of self-regard.

In the late-nineteenth-century Populist revolt, insurgent farmers would have seen it as "plumb silly" to debate whether people are essentially competitive or cooperative. As historian Lawrence Goodwyn notes, "Populists thought of man as being both competitive and cooperative," though they tilted toward cooperation as they desired a generous rather than a selfish society. In a democratic, non-elite society, people would respectfully listen to one another's views of human nature and ideas about the kind of society that brings out the best and worst of people.

A large divide between populists has to do with their views of the US government. Libertarians see the US government as the tyrant, and they seek to drastically eliminate the government's power so that "We the People" can regain liberty. Left populists see giant corporations as the tyrants, and short of eliminating this corporate elite, they seek freedom and social and economic justice by taking back control of government and using it to ensure that the corporate elite will not tyrannize them. While some self-identified libertarian populists rail only against "governmental tyranny," and some self-identified left populists rail only against "corporate tyranny," other populists get that, in the corporatocracy, Americans are being ruled by a corporate-governmental partnership.

Real-deal populism is hurt by those self-identified populists who ignore the reality that the US government is the junior—not the senior—partner of the corporate elite in the corporatocracy. The corporate elite relishes the role of the US government being seen as the tyrant. Every tyrant wants to demonize some other entity—be it an institution or a people—so as to deflect rebellion against itself. In reality, one major role of the US government in the corporatocracy is to serve as a scapegoat to deflect rebellion against the corporate elite.

A great mistake of many heartfelt populists across the political spectrum who share an essential commonality of anti-elitism is to compromise themselves with elitists who *pretend* to have sympathy for their position. The Democratic Party, for example, is replete with elitists who pander to left populists by pretending to believe in social and economic justice and altruism. And the Republican Party is replete with elitists who pander to libertarians by pretending to believe in freedom and autonomy. Wake up, populists—all elitists believe in elite rule.

It is certainly in the interest of the elite and their apologists who believe in elitist rule to dismiss the reality of class war, and to call those who invoke it "demagogues." The corporate-governmental elite work very hard in staying unified. There is public posturing of antipathy between the Democratic and Republican Parties, but behind closed doors on the issue that they care most about—maintaining a government-corporate ruling elite—they work together.

It is in the interest of Americans who are not in the elite ruling class and who do not believe in elitist rule to declare loudly that there is a class war going on, one that the elite are easily winning. It is also in the interest of anti-elitists to understand that they have been divided, and this has made it easy for a small elite class to rule and to break their resistance.

All anti-elitists need to realize that what they share bonds them much more than anything that divides them. It is true that not all anti-elitists have the same views of human nature or the same exact solutions to self-government. In genuine democracy and real-deal populism, people will continue to disagree on issues. However, if we want to defeat the elite, we must come to realize that listening to one another and ironing out differences can be individually strengthening as well as galvanizing for us as a whole. I encounter real-deal populists across the political and ideological spectrum, and I believe it is quite possible for us to learn from one another and work together. In my experience, as long as I listen and speak with respect, other populists and I almost always find more to agree about that is substantive than remains between us as difference—and sometimes we can iron out our differences.

> 66I spent 15 years logging in WA state and Alaska in remote logging camps accessible only by floatplane. I come from a redneck background, and I am proud of it. The people being misled by the right wing conservatives in this country are good hard working people, and progressives need to start respecting them. This Sunday I went out to one of my fav. redneck bars with another redneck liberal friend of mine. The discussion in the bar quickly turned to guns, and then of course to Obama and socialism. Now I'm no big fan of Obama but the outright lies these good people have heard from Glenn Beck and the likes are incredible. After an hour or so my friend and I had made some small headway, and pretty much everyone agreed that the big corporations were screwing us. I decided then and

there that I had to go out there every Sunday night and shoot the shit. Obviously being no scholar I don't have a lot of pretty words to explain why we are all getting screwed by them what got, and no one is doing a whole lot about it. I can however tell you what working class Americans are going through cause I've been there. Progressives need to get off their fucking high horse and learn to show some real honest respect for working folks. If you can't do that, then perhaps what you really need is a good ole fashioned cup of shut the fuck up.**"**

—Undefined, *AlterNet*, March 24, 2010

In addition to agreeing on the general principle of opposition to elite rule, both left and libertarian populists agree on many specific issues. Both opposed the Wall Street bailout; and similar to most left populists, many libertarian populists oppose the US government's wars in Iraq and Afghanistan as well its war on drugs.

There are of course issues that divide many left and libertarian populists, but I believe it's possible to have discussions around these issues that create greater unity. To do so, we must keep in mind that some of these issues are fairly emotional ones that need to be addressed with sensitivity.

Gun control is one such personal issue that divides populists to their detriment. Many libertarian populists will tell you something like, "Hang out in rural America, and you'll see that a gun is just a tool, no different from a hammer or a chain saw, and even among those of us who have stopped hunting, we have fond memories of hunting with our family and buddies, and gun-control liberals are screwing with something very personal here." For many left populists, gun control may also be a very emotional issue, and they might tell you something like, "My dad killed himself with a gun when the bastards took away the job he'd had for twenty years, and I have two close friends who have had family members who also did themselves in with a gun when they probably would still be alive without such an easy way of committing suicide, and, not living in rural America but in urban America, what I see is people using guns not to hunt deer but to hunt one another." However, when both sides stay respectful, I have also seen them reach agreements on reasonable gun policies that don't deprive people of either liberty or life.

Often the most emotional divide between left and libertarian populists is the divide I noted earlier on their view of human nature. All of us have a tendency to focus on one aspect of human nature at the expense of others. Not only can respectful communication on the multiple dimensions of our humanity help unify populists, but it can also strengthen individuals, marriages, families, and communities.

Hillel, the great Jewish scholar who lived around two thousand years ago during the time of the Roman Empire's domination, respected both the libertarian and left understandings of human nature and, in a sense, challenged people to respect both aspects of their own humanity and unify them so as to gain strength. Specifically, Hillel said:

If I am not for myself, who will be for me?

If I am only for myself, what am I?

And, if not now, when?

So libertarian populists are right when they say, "If I don't financially take care of myself and my family, then I will not only lose my self-respect but will be a burden to others." But left populists are also right when they say, "If I am only for myself, then I am some kind of sociopath, like a Wall Street banker ripping off everybody, and if everybody acted completely selfishly, we could never have the cooperation necessary to defeat the elite."

It's my experience that when individuals follow Hillel's advice to care about *both* self and others, they gain greater wholeness and strength, and they are more capable of uniting with others.

Inspiration to Overcome Distrust

66 Back in the day people saw themselves as part of a group. They were more united. The feeling of solidarity allowed them

to fight and rise up and make demands. Americans have been so fragmented that they have lost that sense of unity. They've been twisted into seeing their fellow sufferers as parasites, rather than as allies. Until people start seeing themselves as belonging to a whole, rather than as lone little people trying to take down a mountain with a toothpick, they'll keep getting shafted.**"**

—cultured banana slug, *Reddit*, January 2010

If you doubt that it's possible to find common ground with populists who have different opinions from yours, then consider an event that has for the last century given people hope that even in the midst of the most dehumanizing insanity, human beings can retain their humanity and reach across the divides of fear and hatred.

Battlefields for democracy can emerge in surprising places, even on military battlefields in wars begun by elites vying with one another for control. One such war was World War I, which began in August 1914 and would ultimately result in approximately fourteen million people killed.

On Christmas Eve and Christmas Day in 1914, after the first four months of World War I, in which approximately one million soldiers had already been killed, British and German soldiers and officers in the field spontaneously created their own truce. This truce quickly spread to more than one hundred thousand troops across a good part of the Western Front. Some participants claim that it began when German soldiers placed candles on their trenches and began singing Christmas carols, and British troops responded by also singing carols. All of this inspired soldiers and officers on both sides to take the next step. Captain Josef Sewald of Germany's Seventeenth Bavarian Regiment reports making one gesture:

> I shouted to our enemies that we didn't wish to shoot and that we make a Christmas truce. I said I would come from my side and we could speak with each other. First there was silence, then I shouted once more, invited them, and the British shouted "No shooting!" Then a man came out of the trenches

159

and I on my side did the same and so we came together and we shook hands—a bit cautiously!

Increasing numbers of soldiers from both sides shouted Christmas greetings to one another, and they left the protection of their trenches and strolled out into "no-man's land" (where lay the dead and dying). Both sides retrieved their fallen comrades. Then the Germans and British exchanged small gifts, including food, alcohol, and souvenirs, and they kicked around soccer balls together.

In the following years, the elite took precautions so that such truce making would not recur. Generals made sure that there were artillery bombardments on Christmas Eve and Christmas Day so as to make it too dangerous to come out of the trenches, and troops were rotated so as not to become too familiar with the men opposing them. But the instinct for humanity in the trenches was not yet completely defeated. Again on Christmas Eve in 1915, German and British as well as French troops climbed out of their trenches, declared a truce with each other, and exchanged gifts. However, as the war continued in 1916 and 1917, with increasing savagery, there were no more Christmas truces, and no more fraternizing, gift exchanging, or soccer playing.

What frightened the elite about these truces created by the men in the field was not the truce itself. There is a history of temporary truces being called in wars. What frightened the elite was that the men in the field spontaneously took power and created the truces. That's democracy, and that is terrifying for the elite. If democracy can break out on the elites' strongest turf—the military battlefield—then it can break out anywhere.

The elite will always want hierarchical, top-down decision making with themselves at the top, which is why they are so comfortable with the military, and why the World War I Christmas truces shook them up. The elite will always be afraid of the majority of people having trusting and cooperative relationships with one another, because this is a prelude to the people believing that they—not the elite—can make decisions that will result in a far more humane world. A major point of David Stratman's book *We CAN Change the World* is that the spirit of the Christmas truce is still alive:

> The Christmas Truce story goes against most of what we have been taught about people. It gives us a glimpse of the world as we wish it could be and says, "This really happened once." It reminds us of those thoughts we keep hidden away, out of range of the TV and newspaper stories that tell us how trivial and mean human life is. It is like hearing that our deepest wishes really are true: the world really could be different.

Collective Self-Confidence: Solidarity and Success

While individual self-respect can be gained simply by the effort itself, collective self-confidence is achieved mostly as a result of achievements, and this has significant implications for strategies and tactics. A group of people need not achieve total victory for heightened collective self-confidence, but they must at least be more successful than pessimist naysayers imagined they could be.

At the beginning of the American Revolution, the colonials did not need to decisively defeat the superior British forces, which had been expected to quickly trounce them. Narrow victories and even draws were good enough for collective self-confidence. This was also true for the Confederate underdogs in the Civil War, who by denying victory to their opposition increased their collective self-confidence and reduced the confidence of the larger and better-equipped Federal troops. And the North Vietnamese and their South Vietnamese allies fought with tactics that prevented American forces from achieving the kinds of victories that would have given the US military collective self-confidence.

One need not look only to war. There are countless examples in sports where teams turn small successes into the kind of collective self-confidence that propels them from losers into champions. I grew up watching that happen with the New York Mets, who came into existence in 1962, and that year had one of the worst teams in professional sports history. But by

1968, the Mets were able to field a couple of pitchers who could completely shut down the opposition, and they began beating teams dotted with all-stars. The Mets gained collective self-confidence and won the World Series in 1969.

In athletics, there is no greater focus than on collective self-confidence. Players and coaches try to dismiss past failure as irrelevant and to focus on success. They know that any success breeds the kind of collective self-confidence that can create greater success. So in attempting to do something with the odds stacked against it—such as defeating the corporatocracy—one must be judicious in choosing which battles to take on and which ones to forgo.

The Green Party gambit in 2000 was a risk. Should the Greens have gotten 5 percent of the vote (instead of the 2.7 percent they ended up with) and thus qualified for public funding in the next election, this might have been the kind of success that would have created collective self-confidence in the anti-corporatocracy community. However, given the fact the Green Party not only failed to achieve that 5 percent but were also seen—fairly or unfairly—as responsible for the election of George W. Bush, the result was a loss of collective self-confidence.

Both favorites and underdogs are wise to pick their battles, but it is especially crucial for the underdogs to pick the battlefield that they have the best chance of winning, because they may be only one defeat away from complete surrender. Success boosts morale, morale enhances solidarity, and solidarity gives the strength necessary for greater successes. So skilled organizers care passionately about how to create solidarity and how not to squander it by failure.

Recall the 1936–37 Flint sit-down strike that after forty-four days was victorious. That strike had great solidarity and support. Early on in the strike, the union asked family members and other supporters to gather at Cadillac Square in Detroit as a show of strength. The overflowing crowd of 150,000 supporters surprised and warmed the hearts of the striking workers. In a retrospective article, *The Detroit News* described how this show of support "gave the union the self-confidence they needed to show its power and solidarity over its management 'oppressors.'"

This Flint sit-down strike was a war with real battles in every sense of the word. The most famous of those battles came to be known as "the Battle of the Running Bulls." About two weeks into the strike, the police tried to stop a food delivery to the strikers and a riot ensued, resulting in police using tear gas and riot guns with buckshot that injured several strikers. The strikers fought back, pelting police with bolts, iron nuts, and whatever they had in the factory. Police attacks were twice repulsed, and then the winds shifted, sending police tear gas back to the police officers. The police retreated, and strikers won the battle. Again, solidarity bred success, and success brought more solidarity.

With these strikers locked in the factory, their spouses, family members, friends, and other strike sympathizers passed food and news to them. Inside the factory, the strikers created their own democratic society. Strikers took their turns keeping watch for police assaults, handling and preparing food, and maintaining cleanliness. They also played cards and music on instruments smuggled into the factory. Workers in other states joined in sympathy strikes and closed down plants; within two weeks of the beginning of the Flint strike, approximately 135,000 men from plants in thirty-five cities across fourteen states were striking General Motors. Ultimately, GM signed an agreement with the United Auto Workers, giving it bargaining rights in seventeen GM plants that had been shut down by the sit-down strikes. GM concessions included a 5 percent pay hike—and permission for workers to speak in the lunchroom.

Recall also the victorious postal workers' wildcat strike in 1970. The New York Letter Carriers, Branch 36 Web site details the strike, which they describe as an "uprising of rank-and-file workers who forged what was a true revolutionary act and who acted with courage and conviction despite the resistance of their elected leaders." This wildcat strike was a successful rebellion against both management and national union leadership, and it was about converting frustration and despair into collective successful action.

On July 1, 1969 (prior to the "Great Postal Strike" in March 1970), in reaction to a meager pay increase issued by President Nixon, most of the letter carriers and postal clerks at the Kingsbridge Station and Throggs

Neck in the Bronx, New York City, called in sick, and management suspended them. But the rank-and-file members of Branch 36, as they recall, "were not frightened by the Post Office Department's investigations and suspensions because for the first time in years, they had gained a sense of control and pride."

These actions of the Bronx mail carriers had instilled a sense of euphoria among many New York postal workers, and they began to believe that—with courage and solidarity throughout the New York area and the United States—the rank and file could gain true power with both management and their own unresponsive union leadership. While union leadership accepted the penalties leveled by management against the Bronx suspended workers, the rank and file did not. While their national union leadership sold out this initial small group of wildcatters, the rank and file stood by them, and their solidarity turned out to be the key to the postal workers' success.

The postal rank and file were in conflict with union authorities over the issue of pay for suspended workers, and they rejected union leadership's other agreements with management. Union leadership tried to dissipate the rising militancy of the rank and file by the delay tactic of conducting a "strike survey" and never releasing the results. Rank and file did not buy it, and they voted to strike. Other mail carrier and clerk locals followed.

On March 18, 1970, picket lines sprung up outside post offices in Manhattan and the Bronx, almost immediately followed by strikers in Long Island and New Jersey. By March 23, the strikers numbered almost 250,000. Following Nixon's decision to use army troops to break the strike, many postal workers throughout the country began to return to work, but New York City area strikers remained steadfast—perhaps these mostly ethnic postal workers had been least socialized to compliance. The luck here was that without the New York City area, the entire national post office system could not really function. Ultimately, postal workers achieved victory, receiving full collective bargaining rights and pay increases. An activist at the time who would later become a postal union leader, Vincent Sombrotto, would later say,

One of the things that I more fully understand now is how revolutions are conceived, how governments can be overthrown, and how our nation was founded because a few good men would not stand by when they experienced conditions so intolerable that they were ready to risk everything.

Winning the Battle
Solutions, Strategies, and Tactics

With the psychological and cultural building blocks of individual self-respect and collective self-confidence, democratic movements have the energy to get off the ground. It becomes realistic—and not naive—to believe that people can take the kinds of actions that produce genuine democracy. Next, one must consider what specific strategies and tactics have the highest likelihood for increased democracy, which in a positive cycle further increases self-respect, collective self-confidence, and the energy to carry the battle forward. All actions and inactions entail risk, and so wisdom is required. One must be realistic about one's own and one's adversary's strength and capacity—and then push the envelope.

Lessons from the Great Populist Revolt

The Populist Movement of the late 1800s began when millions of Americans, predominantly farmers, concluded that the new industrial order of their society was working against them.

The source of these farmers' misery was the "crop lien system." Farmers needed credit to acquire the necessities of working and living before they brought in their harvest and received payment. However, farmers themselves couldn't get bank loans, and so they indebted themselves to merchants, often at unclear and exorbitant rates. At the end of harvest season, it was common for merchants to declare that farmers owed more than they could pay. After accumulating enough debt in this fashion, farmers routinely had to sell their farms and become "tenant farmers" or "sharecroppers," often on what had once been their own property. This became increasingly the norm.

In response to their economic difficulties, these hardworking farmers at first simply tried to work even harder, and when that didn't help, some migrated to other places. However, in the 1870s, they began to increasingly talk to one another about their troubles, and they formed economic self-help organizations such as the Grange. But times grew even harder in the 1880s, and as foreclosures increased, they began to consider more radical steps. Historian Lawrence Goodwyn tells us:

> Their efforts, halting and disjointed at first, gathered form and force until they grew into a coordinated mass movement that stretched across the American continent . . . Millions of people came to believe fervently that the wholesale overhauling of their society was going to happen in their lifetimes.

One myth about mass political insurgency is that it will inevitably happen when times get hard enough. The reality is that in the course of human history, most people are more often than not hurting economically or politically or both, but this usually does not produce democratic mass movements. Utilizing the Populist uprising as an example, Goodwyn describes a necessary sequence for a mass democratic movement: "movement forming," "movement recruiting," "movement educating," and "movement politicization."

"Movement forming" is the creation of a new institution that is outside the control of the elite. In this new and autonomous institution, individuals can form their own interpretation of the realities of their lives, and they can reject the interpretations of authorities. They can, for example, stop thinking that their financial misery is caused by bad luck in a fair market. They can mutually validate the fact that elites have disproportionate market power and so are able to use the market to gain increasing advantage over others. Together they gain confidence in a different interpretation for their hard times. For the Populists, this movement-forming institution was the National Farmers Alliance and Industrial Union—commonly called the "Alliance."

Second, for a movement to build in size, it must have specific tactics to attract large numbers of people. This Goodwyn calls "movement recruiting." Pragmatically, one must offer something that people need and that the movement has the capacity to provide. After several years of experimenting with different self-help ideas, the Alliance developed an extremely powerful mechanism for recruitment: America's first large-scale working people's cooperatives, which ultimately attracted hundreds of thousands of farmers. The Alliance cooperatives were large, well thought out, and well organized.

To get better prices, farmers' common sense told them that they needed to "act together in the sale of their product." They created a mechanism called "bulking" in which they brought their crops to their own warehouses. This made it convenient for buyers, especially foreign ones, to give them a good price. When word got out that these cooperatives were effective in gaining a higher price for farmers' products, it not only built great individual self-respect and collective self-confidence but was also a fantastic recruiting tool. Their success spread quickly by word of mouth, attracting thousands of new members.

The lesson is that a radical and bold plan that provides people with what they need—if successful—is the best recruiting tactic to expand membership, which in turn increases power. More cooperative ideas came about. Populists attempted to create cooperative credit institutions, and they also created a cooperative insurance plan that gave farmers a much better deal than that offered by large insurance companies.

Third in this sequence is what Goodwyn calls "movement educating." After hundreds of thousands of farmers were drawn into the Alliance, the now large rank and file could share information, receive mutual validation, and gain confidence in their ability to articulate an alternative analysis for their problems. Alliance members, often with little formal schooling, gained confidence in their ability to analyze the economic and political realities in which they were getting victimized and to articulate solutions.

Ultimately, the Alliance was able to send forty thousand lecturers out across the United States to get the word out to "plain people" who, perhaps for the first time, heard an alternative view of their problems along with fresh solutions. These self-educated and peer-educated lecturers were able to explain sophisticated cooperative systems in a way that plain folks could understand. It is estimated that more than two million people heard these lectures throughout forty-three states. Once dismissed as "stupid hayseeds," these speakers most likely would have been intimidated prior to their success, but with the success of the cooperatives grew their self-respect, which inoculated them against such ridicule.

The Populist Movement began to create its own culture, which included family involvement, twilight suppers, sing-alongs, and group treks to lectures. Imagine looking around you on a Fourth of July celebration and seeing thousands of families who valued what you valued and who were acting on what you believed in.

For a short period, the Populist revolt existed under the radar of the ruling elite, but eventually the elite understood this threat and attempted to destroy the movement. The oligarchy that declared war on the Populists included large banks, grain elevator companies, railroads (which Populists wanted to nationalize along with other public utilities), and exploitative furnishing merchants.

This oligarchy sought every means possible to discredit, sabotage, and destroy the Populist Movement. The elite imposed taxes on warehouses, but the Alliance moved the warehouses out of town and won that battle. However, other battles were more difficult to win. The elite used every means possible to make it difficult for cooperatives to sell their products. The Populists' highly successful livestock marketing cooperative was killed by the Livestock Commission of Chicago, which simply refused to deal with farmer cooperatives.

Ultimately, the key area where the Populists were unsuccessful was providing credit, a necessity for most farmers. The Populists attempted to create their own banks, which they called Exchanges. Most notable among them was the Texas Exchange, which collected notes on farmers' land and stock to use as collateral for bank loans. However, with few exceptions, banks and their business allies unified and refused to advance cash on this collateral. The call went out for farmers to raise the cash themselves, and thousands came to nearly two hundred Texas courthouses and pledged $200,000 but ultimately came up with only $80,000, which was not enough. Populists had other credit ideas but they were up against an American oligarchy that did not want them to succeed, and so the Populists were unable to sustain a non-exploitative credit system.

This resulted in the fourth step in the sequence: the "movement is politicized." The revolting Populists came to believe that without major political transformations, the elite would successfully sabotage their movement and cause it to fail. For the Populists, politicizing the movement first meant the formation of their own political party, the People's Party.

In 1892, the People's Party ran a presidential candidate, James Weaver. Despite Weaver's lack of charisma and despite widespread attempts to suppress the People's turnout, Weaver received more than one million votes, 8.5 percent of the vote. Weaver won the majority of votes in Kansas, Colorado, Nevada, and Idaho and took those states' twenty electoral votes; and he won two more electoral votes (one of the three electoral votes in Oregon and one out of the three in North Dakota) for a total of twenty-two electoral votes. Weaver also won many counties in Nebraska and South Dakota.

However, it became clear to the Populists that the People's Party would never win a national election, so they decided to use their power in 1896 to help elect a more populist Democratic presidential candidate, William Jennings Bryan. Bryan was defeated that year in a close election (and was twice again defeated in later presidential elections). Following Bryan's 1896 defeat, the morale of the two million members of the People's Party collapsed, and the Populists' collective self-confidence never recovered. After Bryan's defeats, the Democratic Party would at times make attempts to curtail the gross miseries produced by the hierarchical economic system, but no longer would the Democratic Party try to transform the American economy to a truly democratic one. As Goodwyn notes, "This conclusion, of course, had the effect of removing from mainstream reform politics the idea of people in an industrial society gaining significant degrees of autonomy in the structure of their own lives."

Americans began to feel that they had no chance to control a government, and thus government itself began to be seen by many as an evil. Government came to be increasingly seen more as something that is controlled by the elite, and the idea that government could actually be "of the people and by the people" began to die in the hearts and minds of anti-elitists after the Populist Movement failed.

While a government that is truly of the people and by the people now seems childishly naive for millions of Americans, real-deal populists once believed it was not naive. The people in the Populist Movement not only believed it, they seized government institutions for their use. In 1888, for example, when the Alliance summoned 250,000 Alliancemen to meet in nearly two hundred courthouses, they did so without notifying anyone in the courthouses. The courthouses, they believed, were *their* courthouses, and they could simply go ahead and use them. This was emblematic of the connection and intimacy between ordinary citizens and their government institutions, an intimacy that seems only a fantasy today.

This real-deal populism—the sense of ownership of government—has been replaced with a bastardized populism that makes government the enemy without recognition that it is the control of the government by large corporations that is the underlying problem. If we are not controlling government, then the corporations will control government; and if there is no government at all, then corporations will directly control us. The real-deal populists at the end of the nineteenth century wanted to control government and to use it to severely restrict or eliminate the power of the financial elite.

What strategic and tactical lessons can be learned from the rise and fall of Populism and the People's Party?

A hugely important lesson is that if one wants to build a large democratic movement, one must do more than simply create an organization of like-minded idealists. One must create democratic institutions such as the cooperatives that actually provide something useful. With institutions such as the cooperative, people can discard a servile deference and regain individual self-respect, which is lost when one is dependent on despised entities.

Another lesson is the importance of success in building collective self-confidence. With the Alliance's initial successes, they gained collective self-confidence in the belief that it is possible to create non-hierarchical democratic institutions in general. The cooperatives were not only a great recruitment tool but also the basis for a restoration of individual self-respect and collective self-confidence—and this in turn created a new culture in which participants were no longer resigned to elitist rule. They began to see genuine democracy as more than a mere desire; it was a real and achievable possibility—for some, even an inevitability.

While it made sense at the time for the Alliance and the Populists to attempt to solve their credit problem by moving into party politics, ultimately this was a failure. And once Populists allied with the Democratic Party and Bryan lost, the Alliance and the Populist Movement virtually disappeared. The Alliance founders tried to keep the spirit alive and spoke of its continuing "educational value," but as Goodwyn points out, "A community cannot persist simply because some of its members have a strong conviction that it ought to persist." Specifically, it must fulfill a clear need in its supporters' lives, and the ability for the Populists to do so disappeared when the cooperatives disappeared.

The Populists did so much right in their formation of cooperatives, and that is what must be remembered. And though society has changed, the essence of these cooperative economic arrangements must remain a beacon.

Another lesson from the Populist revolt is a sobering one about electoral politics. Given the credit roadblocks they ran into, it made sense at the time for the Populists to switch gears and engage in party politics, first forming their own People's Party and ultimately joining with the Democratic Party. However, both experiments failed. Though the People's Party's platform was clearly anti-hierarchical and democratic, within the party a certain elitism emerged that seems to emerge in all party politics. Political squabbles, such as the choice of Bryan's vice presidential candidate, took away some of their energy. And when the Populists focused on national victory but were defeated, this was deeply demoralizing. Ultimately, Goodwyn tells us, "In folklore, it came to be remembered that the Alliance had been 'a great movement' and that it had killed itself because it had 'gone into politics.'"

Did entering electoral politics kill the Populist Movement, or did the combination of entering electoral politics and losing its economic base of power do so? The economic base of power had provided it with individual self-respect and successes, which had created a collective self-confidence. In contrast, the concentration on party politics did not fuel individual self-respect and, when defeated, destroyed collective self-confidence.

Modern Electoral Politics: Wise or Unwise Battlefield?

Nowadays there is a faction of populists who believe in the electoral process and a faction who do not. Among that pro-voting faction on the left, there are a range of beliefs. Some try to reform the Democratic Party. Others abandon the Democratic Party and vote for the Green Party or some other party that is more representative of people and democracy. Some believe that there should be no political parties at all, and that candidates should stand on their own. Then there is another large faction who believe that voting in national elections is simply a waste of time, and that participating in the electoral process gives it a validity that it does not deserve. Though I have an emotional preference in this debate, I see the logic and illogic in all of these perspectives.

My general view toward politicians—quite possibly shared by the majority of Americans—is best described as *cynical*, defined as "scornful of the motives, virtue, or integrity of another." I respect cynics who are cynical not because of a lack of courage but because of a love of truth. Helen Keller courageously overcame blindness and deafness, but because she was a lover of truth, she was cynical of some of the claims put forth by the women's suffrage movement. In 1911, nine years before the Nineteenth Amendment to the Constitution guaranteed women the right to vote, Keller wrote: "Our democracy is but a name. We vote? What does that mean? It means that we choose between Tweedledee and Tweedledum."

The left populist Keller (a supporter of Socialist Party candidate Eugene Debs) knew that the presidential elections were a "stacked deck," and that giving women the right to vote was mostly going to provide an even greater illusion of democracy.

In 1920, there was great celebration over the passage of women's suffrage.

173

However, with only the Democratic Party Tweedledees and Republican Party Tweedledums having a real chance of winning, Americans chose Republican Tweedledums Warren Harding in 1920, Calvin Coolidge in 1924, and Herbert Hoover in 1928—and then suffered the Great Depression beginning in 1929. People such as Helen Keller conclude that it does little good for women to have the civil right of voting if big business controls the election process.

In genuine democracy, one is not forced to choose between the lesser of two evils, each of whom receives millions of dollars from corporations and wealthy individuals. It has been my experience that voting for Tweedledum simply because one loathes Tweedledee harms individual self-respect, and is dispiriting and bad for democracy. I believe that one reason many Americans have come to be docile is their allegiance to the lesser-of-two-evils philosophy, a doctrine that promotes despair.

If the ultimate goal is a more democratic society, then we should respect that each among us needs to do what builds our self-respect the most. Voting versus nonvoting factions need to be more respectful of one another. Election results may make no difference in terms of real power, but results can increase or decrease real suffering for some people, which matters a great deal if you are one of those people.

It is my experience that an attempt to engage in party politics can result in something positive in the creation of bonds with like-minded people—but it has also been my experience that much bad can come from an exclusive focus on party politics. The bad is that people (1) stop focusing on building up individual self-respect and collective self-confidence through economic self-reliance; (2) buy into the elite notion that democracy is all about elections; (3) give away their power when they focus only on getting leaders elected, becoming dependent on those leaders; (4) lose sight of the fact that genuine democracy means having influence over *all* aspects of their lives; and (5) forget that if they have no power in the workplace, in their education, in their buying and selling of goods, in their entertainment, or in all their institutions, then there will never be democracy worthy of the name.

> "If you can control a people's economy, you don't need to
> worry about its politics; its politics have become irrelevant.
> If you control people's choices as to whether or not they will
> work, and where they will work, and what they will do, and how
> well they will do it, and what they will eat and wear, and the
> genetic makeup of their crops and animals, and what they will
> do for amusement, then why should you worry about freedom
> of speech? In a totalitarian economy, any 'political liberties'
> that the people might retain would simply cease to matter. If,
> as is often the case already, nobody can be elected who is not
> wealthy, and if nobody can be wealthy without dependence on
> the corporate economy, then what is your vote worth?"
>
> —Wendell Berry, *Another Turn of the Crank*

In war, intelligent combatants attempt to force the fight onto the battlefield of their choosing, seeking the battlefield that takes advantage of their strengths and minimizes their weaknesses. So in the class war, the elite, who are very small in numbers but very large in cash, try to make the battlefield something they can purchase with their money. It turns out that an American election is easy to buy—especially when you have pockets deep enough to fund candidates of both major parties.

Keeping the struggle on a battlefield where money is so influential is an important reason the corporatocracy wants us to believe that national elections equal democracy. These elections keep Americans thinking that they have a democracy when they don't, and they are an inexpensive way to control that which appears to be democracy. Perhaps most important, these elections distract people from thinking about other "democracy battlefields" that are not as easy for the elite to buy off and control.

Party politics and the "voting versus nonvoting" issue are a narrow part of democracy. Thus, the major strategic problem in focusing on electoral politics is not in itself but in the overfocus on a battlefield where the elite have such an advantage. This results in a lack of focus on democracy battlefields where the rest of us have a better chance of winning.

The Strategy and Tactics of Disruption

For the last generation, mental health professionals have diagnosed young people who do not obey authorities and who create havoc to get their way with "disruptive disorders." However, throughout history, those who resist domination have utilized the general strategy of *disruption* to challenge unjust authority and gain power.

In *Challenging Authority: How Ordinary People Change America*, sociologist Frances Fox Piven details "the nature of disruptive power" and describes the use of disruptive tactics in fomenting the American Revolution, the Abolitionist Movement, and other social and political movements. Piven argues that

> ordinary people exercise power in American politics mainly at those extraordinary moments when they rise up in anger and hope, defy the rules that ordinarily govern their daily lives, and, by doing so, disrupt the workings of the institutions in which they are enmeshed.

Disruption as a strategy of power is essentially about stopping cooperation with authorities in a manner that creates significant deprivation for authorities. One can disrupt with "active aggression," legally, illegally, and even violently. Or one can disrupt with "passive aggression," by a refusal to work, a boycott, and other non-participations. Effective disruptions are often combinations of both active and passive aggression. For example, effective labor union strikes may include both the passive disruption of withdrawal of labor and the active disruption of the business with picket lines and intimidation of scabs.

The American Revolution and its prelude were acts of disruptive power. A violent revolution is the most risky and extreme of all disruption tactics, as it most certainly results in violent reprisals. In violent revolution, one risks the loss of life and the loss of even more power if defeated. So, given the corporatocracy's absolute technological supremacy in the area of violence, that literal battlefield is even more problematic than the metaphoric battlefield of electoral politics. Organizer Saul Alinsky put it bluntly in his criticism of gun-celebrating leftist radicals in the 1960s: "A guy has to be a political idiot to say all power comes out of the barrel of a gun when the other side has the guns."

But a declaration of independence and war is the extreme disruptive tactic. For the American colonials, the prelude to the Revolutionary War was replete with other less extreme disruptive tactics—all designed to gain power over perceived unjust authorities.

In the 1773 Boston Tea Party, colonists boarded ships of the British East India Corporation and destroyed their cargo of tea by throwing it into Boston Harbor. That was not the only disruptive act to stop the taxed tea. There were boycotts against British tea, and colonials smuggled less expensive Dutch tea into the colonies. Outside Massachusetts, other American colonies actually did not have to resort to the destruction of tea because they were able to force ship captains to take their cargo back to England.

Colonial disruption against the British Crown did not start with the Boston Tea Party. During the 1740s, in response to British "impressments" (kidnappings) of colonials to serve on their ships, colonial crowds in Boston attacked a sheriff and destroyed a Royal Navy barge. And in the period between 1765 and 1769, there were 150 riots in response to perceived injustices.

Immediately following the American Revolution, American commoners did not fear the power of the new American elite. One of the most famous disruptive acts came to be known as Shays' Rebellion. Daniel Shays and his fellow rebels, burdened by debt, responded to increased taxes by attempting to seize the arsenal at Springfield, Massachusetts. They were defeated, and many were imprisoned. The ultimate consequences of Shays' Rebellion were a mixed bag. Taxes were lowered, but this violent uprising also provided the elite with a rationale for a more authoritarian state.

Generally in American history, the tactic of armed and violent resistance by people against the elite fails and has been exploited to frighten the public into demanding "law and order," thus leading to greater authoritarianism. There are exceptions to this general rule.

In 1859, John Brown and his followers attempted to seize the federal arsenal at Harper's Ferry in an effort to foment a slave revolt. Though Brown failed in this goal and did create some reactionary authoritarianism, his bold attempt as well as his hanging and martyrdom turned out to be a great disruptive tactic: It helped inspire and energize the Abolitionist Movement.

Prior to John Brown's raid, there were several slave revolts. In 1800, Gabriel and a group of approximately a thousand slaves planned to seize Richmond, Virginia, but were foiled by bad weather and betrayal, and Gabriel and thirty-five others were executed. In 1811, four hundred slaves in the New Orleans area marched from plantation to plantation recruiting an increasing larger army, and were ultimately put down by the US Army and militia forces. Perhaps the most famous slave revolt was led by Nat Turner in Virginia in 1831. Though these revolts failed at their immediate goals, they have provided historical dignity for African Americans.

In the Abolitionist Movement, each act of courageous disruption galvanized others. Northern white abolitionists were inspired by courageous slave revolts, and news of white abolitionists' efforts gave slaves hope. Piven points out, "What was perhaps the most disruptive strategy of all, the Underground Railroad, was a collaborative venture" between slaves and white abolitionists. The Underground Railroad helped free thousands of slaves from the South, weakening the South's slave economy.

There were abolitionists who believed in the more nondisruptive electoral process, and as early as 1840 they formed the Liberty Party. However, William Lloyd Garrison, perhaps the best-known white abolitionist of that era, did not join in this effort because he believed that electoral politics would ultimately lead to compromise on the goal of immediate emancipation of slaves. Since elections were won by majorities, and abolition was a minority view among white Americans (even in the North), people such as Garrison believed that the emancipation of slaves would require other strategies and tactics.

Sometimes outrageous laws radicalize people, and that is what happened when the Fugitive Slave Act of 1850 was enacted. This law made any federal marshal or other official anywhere in the United States who did not capture and arrest an alleged runaway slave liable to a large fine, made any person aiding runaway slaves subject to imprisonment and large fines, and gave significant rewards to those capturing runaway slaves. This law actually incited moderate abolitionists to become lawbreakers.

Following emancipation of the slaves, the general strategy and specific tactics of disruptive power in the United States could best be seen in the labor movement. The 1894 Pullman strike led to a nationwide boycott by workers on all trains carrying Pullman sleeping cars, resulting in the use of twelve thousand federal troops to put down the strike; strike leaders were jailed. The modern corporatocracy had emerged, and by the end of the nineteenth century it was clear that a major role of the US government was to serve the interests of the corporate elite.

The Great Depression of the 1930s resulted in more disruptions by desperate Americans. Crop prices fell by approximately 60 percent, more than five thousand banks failed, and US unemployment reached 25 percent. Hundreds of thousands of Americans were homeless, living in so-called Hoovervilles, and many of them felt desperate with nothing to lose. Throughout the United States, there was organized looting of food. In cities, there were rent strikes, and it was not uncommon for a crowd of neighbors to block evictions. In rural areas, farmers prevented foreclosure sales. World War I veterans marched on Washington, DC, demanding promised payments. Despite high unemployment, there were also an exceptional number of large labor strikes (seventeen strikes of ten thousand or more workers each in 1933; eighteen strikes in 1934; and twenty-six strikes in 1937, with almost two million workers total striking that year).

During the 1930s, fear among the elite of revolution and the abolition of capitalism was significant enough that this era became one of the few times in American history in which non-elites gained substantial economic reforms. These reforms included relief programs reaching 22 percent of the US population, the National Labor Relations Act providing legal protections for strikers, the Fair Labor Standards Act establishing national minimum wages and maximum hours, and Social Security legislation, among others.

If American history teaches anything, it is that disruptive power can work, but that without its continual threat, the gains it produces disappear. Those who signed on to fight the American Revolution believed that they were fighting for democracy. But following the defeat of the British, the American elite created a Constitution and national government with the essential feature being, as Piven notes, "to wall off from electoral influence those parts of government that performed functions essential to a commercial economy." In the Abolitionist Movement, the disruptive tactics of abolitionists and African American slaves were instrumental in the ultimate emancipation of the slaves, but the controlling elite in the South was able to re-create a system of racial apartheid and subordination of African Americans. And in America's labor movement in the twentieth century, with the use of bold and intelligent disruptive tactics, there was increased power and substantive financial gains for working people through the 1970s, but this was followed by an elite counterattack and a loss of power.

Disruptions take a great deal of energy and involve a great deal of risk. There can be a risk of loss of income, economic marginalization, imprisonment, or death. Disruptive tactics can fail and lead to demoralization. And even when disruptive tactics succeed, this can result in the fantasy that the success is permanent, leaving people vulnerable to a counterattack by the elite.

Another problem is that partial victories often entail the kinds of compromises that are de-energizing. Those in control make compromises so as not to relinquish control. The corporatocracy, for example, may give a slightly higher wage but not give workers any control over working conditions. The problem with winning such compromised small concessions is that these can result in the loss of energy. Striving for an ideal is energizing, and settling for certain compromises can sap energy. That's another reason that abolitionist William Lloyd Garrison was unexcited by an abolitionist political party. He knew that all political parties make compromises to gain voters, and he was concerned that if the Abolitionist Movement compromised at all on the total emancipation of slaves, it would lose the moral high ground that energized it.

While the controlling elite would rather not give away any control, one of their common strategies, if threatened enough, is to give away a small amount of power to a subordinate elite that in turn controls people to meet the needs of the elite. This is exactly what the corporatocracy did with labor unions. Workers were granted the right to organize and strike in return for their being controlled by national union leadership, which helped create elaborate procedures designed to prevent production stoppages. When working people forfeit the threat of surprise work stoppages, companies are able to build up production reserves and sit out strikes. By management utilizing union leaders to control workers, management ensures its control at the expense of workers.

Authorities who benefit from the status quo will always condemn, invalidate, criminalize, or pathologize disruptive tactics. To the extent that we take those authorities seriously, disruptions are prevented and the status quo is maintained. The corporatocracy will always label its disrupters with pejoratives such as *criminals, terrorists, insurgents,* or *mentally disordered.* But depending on how the disruption works out, history books may well describe these disrupters as heroes.

Whether a given tactic is productive, unproductive, or counterproductive has a great deal to do with the nature of an oppressive authority. Wise activists are aware of the nature of the authority they are battling against and its likely response to any given disruptive tactic.

A key to successfully exercising disruptive power is understanding the mutual nature of dependency. If workers are easily replaceable, then the employer's dependency on them is low, and the disruptive tactic of a strike will be ineffective.

Even when dealing with repressive and violent regimes, if a group understands the mutual nature of dependency and exercises wise tactics, it can succeed, at least partially. As mentioned earlier, in July 2010 in Iran, following President Mahmoud Ahmadinejad's 70 percent tax increase on businesses, Iranian merchants struck Tehran's Grand Bazaar, shutting down their enterprise. This put the government in the position of either collecting 70 percent of zero sales—nothing—or reducing the tax. The merchants understood the mutual nature of dependency between themselves and the government, but they also understood that certain tactics would lead to the kind of violent struggle that they could not win. They chose the correct tactic. The Iranian government retreated from its original tax plan and raised taxes only 15 percent, which ended the strike. Was this an energizing success or a de-energizing compromise? Merchants debated this, and I will later discuss the difficulty—at least sometimes—of evaluating such matters.

The desire to rebel against unjust, disrespected, and oppressive authority is valid, and the strategy of disruption is a legitimate one. However, the specific tactics of disruption may or may not be wise ones given the nature of the authority. When people lack self-respect or are depressed, they tend to either do nothing or flail out without wisdom. Research shows that significantly depressed parents are more likely to create additional problems rather than solve them when parenting (such parents routinely underreact or overreact to their children's behaviors). Absent morale and healing, human beings tend to be reactive rather than proactive; they tend to be impulsive rather than strategic. Depressed people may be passive or they may be agitated. They may do nothing, or they may flail out and create blowback that makes matters worse.

Similar to depressed individuals, when a group is demoralized and lacks individual self-respect and collective self-confidence, it can also tend to either do nothing or flail out without wisdom. Thus, there are interplays among self-respect, success, morale, confidence, and the wisdom to size up a situation and select the right strategy and tactics that gain the most power.

Are Protest Demonstrations Effective?

Nowadays, do protest demonstrations do any good? Yes and no. Recent history shows that it depends on what the protest demonstration is about.

A major role of the US government in a corporatocracy is to deflect people's anger from the corporate elite. The corporate elite need elected officials to be taken seriously by the populace. Thus, a demonstration against government is actually a statement that the people are taking their elected officials seriously, which is exactly what the corporate elite want, though of course the elite don't want demonstrations to actually alter government policy in ways that negatively affect the elite.

In a corporate-controlled government, there is mutual dependency between the corporate elite and elected officials. Elected officials are dependent on the corporate elite for financial support, and the corporate elite depend on government institutions to squash those demonstrations that actually threaten their wealth and power. In this sense, government institutions, to justify their existence to the corporate elite, gain power with the corporate elite if government forces are necessary to put down certain protests.

Thus, when demonstrations are aimed at policies that the corporate elite care about, there is a certain impotence protesting against elected officials who are controlled by the corporate elite. This impotence is caused by the reality that both Democrats and Republicans not only are dependent on the corporate elite for campaign contributions, but also rely on the elite's capacity to make a stock market rise and fall and thus affect their political fortunes.

For mainstream pundits, it is an exaggeration to argue that most elected officials are under the control of the corporate elite. These pundits argue, for example, that while some corporations might want a war, only the government actually declares the war and sends in the troops, and so protesting against elected officials' policies is totally sensible.

Recall that on February 15, 2003, several million people around the world in more than six hundred cities came out in force in huge demonstrations against the imminent invasion of Iraq. On that day, organizers estimate as many as five hundred thousand people demonstrated in New York City, with other significant protests in 150 other cities in the United States. Protesters believed that the Iraq War was not about national security but about the needs of the corporatocracy (and there has been a great deal of evidence to confirm this view). These huge protest demonstrations were completely ignored by the US government and its junior partner in the invasion, Great Britain (where elected officials ignored the largest demonstration ever in London). It appears that if major corporate interests are at stake, regardless of how many people take to the streets, such protests will fall on deaf ears of elected officials.

Major corporate interests were at stake in the Iraq invasion, especially those of the energy-industrial complex and the military-industrial complex. Another role of the US government—along with deflecting criticism from corporations and putting down uprisings—is to wage wars deemed useful to the corporate elite. Despite the large demonstrations against the Iraq War, the resistance offered was not disruptive to a government that is dependent on the corporate elite rather than on the people it supposedly represents.

The failure of these large demonstrations against the Iraq invasion to have any impact is perhaps one reason for the decline in protest demonstrations in the United States against the wars in Iraq and Afghanistan despite decreased public support for both wars. It may also be part of the reason there were so few people demonstrating for single payer/Medicare for all or a public alternative to insurance companies despite Americans' support for these health insurance reforms. People know that on the issue of health care reform, there are trillions of dollars at stake for the corporatocracy, especially for insurance and pharmaceutical corporations. Americans increasingly know that the elite are not going to allow a government (which the elite has paid to own) to create legislation that would lose the corporatocracy serious money. And so it is quite possible that even if five million Americans had filled the streets of Washington, DC, demanding single payer/Medicare for all, it would have made no difference. It is far more likely that Americans will finally get something close to single payer/Medicare for all when other elite members of the corporatocracy conclude that the insurance and pharmaceutical companies are taking too much from the elite pie.

Does this mean that mass demonstrations directed at government are useless? Not necessarily. Recall the Latino-dominated protests against crackdowns on illegal immigrants in the United States, including half a million demonstrating in Los Angeles on March 25, 2006. The specific target of the protest was the anti-immigrant legislation HR 4437, passed by the House on December 16, 2005. Following these demonstrations, the

Senate never voted on HR 4437, and so it never became law. Thus these demonstrations can be seen as very effective.

The reality is that not only are illegal immigrants no threat to the corporatocracy, but they're actually good for agribusinesses, meatpacking corporations, the restaurant industry, and other businesses that employ illegal immigrant workers at low wages and often with substandard, even dangerous, working conditions. However, for most of the corporatocracy, the illegal immigrant issue is inconsequential because it can utilize inexpensive labor anywhere in the world, and so much of the corporatocracy is not all that concerned should a few states crack down on immigrant workers.

The corporatocracy is most delighted to see demonstrations against government policies in which there are no corporate interests at stake— issues such as abortion rights and same-sex marriage. These are issues that divide Americans into distrusting camps so that they can be easily conquered on the issues that the corporatocracy does care about. So it's possible to demonstrate for certain civil and human rights and to be successful, as long as those rights are not in conflict with the needs of the corporatocracy.

In the 1960s, huge civil rights demonstrations were far more effective than huge anti-war demonstrations. The corporatocracy benefited by the money made from war; but the corporatocracy actually favored a transformation of the South in the 1960s. The quasi-feudal nature of the South had made it more difficult to create corporate agribusinesses, manufacturing, and an expanded consumer market. So there was big money to be made in bringing the US South into the modern world, and money is what the corporatocracy cares about. Moreover, the corporatocracy loves to divide and conquer, and racial strife makes it difficult for the poor and working class to unify and fight together against the elite. Protest demonstrations against the government are likely to be effective only to the extent that major segments in the corporate elite are in favor of (or at least not opposed to) the goals of the protest.

The corporatocracy cares about issues that gain money or cost money. On money issues, the corporatocracy's hope is that people either don't demonstrate at all or demonstrate only against elected officials who are beholden to the corporatocracy and thus will be unmoved. The corporatocracy fears those demonstrations and other activism directed against the corporations that will actually cost them money.

Instead of directing protests against the government, some have tried focusing directly on the corporations. Such activism against corporations, done intelligently, can be quite effective even if the size of the protests are relatively small.

Consider the David-versus-Goliath contests of City Life/Vida Urbana. City Life has won victories over some of America's largest banks, including the Bank of America, and prevented many foreclosures and evictions. City Life is a small organization based in the Boston area and uses a strategy it calls "the sword and the shield." The "shield" consists of legal services; the "sword" includes small but intelligently targeted demonstrations. City Life states:

> We organize blockades, vigils and other public actions to exert public pressure on the banks. We then draw on the potential of a non-profit bank, Boston Community Capital, to purchase at current real value the homes of foreclosed residents and where possible to resell it to them.

According to City Life organizer Steve Meacham, "People who come to us generally don't get evicted." City Life's canvassing shows that nearly 95 percent who seek their help do not get evicted, while most people without legal assistance do get evicted. How can a small organization with limited resources be effective? It comes down to understanding what the corporatocracy cares about.

City Life is well known for eviction blockades in front of the home of the person being evicted. Meacham notes, "One reason we do the blockades is because they get a lot of publicity. If 50 or 75 people come and sit in front of a building and they're folks willing to be arrested, that is dramatic and it gets a lot of publicity." Corporations hate bad publicity, which affects their profits and stock price. What Meacham and City Life are using against the banks is the banks' own bottom-line mentality. Even small numbers of people blockading an eviction create a public relations battle that the banks almost always lose. So, Meacham notes, "The banks are very often choosing to negotiate and settle with us."

Similar to City Life, the Neighborhood Assistance Corporation of America (NACA) also has used targeted demonstrations against banks to save homes. NACA, with even greater resources behind it than City Life, is another nonprofit advocacy group that helps troubled borrowers renegotiate predatory mortgages. Bruce Marks, the chief executive of NACA, is a self-proclaimed "bank terrorist." Marks says:

> We wear that as a badge of honor. Bank terrorism is a nonviolent way we personalize the consequences of CEOs' actions. When someone loses their home, they lose their neighbors, they lose their community, and their kids lose their friends and their schools. It's personal. Lives have been devastated. We go to the CEOs' homes, usually on Sunday morning, which is family time, in their gated communities. We are relentless and we go after them everywhere they go.

In March 2009, NACA demonstrated at the Greenwich, Connecticut, home of William Frey, chief executive of Greenwich Financial Services, as well as at the Rye, New York, home of John Mack, chief executive of Morgan Stanley. NACA says Frey and Mack have opposed loan modifications designed to help homeowners avoid foreclosure by reducing their interest rates or, in some cases, the principal balance on loans. Frey's Greenwich Financial Services, which deals in mortgage-backed securities, actually sued a mortgage lender over loan modifications that benefited distressed homeowners. This appalled NACA and Bruce Marks, who reacted, "The greed they are showing is just beyond the pale. To sue lenders who are trying to do the right thing is outrageous."

NACA has signed agreements with JPMorgan Chase, Bank of America, Wells Fargo, and Citigroup, in which these four giant banks agreed to work with borrowers to lower mortgage payments. However, according to NACA, JPMorgan Chase reneged on its agreement, as its modifications were not sufficient; in December 2009, approximately one thousand NACA protesters demonstrated in front of JPMorgan Chase. This gained media attention and pressured JPMorgan Chase to reconsider.

This battle against banks has also been successful because other players in corporate America are being hurt by unnecessary foreclosures of greedy lenders who refuse to renegotiate loans. The real estate lobby, for example, desperately wants to stop foreclosures, which contribute to falling property values, fewer home buyers, and a stagnant real estate market. Newspapers, which depend on real estate advertising revenue, actually have some incentive to give attention to even small demonstrations against these banks. As previously noted, the corporatocracy is not a monolith, and the profits of one industry can affect another. Thus, on some issues, activists can themselves utilize a "divide and conquer" strategy.

The success and failure of a protest demonstration cannot always be measured by whether or not it is successful in its immediate and concrete goals. For example, the Battle of Seattle brought attention to corporate-dominated, anti-democratic globalization efforts of such organizations as the World Trade Organization. And in demonstrations and rallies, even those that fail to produce identifiable success, many people can, perhaps for the first time, feel validated by others, less alienated, and more energized.

In the end, successful activism requires pragmatism, common sense, and wisdom. In concrete terms, this means assessing the consequences of a specific action—and taking action based not on emotional impulses or ego attachments. One might feel rage toward a specific politician, government institution, or corporation, but one must keep in mind how the corporatocracy can easily exploit any violence to marshal support for more authoritarian policies. Demonstrations, protests, and rallies are weapons, and like all weapons, they must be used wisely.

The Power of Divorce

66 Each one of us, as long as life stirs in him, may play a part in extricating himself from the power system by asserting his

primacy as a person in quiet acts of mental or physical withdrawal . . . Though no immediate and complete escape from
the ongoing power system is possible, least of all through
mass violence, the changes that will restore autonomy and
initiative to the human person all lie within the province of each
individual soul, once it is roused.**

—Lewis Mumford, *The Myth of the Machine: The Pentagon of
Power* (1970)

**I know many people who have given up. They consider what
happens back east to have nothing to do with them. They don't
vote, pay taxes, or have driver's licenses. They work under the
table and barter. This country has been on the slippery slope
for years. Maybe it has already slid too far down to recover.**

—Miklkit1, *Propeller*, December 16, 2009

I am essentially conservative when it comes to relationships. In every relationship, there will be conflicts and frustrations that can result in an individual, at any given moment in time, wanting to exit. However, whether
the bond is a friendship, a marriage, or some other familial relationship, I
believe it does not serve one's interest to dissolve that relationship based
on the passion of the moment. I am also essentially conservative when
it comes to divorcing from a community, a society, a culture, or a nation.
One can exaggerate the problems of what one knows and minimize the
problems of what one doesn't know.

While I am essentially conservative when it comes to divorce and
dissolving relationships, there are times when unpleasant tension can
go well beyond frustrated needs that can be resolved through dialogue.
There are times when unpleasant tension is caused by deep resentment,
disrespect, and distrust. What if, after extensive experience, you have
come to the conclusion that your spouse does not care at all about you?
That your spouse has been completely dishonest with you? Has taken
huge amounts of family money to use selfishly? Has had multiple hurt-
ful affairs? Has exploited you? What if your unpleasant tension with

your spouse has lasted for several years and you have come to have deep resentment, disrespect, and distrust? Even religions that ostensibly forbid divorce provide loopholes that allow for dissolution of a marriage that has come to be destructive.

There are even times when children and their parents need to part ways to avoid irreversible damage. When a child has zero respect for his or her parents, when parents have zero trust for their child, and when there is physical and emotional abuse, it is often safer for all concerned if that child is separated from his or her parents.

If one can honor the sanctity of a marriage and a family but still recognize that there are times when their dissolution is necessary, it seems reasonable that the option of divorce from a society, culture, or nation should also be a legitimate last resort.

Immigrants to the United States have essentially seceded from their original societies, cultures, and nations. And within the United States prior to the Civil War, millions of African Americans living in the South had bitter resentment and no confidence that reform in the South was possible, and thousands of them fled. Their self-emancipation was of course "self-help," but it also inspired abolitionists, drained the South of labor, and made it more likely the South would be defeated. And when de facto apartheid reemerged in the South, another exodus not only freed those who emigrated but also deprived the South of labor.

In addition to mass emigrations, there is a long history of people within the confines of the United States creating alternative societies and cultures that they believe better meet human needs. Experiments in communal living did not begin with hippies in the 1960s but date back hundreds of years. For example, the Amish, Mennonites, Shakers, and many other groups rejected societal and cultural norms and created their own societies.

Regardless of whether one believes in the values of any given alternative society, such creations remind us that it is quite possible to build a very different way of life. These alternative societies can be seen as experiments for all of us in which we can learn something. We can judge which aspects were and were not successful in generating increased individual self-respect, collective self-confidence, and democracy. The Amish and Mennonites produce, and Shakers in their time did produce, the kind of skilled craftsmanship that creates a great deal of self-respect. Some of these communities have had economic successes that have created collective self-confidence, while others had practices that led to their dissolution. While the Amish and the Mennonites are still vital, the once large Shaker communities have all but disappeared (largely because of economic competition following the Industrial Revolution). I have made several visits to the preserved Shaker grounds in Pleasant Hill, Kentucky, and I always get energized by my visits. Though the Shakers were, as all societies are, imperfect, I get inspired by what they did right.

The spirit of intentional communities, communes, and other withdrawals from mainstream culture is still alive. If you are curious, check out the Fellowship of Intentional Communities, which provides directories and descriptions of several hundred such communities in the United States and around the world.

I am also energized by models of "private seceders" who may have remained within the United States but exited as much as possible from the dehumanizing aspects of society and culture. With courage, intelligence, and a modest side-cash income, both the Nearings and the Hubbards were successful.

Scott Nearing was a Wharton University economics professor who in the 1920s spoke out against child labor and was fired. At age forty-seven, in the middle of the Great Depression, Scott and his wife, Helen, began homesteading in Vermont, and at age sixty-five he and Helen picked up their compost and began a new homesteading life in Maine. At ninety, Scott was still mixing cement for one more of his beloved stone homes, and he died at one hundred. Helen was going strong at age ninety-five when she died in a car accident in 1994. Scott and Helen Nearing's *The Good Life* has sold hundreds of thousands of copies to those who long for a simpler and more rehumanized life.

Harlan Hubbard, unlike Scott Nearing, was no political ideologue. He was an artist and writer, and also a handyman, who lived a solitary existence until middle age. At forty-three, he met and married Anna, a

Cincinnati librarian, and the following year they built a shantyboat on which they voyaged down the Ohio and Mississippi Rivers. From 1951 to 1986, they lived in a house they built themselves in northern Kentucky beside the Ohio River, where they gardened, read aloud to each other, played music, cut firewood, tended a herd of goats, fished, painted, and created their own good life.

Another form of individual secession is the route of becoming an expatriate, living much if not all of one's life abroad. My sense is that for many Americans, becoming an expatriate is seen as an increasingly reasonable choice. Expatriates routinely move down this path through their travels, going to school abroad, or working in a foreign country. One vehicle to ultimately becoming an expatriate is World Wide Opportunities on Organic Farms, in which one can exchange work for room and board in many locations on the planet.

Among left and libertarian populists, there are those decentralization activists who believe a nation's population size can be its essential impediment to achieving and sustaining democracy. They argue that once a nation has too many people, genuine democracy—in which people have a sense of real power over their lives—is impossible. So, for example, if your nation had six billion people, would you really feel that your vote had any impact in an election? How about one billion people? How about three hundred million? Thus, such decentralization activists take seriously the idea that when nations become too large for democracy to function, secessions are necessary.

The mainstream press labels secession movements in the United States as "crazy" and "extremist." Deriding such movements in the United States is made easier because of secession's unfortunate association with slavery. Following the American Revolution—a hugely successful secessionist movement that created the United States—the largest secession movement in US history was the failed movement by southern states organized into the Confederacy. However, how would Americans look at the idea of secession had New England, following the 1854 passage of the Kansas-Nebraska Act (a major setback for the Abolitionist Movement), attempted to secede from the United States in order to establish a nation that prohibited slavery?

While the Alaskan Independence Party and its aspiration of an "independent nation of Alaska" has received attention from the press because of its link to Sarah Palin's husband, another significant movement is the Second Vermont Republic, Vermont's secessionist movement, which was given some ink by *Time* magazine in 2010. Vermont was not one of the original thirteen colonies, having first been part of the colony of New York. Vermont came into existence in 1777, when it declared its independence from both New York and England, and remained independent until 1791, a period historians now call the era of the Vermont Republic, during which it coined its own currency and operated its own postal system. According to a 2007 poll, the Vermont secessionist movement has support from 13 percent of Vermont voters, and the *Vermont Commons*, a secessionist monthly newspaper, has a circulation of ten thousand.

While at the present time, these and other US secession movements have low probability of success, they remain interesting for the cause of democracy. Some of these movements, most notably Vermont's, comprise a mix of both left and libertarian populists and are decidedly anti-war and anti-corporate-control.

A few years ago, I interviewed historian and decentralization activist Kirkpatrick Sale about secessionist movements. Sale pointed out that while secession may not seem realistic to many Americans, "In today's world, that's what's happening." He reminded me of the breakup of the Soviet Union and several other countries and noted, "Just look at what's happened in the last 60 years—the United Nations started with 51 nations in 1945, now has grown to 193 nations." I asked him if simply having the "balls" to bring up the topic of secession creates energy. He responded that some think that it is just "plain nutsy" but added:

> I certainly have found that the idea of secession resonates
> with quite a number of people . . . Once you reject acquies-
> cence and reform and revolution as political responses to the
> empire, there's not a lot left . . . It certainly makes a lot more
> sense than trying to make change by voting or writing your

senator or marching and demonstrating or sitting around piss-ing and moaning.

What can be said of the value of dissolution, divorce, extrication, and secession? First, their threat can be a disruptive tactic that can get an oppressor's attention. Second, as a backup plan, these can provide the calm and wisdom necessary to create other tactics. Third, when success-fully executed, they become models that inspire others.

Twenty-first-Century Abolitionism: Ending Student-Loan Debt Servitude

Young people and their families are often told that if one lacks a college education, one will be among society's "losers." At the same time, govern-ment funding of public universities has been drying up; both public and private higher education are now so expensive that most young people are forced to take out large loans. While elitists can afford—without loans—to shell out whatever money is necessary for college, almost everyone else is saddled with debt—for many, a "debt sword" that hangs over their heads for a significant part of their lives.

Enraged? Good. Anger can be a good starting energy to rethink how you or your children may want to gain an education and a livelihood.

Maybe one day, when enough of us regain collective self-confidence, "no tuition" will be restored at excellent public university systems such as the City University of New York, and no tuition in public universities will be the rule throughout the United States. No young person should have to deal with student-loan debt. It would be a simple matter of govern-ment shifting the money that it is now spending on private contractors in unnecessary wars.

Maybe one day, student debtors and their friends and family—an increasingly large group—will form a movement to gain debt forgiveness. Debt forgiveness would not only be a major "stimulus package" (costing about the same as a recent stimulus package) but would also help liberate an entire generation.

However, even before these "maybe days" come about, there are some ways that people, at an individual and family level, can begin to fight back against student-loan debt and contemporary servitude.

First, the math. The mainstream number that we hear repeatedly is that those who graduate college make a million dollars more in their lifetime than those who don't. However, half of those who attend college don't graduate. And while on average, a college degree may increase lifetime earnings, in individual cases (for example, depending on whether one really had wanted to go college, and what one then did with one's college degree), a degree may ultimately be a waste of time and money. Moreover, for that majority of young people who must take on increasingly steep student loans, even if that degree does help them make more money over the course of their lifetime, major debt in their twenties and thirties (or longer) will likely curtail all kinds of life possibilities.

There is another kind of math to consider. In this math, it may make sense to go college, or it may not. And it may make sense to go to a college with a high sticker price, but it probably does not.

The College Board in 2010 reported that for tuition alone, private colleges average $26,273 per year and public colleges average $7,020. While the majority of students receive grants and aid to make up some of that price, they also have living expenses. So, at Ohio State University, a public university, tuition is $10,440 for in-state residents and $25,302 for out-of-state residents, and the additional "estimated annual expenses for room, board, insurance, books and supplies" is $13,764.

Recently, I counseled parents who had shelled out $55,000 for their daughter's *first year* at a private college, only to come to resent her for partying and flunking out. Although this upper-class family could afford the financial hit, by falling victim to the notion that they would be considered "bad parents" if their child did not go to college, they denied the fact that their daughter was not ready for college, and so paying their daughter's college costs created needless family acrimony.

When considering college, here's the math that you might want to take more seriously. Add up the money that will be spent on college. Add that to four years' lost income from not working. What's your total? $75,000? $100,000? $150,000? More? Then consider your financial resources—specifically, how much debt are you are likely to accrue? Then consider: How much money per month will that debt cost you? How long will you have that debt? If your parents have the money, what could you do with it instead of going to college? Could your parents hold on to that money and allow you to try surviving out in the world for a few years until you mature? Could you then use that money for a start-up business? Or use it to buy a home to live in free and clear? Or could you use a year's worth of college expenses to travel and gain knowledge, experiences, and maybe even connections to help you make a buck?

The point here is not ruling out college. College may make sense, especially if you want to make a living at something that requires college-level certification, but it may not be necessary to spend as much as people are now spending to get such certifications. And college may not make any sense at all, especially if you are not motivated for it.

Exiting from the modern world-religion view that not attending college is sinful and shameful, let's look at it soberly. Colleges offer (1) learning—usually more information than skills; (2) certifications and accreditation; and (3) partying and potential for meeting people.

While learning does take place in college, it is just as easy to gain knowledge outside of college, even the kind of knowledge that is specific to quality colleges and universities. Most college learning is book learning, and one need not go to college to read books. Most of us have learned much of what we utilize to make a living and survive through experience, not through coursework. But what if you want the kind of course work that is specifically given at a prestigious university?

In 2001, the Massachusetts Institute of Technology put nineteen hundred of its courses online *for free*. While not all courses offer complete syllabi, lecture notes, class exercises, tests, video, and audio, many do. For instance, I checked out "7.012 Introduction to Biology," where I scrolled down to "video/lectures" and listened to the professor deliver the actual class lectures as well as read a complete transcript; and there was everything else routinely available in a college course, such as reading assignments and exams. All this is part of what is called the "open education movement," which is rapidly growing.

It is true, however, that without a college degree and specific certifications, one simply will not be hired for certain jobs. What if you really want to become a teacher and you need to have a degree and certifications, but you have little money and you don't want to be a debt slave?

I strongly advise you to get that degree as inexpensively as possible. I needed degrees to get licensed, but in twenty-five years of private practice no client has cared that I went to public universities. Furthermore, no publisher has ever asked me where I received my education. So if you need to get some certification, shop around, and you may well be able to do so without accumulating debt.

At the College of the Ozarks in Missouri, 95 percent of students graduate debt free. All students must work fifteen hours a week to help pay for their tuition. The College of the Ozarks is one of seven members of the Work College Consortium, mostly small rural private schools, which all make work part of the deal to get a degree either at very low cost or tuition free. The others are Blackburn in Illinois, Ecclesia in Arkansas, Sterling in Vermont, Warren Wilson in North Carolina, and Alice Lloyd and Berea in Kentucky. The quaint crafts town of Berea is not far from where I live, and I have visited it several times and chatted with Berea's intelligent and hardworking students, all of whom are enthusiastic about their educational deal.

Robin Taffler is director of the Work College Consortium and has also worked at public universities in Massachusetts and Kentucky. Taffler describes how these work colleges are different. "I have to say they're joyous campuses . . . The students take a lot of ownership at these schools. They are tolerant, respectful, and they learn to depend on one another very early on." At these colleges, students maintain the grounds, run the library, admissions, and registrar's offices, answer the president's phones, and on some campuses farm. Berea College has a restaurant and craft shops that students staff. These Work College Consortium schools are not for everyone. Berea College, for example, was founded by ardent abolitionists and radical reformers and has a religious mission.

What if you don't need the social scene of college and just want to get an accredited degree online that will leave you with little or no debt?

Western Governors University (WGU) is an online university that has the necessary accreditations and is relatively inexpensive. Basic tuition for most programs such as a teaching degree is $2,890 every six months. This is about one-third of the cost of the better-known online universities such as University of Phoenix. Moreover, the WGU tuition is a flat rate, and because of its competency-based approach, if one is industrious, one can get a degree and certifications in significantly less than four years. Instead of requiring that students take specific courses or amass a certain number of credit hours, WGU asks only that students demonstrate mastery of the subject matter via online exams or papers. There are also grants and aid available, and one can remain at one's day job, so it is very possible to get necessary credentials without accruing any debt. WGU has four career paths—education, information technology, business, and health care. If you want to become a certified teacher, WGU has accreditation from both regional standard-bearers and the National Council for Accreditation of Teacher Education, the professional body recognized by the US Department of Education for certifying teacher-preparation programs. Kevin Kinser, a professor at New York's University at Albany who studies online learning (and is not affiliated with WGU) told *Time* magazine in 2008, "[WGU] has earned a reputation for producing high-quality graduates, particularly in education." WGU has about 250 full-time faculty members who work as mentors, checking in with students by phone every couple of weeks to ensure that they are making progress in their courses and to recommend additional resources. Alisa Izumi, a business professor at WGU who previously taught at the University of Massachusetts–Amherst, said, "I get to know each of my students much better than I did when I lectured to them once a week in class." Students can also interact with one another online.

A good place to start looking for alternatives to standard college education and enslaving debt is Anya Kamenetz's *DIY U: Edupunks, Edupreneurs, and the Coming Transformation of Higher Education*, which provides details on the open education movement, the Work College

Consortium, and inexpensive online universities such as WGU; it also offers a lengthy list of Web sites that will help you get self-educated on the topic.

Besides learning and credentialing, colleges do offer a certain kind of socializing and partying that one does not get via independent study. However, again, let's get back to the math and common sense. Is the typical college partying worth the price tag? How expensive is the typical socializing that goes on at colleges compared with many other ways of mixing it up with the world that are less expensive?

What if you are young, have no money, do not want to go directly from high school to college, and want to gain life experience and not accrue any debt? One option is AmeriCorps. AmeriCorps NCCC (National Civilian Community Corps) is a residential, team-based, national service program in all fifty states and US territories for young adults ages eighteen through twenty-four. AmeriCorps members help local communities address their needs. They perform team-based service projects in five different areas: natural and other disasters, infrastructure improvement, environmental stewardship and conservation, energy conservation, and urban and rural development. AmeriCorps members receive a living allowance of approximately $4,000 for the ten months of service as well as housing, meals, and limited medical benefits. Some young people have a great experience in AmeriCorps, while others do not, but all get some kind of life experience that does not create debt.

Working with teenagers, young adults, and their families, I have discovered that mainstream society has given many of them a distorted sense of life with regard to risk. Specifically, many of them have been socialized to believe that the least risky path is the most prestigious college that one is admitted to. This path can work out fine for some people, but it does not make sense for everyone. In addition to the young woman who flunked out her first year, blowing $55,000, then feeling like a "loser" and creating resentment, there have been other cases where the most prestigious college has not been the best choice. I know of one intelligent man who grew up working class and was admitted to Harvard, but he felt alienated and had a psychotic break. And while young people have been socialized to be terrified of not having a college education or not receiving a degree from a prestigious institution, they have not been told about the risk of carrying huge debt. They also have not been told that risk is inescapable in life, and that often authorities' idea of the least risky path turns out to be the most risky one.

Workplace Democracy: Worker and Other Co-operatives

There is a saying: "The real problem with corporations is not what they do but what they are." It means that there is something *essentially* anti-democratic about gigantic corporations in which major decisions are made by executives and a board of directors solely on the basis of profit. There is, for example, something terribly wrong when worker misery can result in increased shareholder profits, which is routinely the case when Wall Street pushes up the stock price of a corporation that is laying off thousands of its workers.

In dramatic contrast to such giant corporations is Union Cab Cooperative in Madison, Wisconsin. Union Cab is a *worker coopera-tive*, defined by the US Federation of Worker Cooperatives as "a business entity that is owned and controlled by the people who work in it." Union Cab was founded in 1979 by a group of drivers, dispatchers, and mechanics after a failed labor struggle against the Checker Cab company. Union Cab's Web site states:

> Since day one, we have operated as a democratic workplace with one member/one vote. A board of directors consisting of an elected group of drivers, mechanics and dispatchers governs Union Cab. We believe that our structure helps customers have a voice at all levels of our organization.

Workers owning their business collectively usually means that they all invested with a "buy-in" when they began working at the cooperative. Worker-owners share profits—the surplus money left after expenses—as well as financial risks. Fundamental to a worker cooperative is that decisions are made democratically by the people who do the work, usually according to the principle of "one worker, one vote." Some worker cooperatives, depending on the size and decision making required, have elected boards of directors or elected managers—or they may have no managers at all. In some worker cooperatives, decisions are made by consensus and complete agreement, while in others, decision are made by a simple majority.

Several types of businesses are worker-owned and -controlled. The US Federation of Worker Cooperatives reports that the majority of worker cooperatives in the United States are small businesses, with a few larger enterprises. It estimates that there are "over 300 democratic workplaces in the United States, employing over 3,500 people and generating over $400 million in annual revenues."

One of the largest members of the US Federation of Worker Cooperatives is Alvarado Street Bakery, located just north of San Francisco in Petaluma. It began by producing whole-grain organic baked goods in 1979. Alvarado Street Bakery traces its roots back to the "Food for People, Not for Profit" movement in the San Francisco Bay Area, and was originally part of a nonprofit organization called Liberty Clover Worker's Brigade. In 1981, five brigade workers formed a worker cooperative and purchased a bakery.

Alvarado Street Bakery, according to a report by Petaluma's *Press Democrat* in October 2009, has 117 workers with $24 million annual revenue. Each worker "member" of the cooperative is given one share a year in the company. That share grants each member a right to an equal vote on matters ranging from reinvesting profits, to salaries, to health and other benefits. All members relinquish their share at the end of the year and are granted a new one; and each member gets only one share. All salaries are not equal, but production workers earn between $18 and $22 an hour, the average worker earns between $65,000 and $70,000 a year, and the ratio of executive to worker compensation is less than three to one. The majority of employees have been with the company for more than fifteen years. The *Press Democrat* spoke with Ronnie Bell, an Alvarado Street Bakery bread line quality control supervisor, who said, "There's no big I's and little You's. Everything is shared."

In the spirit of the nineteenth-century Populist Alliance cooperatives, there continue to be American "producer cooperatives" that provide more power to small businesses. By banding together, producer cooperatives are not at the mercy of giant corporations and have greater bargaining power with buyers. These producer cooperatives combine resources to more effectively market their products, improving the incomes of their members.

One such example of a producer cooperative is the organic farming cooperative called the Coulee Region Organic Produce Pool (CROPP). In 1988, with increasing numbers of family farms folding and others being threatened with extinction because of the low prices farmers were receiving for their goods, seven Wisconsin farmers created CROPP. These farmers shared a belief that a new, sustainable approach to agriculture was needed if family farms and rural communities were to survive. CROPP has grown into the largest farmers' cooperative in North America. It started with organic vegetables but soon moved into organic dairy products. Eventually, the CROPP cooperative developed its own brand name, Organic Valley, and has become the largest source of organic milk in the United States. CROPP has grown to approximately fourteen hundred farmers across thirty-three states. One of those farmers is Travis Forgues from Alburg Springs, Vermont.

Travis Forgues grew up on his father's conventional farm and was always aware of the stress that his parents were under trying to make ends meet. His parents, believing there was no future in farming, encouraged Travis to go to college and find a career away from the farm. Travis married his high school sweetheart Amy, moved to Burlington, Vermont, and began working with high-risk youths, but he longed to get back to the rural life and farming. Since his father's farm had not been worked for many years—and was not chemically treated—it was an ideal place to try organic farming. The Forgues received a visit from Jim Wedeberg from Organic Valley, who encouraged them to convert to organic farming and become farmer-owners in CROPP. The Forgues family signed up, and Travis convinced two neighboring farm families to join as well, which guaranteed there would be enough milk to justify a steady truck run to northern Vermont. Other Vermont farmers have since joined.

Today the Forgues family farm—240 acres with seventy milking cows—is able to support two families because they converted to organic farming and joined CROPP to get better prices for their product. As a result of the Forgues's efforts and CROPP, there are now Vermont farm families whose land might otherwise have been cut up for house lots, who are living and working on their farm, able to make a living at it, and producing a product that they are proud of.

In addition to worker cooperatives and producer cooperatives, there are also consumer cooperatives and purchasing/shared service cooperatives. Consumer cooperatives are owned by the people who buy the goods or use the services of the cooperative. Such cooperatives can be food cooperatives, housing cooperatives, or credit unions. Purchasing and shared services cooperatives are owned and governed by independent business owners, small municipalities, and, in some cases, state governments that band together to enhance their purchasing power, lowering their costs and improving their competitiveness and ability to provide quality services.

The National Cooperative Business Association (NCBA) explains that "Co-ops are formed by their members when the marketplace fails to provide needed goods or services at affordable prices and acceptable quality." What makes something truly a cooperative of any kind, according to NCBA, is that it's owned and democratically controlled by its members, the people who use the cooperative's services or buy its goods—not by outside investors; and it's motivated not by profit, but by the desire to meet members' needs for affordable, high-quality goods or services. NCBA reports that US cooperatives of some kind serve some 120 million members; worldwide, some 750,000 cooperatives serve 730 million members.

A bold step toward a genuinely democratic society is to democratize the work world. Central to people's lives are personal relationships and work. If their work lives are democratic, it is difficult to imagine that they would put up for too long with a society that is not so. Whether a mom-and-pop independent or a worker cooperative, it is democracy when the people who are working the business are making the decisions.

Helpful and Harmful Small Victories and Compromises

A major divide among anti-elitists is over what magnitude of change should be worked for and celebrated.

On one extreme are people who think that *anything* is better than nothing at all. They, for example, don't consider that sometimes agreeing to a small gain can, in the big picture, be more of a defeat than a triumph.

At the other extreme are people who reject any incremental change and hold out for total transformation. Self-described "unrepentant Marxist" researcher, activist, and writer Louis Proyect is critical of the celebration of worker cooperatives such as the Alvarado Street Bakery because, he believes, worker cooperatives lack the power to transform the American economy and that "they would be nothing but tokens in a vast system operating on the basis of profit."

I believe that there is a simple criterion that can be applied here: Does the change increase individual self-respect and collective self-confidence, and does it increase one's energy level to pursue even greater democracy? Or does it feel like a sellout that decreases individual self-respect and collective self-confidence and de-energizes individuals and groups?

It is difficult to imagine how a successful worker cooperative fails to increase individual self-respect and collective self-confidence—not only for participants but for people looking for inspiration. However, it also seems clear that settling for small crumbs when the time is ripe for a major victory can certainly be de-energizing.

Anything is not necessarily better than nothing at all; but perfection, as the saying goes, can be the enemy of the good. A change that seems likely to increase individual self-respect and collective self-confidence so that there is increased energy to create democracy is the kind of change that I can get excited about.

Utilizing the criterion of increased self-respect and collective self-confidence, those of us who believe in genuine democracy can more constructively debate the wisdom of what is truly a victory. Is the change going to increase strength to gain democracy, or is the small gain going to take the steam out of a democratic movement? People will have different opinions, especially with regard to what is crucial for their self-respect—that is the nature of democracy—so this criterion doesn't necessarily make for easier decisions, but staying focused on it makes debate more fruitful.

With respect to compromise, there is a huge difference between those compromises that violate our core being and those that do not. To remain alive, virtually all of us would compromise our body to the extent of having a gangrened toe amputated, but most of us would reject the compromised life provided by life-support machines. When it comes to our core values, it is often less clear what type of compromise violates an individual's or a group's essential integrity so as to be worse than death.

In 1877, after a series of land concessions followed by broken promises on the part of the US government, a group among the Nez Perce were not willing to compromise again and accept the US government's latest and even smaller land promises. It was clear to them that the US government was not negotiating in good faith and that the Nez Perce were being forced to compromise their essential way of life as they knew it. So this group of Nez Perce refused to submit and surrender. They outmaneuvered a far larger US army force for more than three months, over approximately eighteen hundred miles, from their homelands in what is now eastern Oregon through Montana—not in any attempt to defeat the United States but simply to escape it. Ultimately they were unsuccessful. Casualties mounting, Joseph, one of their chiefs, surrendered with these words:

> . . . It is cold and we have no blankets. The little children are freezing to death. My people, some of them, have run away to the hills, and have no blankets, no food; no one knows where they are—perhaps freezing to death. I want to have time to look for my children and see how many of them I can find. Maybe I shall find them among the dead. Hear me, my chiefs. I am tired. My heart is sick and sad. From where the sun now stands, I will fight no more forever.

How should we view such a surrender? Among contemporary Nez Perce, according to Kent Nerburn's *Chief Joseph and the Flight of the Nez*

Perce, there is ambivalence toward Joseph. One unnamed Nez Perce told Nerburn, "Many of our people even see him as a coward and traitor for surrendering. But without him no one pays any attention to us."

During the flight, there was debate among the Nez Perce at almost every stage, especially on their speed, as some believed that Looking Glass, their initial flight strategist, directed them to move too slowly. Forty miles from the Canadian border, US troops trapped them, and this forced a debate among the Nez Perce as to what to do next. White Bird, another chief, had no trust for the promises of white people and refused to surrender. So when Joseph did surrender—saving the lives of many children, the elderly, and other nonwarriors—it was agreed among them that he would do so in a manner that provided White Bird and his followers a chance to slip through enemy lines, which they did, successfully getting to Canada, where they were outside the reach of the US forces.

Joseph's later success at gaining publicity for the plight of the Nez Perce was vital to their survival as a people, and Nerburn's account of Joseph reveals not a coward but a man of integrity who genuinely believed his decisions to be in the best interest of his people. It seems to me that there was a great wisdom among the Nez Perce that enabled Joseph and White Bird to take their followers on different paths. Joseph and White Bird, each retaining their core values, both created a historical dignity and energy for the Nez Perce's survival as a people.

Compromising core values, however, is quite a different matter. Abolitionists such as William Lloyd Garrison knew that compromising their movement's core value of a complete abolition of slavery by accepting some kind of compromised solution would strip the movement of the moral energy that powered it. Most civil rights activists understand that accepting an agreement that does not provide *full* equality is a violation of core values of the movement, and would de-energize it.

But compromises in which core beliefs are not violated are another matter. Recall that when the Iranian government raised taxes 70 percent on businesses, Iranian merchants struck Tehran's Grand Bazaar, ultimately forcing the government to retreat to only a 15 percent increase.

What was at issue was not whether or not any taxes should be paid, it was merely a question of how much, and so a compromised solution was not a violation of core beliefs and values. Instead, such a compromise should only be evaluated as a good or poor negotiation, and there was in fact disagreement among Iranian merchants over whether or not their victory was large enough to be an energizing one. From what Americans are told about Iranian president Mahmoud Ahmadinejad, it would seem that the merchants' standing up to a ruthless dictator and significantly reducing taxes should be an energizing victory. But for those Iranian merchants who believed Ahmadinejad was not all that powerful—and there were such merchants—the tax increase compromise was somewhat de-energizing.

Crossing the Final Divide

There is one more divide, I believe, that not only divides true populists from one another but also divides many of us internally. That divide is about the belief in the possibility or impossibility of our actually defeating the corporatocracy. By the looks of things, it seems remote. But just how seriously should we take the looks of things?

Less than a decade before African American slavery ended in the United States, the idea of abolishing slavery seemed like an impossibility for most Americans, including Abraham Lincoln, who even doubted whether it would be possible to stop the spread of slavery. In 1856, he stated:

> The slaves of the South, at a moderate estimate, are worth a thousand millions of dollars. Let it be permanently settled that this property may extend to new territory, without restraint, and it greatly enhances, perhaps quite doubles, its value at once. This immense, palpable pecuniary interest, on the question of extending slavery, unites the Southern people, as one man. But it can not be demonstrated that the North will gain a dollar by restricting it. Moral principle is all, or nearly all,

that unites us of the North. Pity 'tis, it is so, but this is a looser bond, than pecuniary interest. Right here is the plain cause of their perfect union and our want of it.

That slavery would be abolished in the United States less than a decade after Lincoln's pessimistic analysis of the difficulty of merely stopping its spread was one of those seeming impossibilities that became possible because of unforeseen historical events. In the North, there was certainly not enough concern for African Americans to end slavery, and few could have predicted that Southerners would fire on Fort Sumter and the federal troops inside, helping provide Lincoln with a justification to invade the South. And had not General William Tecumseh Sherman succeeded in taking Atlanta in September 1864, Lincoln may well have been defeated in that year's presidential election by the Democratic candidate, who would have likely worked out a deal with the Confederates not to abolish slavery. A close look at much of history tells us that all kinds of seeming impossibilities actually occur, and all kinds of seeming inevitabilities were not inevitable at all.

In my lifetime, as a result of unforeseen variables, what had previously seemed impossible has in fact occurred. Until shortly before it occurred, the collapse of the Soviet empire seemed an impossibility to most Americans, who saw only mass resignation within the Soviet Union and its sphere of control. But the shipyard workers in Gdansk, Poland, did not see their Soviet and Communist Party rulers as the all-powerful forces that Americans did. And so Polish workers' Solidarity, by simply refusing to go away, provided a strong dose of morale across Eastern Europe at the same time other historical events weakened the Soviet empire.

The lesson from history is that tyrannical and dehumanizing institutions are often more fragile than they appear, and with time, luck, morale, and the people's ability to seize the moment, damn near anything is possible. You never really know until it happens whether or not you are living in that time when historical variables are conspiring to create opportunities for seemingly impossible change. Maybe in your lifetime, or your kids' lifetime, or their kids' lifetime, there will be a realistic chance to defeat the corporatocracy. And when that opportunity presents itself, victory may well rest on whether there are enough of us who are capable of seizing that opportunity and starting the ball rolling. So if not now, when will individuals begin regaining their self-respect? If not now, when will we begin restoring collective self-confidence? If not now, when?

NOTES

Chapter 1: The People Divided Versus the Corporatocracy in Control

1 **"Are Americans a Broken People?"**: Bruce E. Levine, "Are Americans a Broken People?" *AlterNet*, December 11, 2009, www.alternet.org/story/144529 (accessed December 18, 2009). Earlier versions of the article: "Liberation Psychology for the US: Are We Too Demoralized to Protest?" *Z Magazine*, November 2009, 27–30; and "Are Americans Too Broken for the Truth to Set Us Free?" *CounterPunch*, December 4–6, 2009, www.counterpunch.org/levine12042009 .html (accessed December 6, 2009).

1 **reaction comments**: Reader comments throughout the book are taken from responses to the above articles as well as to follow-up articles: Don Hazen, Les Leopold, and Bruce E. Levine, "Are Progressives Depressed or Too Privileged to Produce Social Change? Or Are We Just Failing to Organize Effectively," *AlterNet*, January 7, 2010 (in which Leopold responded to my first article, I responded to Leopold, and Hazen to both), www.alternet.org/story/144982; Bruce E. Levine, "How Teenage Rebellion Has Become a Mental Illness," January 28, 2008, *AlterNet*, www.alternet.org/health/75081; Nan Mooney, "College Loan Slavery: Student Debt Is Getting Way Out of Hand," *AlterNet*, November 12, 2008, www .alternet.org/economy/106445. Comments are also taken from re-publications of the above articles at *Democratic Underground*, December 13, 2009, www .democraticunderground.com/discuss/duboard.php?az=view_all&address=103x 502317; *Capital Hill Blue*, December 15, 2009, http://readerrant.capitolhill blue.com/ubbthreads.php?ubb=showflat&Number=135248&fpart=1; Reddit .com, January 25, 2010, www.reddit.com/r/reddit.com/comments/aj7cw/are _americans_a_broken_people_have_consumerism; *Propeller*, December 16, 2009, www.propeller.com/story/2009/12/16/are-americans-a-broken-people (site discontinued); TheSurvivalistBlog.net, December 17, 2009, www.thesurvivalist blog.net/2009/12/are-americans-broken-people.html; *Video Café*, December 23, 2009, http://videocafe.crooksandliars.com/heather/ed-schultz-show-bummed-base; *Prison Planet*, December 17, 2009, www.prisonplanet.com/are-americans-a-broken-people-why-weve-stopped-fighting-back-against-the-forces-of-oppression.html; Atheistnexus.org, December 14, 2009, www.atheistnexus.org/group/consumereth ics/forum/topics/are-americans-a-broken-people?commentId=2182797%3ACom ment%3A647712&xg_source=activity&groupId=2182797%3AGroup%3A264752 (site discontinued); ThomHartmann.com, December 14, 2009, www.thomhart mann.com/board/viewtopic.php?f=17&t=2692; and *Information Clearing House*, December 15, 2009, http://js-kit.com/api/static/pop_comments?ref=http://infor mationclearinghouse.info&path=%2Farticle24184_htm (site discontinued). Sites accessed between January 28, 2008, and January 30, 2010.

3 **Goodwyn writes in *The Populist Moment***: Lawrence Goodwyn, *The Populist Moment: A Short History of the Agrarian Revolt in America* (Oxford, London, New York: Oxford University Press, 1978), xix.

5 **Lawrence Summers**: John D. McKinnon and T. W. Farnam, "Hedge Fund Paid Summers $5.2 Million in Past Year," *Wall Street Journal*, April 5, 2009, http://online.wsj.com/article/SB123879462053487927.html (accessed May 10, 2010).

5 **Neal Wolin . . . *Mother Jones***: Andy Kroll, "The Bankers on Obama's Team," *Mother Jones*, January–February 2010, http://motherjones.com/politics/2010/01/henhouse-meet-fox-wall-street-washington-obama (accessed April 20, 2010). An excellent article on the revolving door is Zach Carter, "America's Ten Most Corrupt Capitalists," *AlterNet*, May 13, 2010, www.alternet.org/economy/146819 (accessed May 13, 2010).

5 **Billy Tauzin**: Jacob Goldstein, "Wanted: Ex-Congressman. Must Love Drugs. Good Pay," *Wall Street Journal*, February 12, 2010, http://blogs.wsj.com/health/2010/02/12/wanted-ex-congressman-must-love-drugs-good-pay/tab/article (accessed May 15, 2010); Jim Drinkard, "Drugmakers Go Furthest to Sway Congress," *USA Today*, April 25, 2005, www.usatoday.com/money/industries/health/drugs/2005-04-25-drug-lobby-cover_x.htm (accessed May 15, 2010). *60 Minutes* reported on April 1, 2007, that Tauzin's salary at PhRMA was $2 million a year.

6 **Mitch Daniels, Eli Lilly, and Bush family**: "Mitch Daniels: Indiana's 49th Governor," *The Indianapolis Star*, January 11, 2005, http://www2.indystar.com/library/factfiles/people/d/daniels_mitch/daniels.html (accessed December 3, 2010); Alexander Cockburn, *The Golden Age Is in Us* (London: Verso, 1995), 297–298; Peter R. Breggin and Ginger Ross Breggin, *Talking Back to Prozac: What Doctors Aren't Telling You About Today's Most Controversial Drug* (New York: St. Martin's Press, 1994), 207; Bob Herbert, "Whose Hands Are Dirty?" November 25, 2002, *New York Times*, www.nytimes.com/2002/11/25/opinion/25HERB.html (accessed May 10, 2010); Miriam Hill, "Whistle-Blower's Perspective on Lilly Case," *Philadelphia Inquirer*, January 19, 2009, www.philly.com/inquirer/breaking/business_breaking/20090119_Whistle-blowers_perspective_on_Lilly _case.html (accessed January 20, 2009—site discontinued) information currently available at http://tmap.wordpress.com/2009/01/19/629/; Sharyl Attkisson, "Eli Lilly's $1.4 Billion Crime," CBS News, January 16, 2009, archived at www .cbsnews.com/video/watch/?id=4726046n (accessed May 11, 2010); Bruce E. Levine, "The Case for Giving Eli Lilly the Corporate Death Penalty," *AlterNet*, March 3, 2009, www.alternet.org/story/129709 (accessed March 3, 2010).

7 **mass media . . . a handful of large corporations**: "Ownership Chart: The Big Six," Freepress.net, www.freepress.net/ownership/chart/main (accessed April 22, 2010).

Chapter 2: Are the People Broken?

14 **presidential election of 1892 . . . presidential election of 1912**: David Leip, "United States Presidential Election Results," *Dave Leip's Atlas of US Presidential Elections*, http://uselectionatlas.org/RESULTS (accessed October 2, 2010).

14 **Teddy Roosevelt's Progressive Party**: Patricia O' Toole, "The War of 1912," *Time,* June 25, 2006, www.time.com/time/magazine/article/0,9171,1207791-2,00 .html (accessed October 15, 2010).

15 *Advertising Age* **"Marketer of the Year"**: Nikki Gloudeman, "Barack Obama: Marketer of the Year," *Mother Jones,* October 20, 2008, http://motherjones.com/ riff/2008/10/barack-obama-marketer-year (accessed February 6, 2010).

16 **United States Social Forum**: Sally Kohn, "15,000 Progressive Activists in Detroit: Why No Media or Respect?" *AlterNet,* June 26, 2010, www.alternet.org/ story/147341 (accessed June 26, 2010).

16 **City Life/Vida Urbana**: *Bill Moyers Journal,* December 18, 2009, www.pbs.org/ moyers/journal/12182009/transcript2.html (accessed January 10, 2010).

16 **Margaret Flowers**: *Bill Moyers Journal,* February 5, 2010, www.pbs.org/moyers/ journal/02052010/transcript5.html (accessed February 7, 2010).

16 **The Battle of Seattle** : For crowd estimates: Anup Shah, "WTO Protests in Seattle, 1999," *Global Issues,* February 18, 2001, www.globalissues.org/article/46/ wto-protests-in-seattle-1999; Patrick F. Gillham, "Complexity & Irony in Policing and Protesting: The World Trade Organization in Seattle," *Social Justice* 27, no. 2 (2000), 212–236, http://web.mit.edu/gtmarx/www/seattle.html; Saint Schmidt "Remembering Seattle," October 30, 2009, *Anarchist News,* www.anarchistnews .org/www.anarchistnews.org/?q=node/9981; Joseph Young, "Lessons from Seattle: Resistance to Globalization, the Media, and the State's Response," paper prepared for delivery at the Annual Conference of the Global Studies Association, Boston, MA, April 23–25, 2004, www.net4dem.org/mayglobal/Events/Conference%20 2004/papers/JoeYoung.pdf (all accessed March 10–12, 2010).

17 **April 2000 . . . protests in Washington, DC**: Anup Shah, "IMF & World Bank Protests, Washington DC," *Global Issues,* July 13, 2001, www.globalissues.org/ article/23/imf--world-bank-protests-washington-dc (accessed October 14, 2010).

17 **TransAtlantic Business Dialogue (TABD)**: Janice Morse and Cliff Peale, "Leaders Tackle Need to Improve Message: Conferees Acknowledge 'Dislocations,'" *Cincinnati Enquirer,* November 18, 2000, www.enquirer.com/ editions/2000/11/18/fin_conferees.html (accessed January 6, 2010).

18 **reported that since the election**: Robin Tone, "Disdain for Bush Simmers in Democratic Strongholds," *New York Times,* August 4, 2003, www.nytimes .com/2003/08/04/politics/campaigns/04DEMS.html?pagewanted=1 (accessed February 21, 2010).

18 **widely reported . . . dissenting comment of Justice John Paul Stevens**: *CyberAlert* 5, no. 267 (December 13, 2000), www.mediaresearch.org/ cyberalerts/2000/cyb20001213_extra.asp (accessed February 22, 2010).

18 **Bush's Inauguration Day**: Angela Couloumbis, "Inauguration Protests Largest Since Nixon in 1973," *Philadelphia Inquirer,* January 21, 2001, reported in www .commondreams.org/headlines01/0121-01.htm (accessed February 22, 2010).

19 **disputed presidential election in Iran**: Nahid Siamdoust, "Tehran's Rallying Cry: 'We Are the People of Iran,'" *Time*, June 15, 2009, www.time.com/time/ world/article/0,8599,1904764,00.html?xid=rss-topstories (accessed February 24, 2010); Laura Secor, "The Iranian Vote," *New Yorker*, July 13, 2009, www.newy orker.com/online/blogs/newsdesk/2009/06/laura-secor-irans-stolen-election .html?printable=true (accessed February 24, 2010); "Iranian Public on Current Issues," World Public Opinion, September 19, 2009, www.worldpublicopinion.org/ pipa/pdf/sep09/IranUS_Sep09_quaire.pdf (accessed February 24, 2010).

19 **disputed Mexican presidential election**: Ceci Connolly, "Mexico Votes 2006: Mexico Restless for a Result," *Washington Post*, July 18, 2006, http://blog .washingtonpost.com/mexicovotes/2006/07/post_3.html (accessed February 23, 2010); "Global Exchange Final Report on Electoral Observations in Mexico," Global Exchange, July 12, 2006, www.globalexchange.org/countries/americas/ mexico/electionreports.html (accessed February 23, 2010); Michael Collins, "The Mexican People: Heroes of Democracy," *Scoop*, August 23, 2006, www .scoop.co.nz/stories/HL0608/S00269.htm (accessed February 23, 2010).

20 **the "Orange Revolution"**: Wikipedia, http://en.wikipedia.org/wiki/Orange _revolution#cite_note-9 (accessed October 17, 2010).

21 **increase of thirty thousand**: "Obama Details Afghan War Plan, Troop Increases," Associated Press (reported on MSNBC), December 1, 2009, www .msnbc.msn.com/id/34218604 (accessed February 26, 2010).

21 **Afghanistan . . . American people actually opposed the war**: Jennifer Agiesta and Jon Cohen, "Public Opinion in US Turns Against Afghan War," *Washington Post*, August 20, 2009, www.washingtonpost.com/wp-dyn/content/ article/2009/08/19/AR2009081903066.html (accessed February 26, 2010); "CNN Poll: Afghanistan War Opposition at All-Time High," *CNN Politics*, September 1, 2009, http://politicalticker.blogs.cnn.com/2009/09/01/cnn-poll-afghanistan-war-opposition-at-all-time-high (accessed February 26, 2010).

21 **"Do you favor or oppose"**: PollingNumbers.com, www.pollingnumbers.com/ poll-of-polls/afghanistan-war-support.html (last updated February 1, 2010).

22 **twenty thousand . . . against the impending invasion of Afghanistan**: "Thousands Take to the Streets in San Francisco and Washington, D.C. to Call for Peace and Justice," *Democracy Now*, October 1, 2001, www.democracynow .org/2001/10/1/thousands_take_to_the_streets_in (accessed March 1, 2010).

22 **overwhelming majority . . . favored taking military action in Afghanistan**: "America and the War on Terrorism," *AEI Studies in Public Opinion*, 45. In response to the question, "Do you favor or oppose the United States taking direct military action in Afghanistan?," on September 21–22, 2001, 82 percent favored, while 13 percent opposed. Gallup/CNN/USA, www.aei.org/docLib/20050805_ terror0805.pdf (accessed March 2, 2010).

22 **far more protest by Americans against the imminent invasion of Iraq**: CNN, "Cities Jammed in Worldwide Protest of War in Iraq," February 16, 2003, www

.cnn.com/2003/US/02/15/sprj.irq.protests.main (accessed March 3, 2003); "Massive Anti-War Outpouring," CBS, February 15, 2003. CBS News correspondent Jim Acosta says New York organizers claim the rally drew five hundred thousand people and that there were certainly several hundred thousand: www .cbsnews.com/stories/2003/02/16/iraq/main540782.shtml (accessed March 3, 2003); "Anti-War Rally Makes Its Mark," BBC News, February 19, 2003, http:// news.bbc.co.uk/2/hi/uk_news/2767761.stm (accessed March 3, 2010).

23 **Once the Iraq War commenced**: Michael Ruane and Fredrick Kunkle, "Thousands Protest Bush Policy," January 28, 2007, www.washingtonpost.com/ wp-dyn/content/article/2007/01/27/AR2007012700629.html (accessed March 3, 2010); Michelle Boorstein, V. Dion Haynes, and Allison Klein, "Dueling Demonstrations," *Washington Post*, September 16, 2007, www.washingtonpost .com/wp-dyn/content/article/2007/09/15/AR2007091500826.html (accessed March 3, 2010).

23 **March 20, 2010 . . . Kathy Hoang**: "Thousands Rally on Anniversary of Invasion of Iraq," Associated Press (reported in *USA Today*), March 20, 2010, www.usatoday.com/news/washington/2010-03-20-iraq-war-protest_N.htm (accessed March 3, 2010).

23 **Bill Moyers's pained questions**: *Bill Moyers Journal*, December 11, 2009, www. pbs.org/moyers/journal/12112009/transcript2.html (accessed December 12, 2009).

24 **Pew Research Center**: The Pew Research Center, September 23, 2008, http:// people-press.org/reports/pdf/452.pdf (accessed March 14, 2010).

24 **Wall Street bailout . . . most other polls**: PollingReport.com, www.polling report.com/business3.htm (accessed March 14, 2010).

25 **not only did the majority of Americans disapprove**: CBS News Poll, "Bailing Out Banks and Financial Institutions," March 12–15, 2009, released March 16, 2009, www.cbsnews.com/htdocs/pdf/MAR09A-Banks.pdf (accessed March 14, 2010); CBS News Poll, "Bailouts, the Economy and the President," March 12–16, 2009, released March 17, 2009, www.cbsnews.com/htdocs/pdf/poll_031709.pdf (accessed March 14, 2010).

26 **protests against the Wall Street bailout**: Christian Wiessner, "Labor Unions Protest in New York Against Bailout," Reuters, September 25, 2008, www.reuters .com/article/idUSTRE4808KJ20080925 (accessed March 15, 2010).

26 **AFL-CIO-led protest**: Alexander Zaitchik, "Thousands Rally in New York for Showdown with Wall St.," *AlterNet*, April 30, 2010, www.alternet.org/ story/146678 (accessed April 30, 2010).

26 *The Wall Street Journal* **reported**: Luca Di Leo and Maya Jackson, "Fed Data Show Firms on the Brink," *The Wall Street Journal*, December 1, 2010, http:// online.wsj.com/article/SB10001424052748704594804575648740948074042.html (accessed December 2, 2010).

27 **July 2009 Kaiser Health Tracking Poll**: Kaiser Health Tracking Poll, July 2009, www.kff.org/kaiserpolls/upload/7943.pdf (accessed January 8, 2010).

27 **February 2009 CBS News/New York Times Poll**: CBS News/New York Times Poll, February 1, 2009, www.cbsnews.com/htdocs/pdf/SunMo_poll_0209.pdf (accessed January 8, 2010).

27 **December 2009 Reuters poll**: "Most in US Want Public Health Option: Poll," Reuters, December 3, 2009, www.reuters.com/article/idUSTRE5B20OL20091203 (accessed January 8, 2010).

27 **Time Magazine/ABT poll**: Time Magazine/ABT SRBI, July 27–28, 2009 Survey, www.srbi.com/TimePoll4794_Final_%20Report.pdf (accessed January 8, 2010).

29 **Robert Reich**: Robert Reich, "The Final Health Care Vote and What It Really Means," *Huffington Post*, March 22, 2010, www.huffingtonpost.com/robert-reich/the-final-health-care-vot_b_507596.html (accessed March 22, 2010).

30 **put out a joint statement**: John McCain and Barack Obama, "In Their Own Words: The Debate Dispute: Joint Statement of Senators John McCain and Barack Obama," *New York Times*, September 24, 2008, www.nytimes.com/2008/09/25/us/politics/25words.html (accessed February 6, 2010).

30 **Did candidate Obama threaten the military-industrial complex**: Chris Hedges, "The Obama Brand: Feel Good While Overlords Loot the Treasury and Launch Imperial Wars," January 25, 2010, www.alternet.org/story/145358 (accessed January 25, 2010).

30 **Obama asked Congress to hike defense spending**: Robert Reich, "Our Only Existing Jobs Program Is the Military—an Insane Way to Keep Americans Employed," August 12, 2010, www.alternet.org/economy/147831 (accessed August 13, 2010).

30 **also made the energy-industrial complex smile**: "Remarks by the President in State of the Union Address," White House, January 27, 2010, www.whitehouse.gov/the-press-office/remarks-president-state-union-address (accessed January 28, 2010).

31 **Ezra Klein**: Ezra Klein, "Yes, Obama Did Campaign on the Public Option," *Washington Post*, December 23, 2009, http://voices.washingtonpost.com/ezra-klein/2009/12/yes_obama_did_campaign_on_the.html (accessed December 23, 2009).

31 **reported an unemployment rate at 10.0 percent**: *Dollars and Sense*, January 8, 2010, www.dollarsandsense.org/blog/2010/01/december-job-numbers-bls.html (accessed February 21, 2010); other statistics found at Bureau of Labor Statistics, www.bls.gov/news.release/pdf/empsit.pdf (accessed February 21, 2010); also see David Goldman, "Worst Year for Jobs Since '45," CNNMoney.com, January 9, 2009, http://money.cnn.com/2009/01/09/news/economy/jobs_december (accessed February 21, 2010).

32 **inequality between the rich and poor**: James Park, "Global Wages Decline; US Income Gap Worst of Developed Countries," *AFL-CIO Now*, November 25, 2008, http://blog.aflcio.org/2008/11/25/global-wages-decline-us-income-gap-worst-of-developed-countries (accessed February 21, 2010).

32 **Moyers asked Richard Trumka**: *Bill Moyers Journal*, January 29, 2010, www.pbs .org/moyers/journal/01292010/transcript4.html (accessed January 30, 2010).

33 **story about the Chicago workers**: Chris Spannos, "How to Occupy Your Workplace," Z *Magazine*, July–August 2010, 18–19; "Chicago Workers End Window Plant Sit-In," CNN, December 10, 2008, www.cnn.com/2008/US/12/10/ illinois.labor.protest (accessed February 22, 2010).

33 **In October 2009 in Puerto Rico**: Damien Cave, "Puerto Rico Unions Protest Job Cuts," *New York Times*, October 15, 2009, www.nytimes.com/2009/10/16/ us/16puerto.html (accessed February 22, 2010).

33 **120,000 Irish workers protested**: "Protesting Economy, Irish Workers Take to the Streets," *Employment Spectator*, February 23, 2009, www.employmentspec tator.com/2009/02/protesting-economy-irish-workers-take-to-the-streets (accessed February 22, 2010).

33 **In Scotland in 2009**: Simon Johnson, "More than 20,000 Take to Streets to Protest Johnnie Walker Plant Closure," *Telegraph UK*, July 26, 2009, www .telegraph.co.uk/news/newstopics/politics/scotland/5913043/More-than-20000 -take-to-streets-to-protest-Johnnie-Walker-plant-closure.html (accessed February 22, 2010).

33 **French government's plan to raise**: Greg Keller, "French Strikes Disrupt Country," Associated Press, October 12, 2010, http://ca.news.finance.yahoo .com/s/12102010/2/biz-finance-french-strikes-disrupt-life-shut-eiffel-tower-battle .html (accessed October 19, 2010—site discontinued) Associated Press article with revised title is currently available at http://finance.yahoo.com/news/French -strikes-disrupt-life-apf-2749688445.html?x=0&.v=12.

34 **"umbrella demonstration" . . . 'One Nation Working Together'**: Krissah Thompson and Spencer Hsu, "Tens of Thousands Attend Progressive 'One Nation Working Together' Rally in Washington," *Washington Post*, October 2, 2010, www.washingtonpost.com/wp-dyn/content/article/2010/10/01/AR20101 00104440.html (accessed October 3, 2010); Steven Greenhouse, "Liberal Groups Rally, Challenging Tea Party," *New York Times*, October 2, 2010, www.nytimes .com/2010/10/03/us/03rally.html (accessed October 3, 2010); "One Nation Working Together Official March Release," October 2, 2010, www.onenation workingtogether.org/news/entry/one-nation-working-together-official-march -release (accessed October 4, 2010).

35 **Tea Party Patriots . . . mission statement**: "Tea Party Patriots: Mission Statement and Core Values," www.teapartypatriots.org/Mission.aspx (accessed April 22, 2010).

35 **positive view of the Tea Party**: David Brooks, "The Tea Party Teens," *New York Times*, January 4, 2010, www.nytimes.com/2010/01/05/opinion/05brooks.html (accessed January 4, 2010).

35 **CBS reported that 29 percent**: Stephanie Condon, "Poll: Nearly 3 in 10 Support Tea Party," CBSNews.com, August 26, 2010, www.cbsnews.com/8301 -503544_162-20014854-503544.html (accessed October 15, 2010).

35 **New York Times/CBS poll**: Kate Zernike and Megan Thee-Brenan, "Poll Finds Tea Party Backers Wealthier and More Educated," *New York Times*, April 14, 2010, www.nytimes.com/2010/04/15/us/politics/15poll.html?pagewanted=print (accessed April 22, 2010).

35 **Fox News reported**: Dana Blanton, "Fox News Poll: Voters Use Midterm Elections to Send Message to White House," FoxNews.com, September 30, 2010, www.foxnews.com/politics/2010/09/30/fox-news-poll-voters-use-midterm-elections-send-message-white-house (accessed October 17, 2010).

36 **750 Tea Party demonstrations**: Liz Robbins, "Tax Day Is Met with Tea Parties," *New York Times*, April 15, 2009, www.nytimes.com/2009/04/16/us/politics/16taxday.html (accessed April 15, 2010).

36 **Taxpayer March on Washington**: Jack Sherman, "Protesters March on Washington," *Wall Street Journal*, September 12, 2009, http://online.wsj.com/article/SB125276685577405975.html (accessed April 22, 2010).

36 **Restoring Honor**: Brian Montopoli, "Glenn Beck: My Rally Had 'Minimum of 500,000 People,'" CBSNews.com, August 30, 2010, www.cbsnews.com/8301-503544_162-20015115-503544.html (accessed September 1, 2010).

36 **high-profile Republican Sarah Palin**: Steven Portnoy, "Whose Tea Party Is It? Nashville Convention Stirs Debate," ABC News/Politics, February 4, 2010, http://abcnews.go.com/Politics/tea-party-nashville-convention-stirs-debate/story?id=9741637 (accessed February 5, 2010).

37 **Koch Industries**: Jane Mayer, "Covert Operations: The Billionaire Brothers Who Are Waging a War Against Obama," *New Yorker*, August 30, 2010, www.newyorker.com/reporting/2010/08/30/100830fa_fact_mayer (accessed October 14, 2010).

37 ***The Atlantic* asked**: Chris Good, "The Tea Party Movement: Who's in Charge?" *The Atlantic*, April 13, 2009, http://politics.theatlantic.com/2009/04/the_tea_party_movement_whos_in_charge.php (accessed April 22, 2010).

38 **protested against crackdowns on illegal immigrants**: "Immigration Issue Draws Thousands into Streets: LAPD Estimates 500,000 at Protest," Associated Press (reported on MSNBC), March 26, 2006, www.msnbc.msn.com/id/11442705 (accessed March 24, 2010); Joel Robberts, "500,000 in the Streets on Immigration," CBS News, March 25, 2006, www.cbsnews.com/stories/2006/03/25/politics/main1439527_page2.shtml (accessed March 24, 2010).

38 **HR 4437**: HR 4437: "Border Protection, Antiterrorism, and Illegal Immigration Control Act of 2005," GovTrac.us, www.govtrack.us/congress/bill.xpd?bill=h109-4437 (accessed March 24, 2010).

39 **Robert Martinez . . . Juan Gomez . . . Orlando Fernandez**: Robert D. McFadden, "Across the US, Growing Rallies for Immigration," *New York Times*, April 10, 2006, www.nytimes.com/2006/04/10/us/10protest.html?_r=2&th&emc=th (accessed March 24, 2010).

39 **On March 21, 2010, they rallied**: Julia Preston, "At Rally, Call for Urgency on Immigration Reform," *New York Times*, March 21, 2010, www.nytimes

.com/2010/03/22/us/politics/22immig.html?hpw (accessed March 21, 2010); Douglas Rivlin, "200,000 March for Immigration Reform in Massive DC Rally," *AlterNet*, March 21, 2010, www.alternet.org/immigration/146119 (accessed March 21, 2010).

39 **fueled by new anti-illegal-immigrant law**: Julia Preston, "Immigration Advocates Rally for Change," *New York Times*, May 2, 2010, www.nytimes .com/2010/05/02/us/02immig.html?hp (accessed May 2, 2010).

40 **Center for Economic and Policy Research**: Jeanne Sahadi, "Who Gets the Most (and Least) Vacation," CNNMoney.com, June 14 2007, http://money.cnn .com/2007/06/12/pf/vacation_days_worldwide (accessed April 4, 2010).

40 **Germans have six weeks of federally mandated vacation**: Terrence McNally, "Why Germany Has It So Good—and Why America Is Going Down the Drain," *AlterNet*, October 14, 2010, www.alternet.org/story/148501 (accessed October 14, 2010).

40 **The Work, Family, and Equity Index**: "The Middle-Class Squeeze 2008: A Drum Major Institute for Public Policy Overview," Drum Major Institute, www .drummajorinstitute.org/library/report.php?ID=74 (accessed April 4, 2010).

41 **Institute for Women's Policy Research**: Ibid.

41 **United States joins Liberia**: Ibid.

41 **Thousands of Americans die**: Stan Dorn, "Uninsured and Dying Because of It," Urban Institute, www.urban.org/publications/411588.html (accessed October 5, 2010).

41 **have not gone to the doctor**: Rockefeller Foundation, reported in "The Middle-Class Squeeze 2008," Drum Major Institute.

41 **Health care premiums**: Health Affairs and National Coalition on Health Care, reported in ibid.

41 **Contrary to the urban myth**: Aaron Carroll, "Phantoms in the Snow," *Incidental Economist*, October 11, 2010, http://theincidentaleconomist.com/ wordpress/phantoms-in-the-snow (accessed November 4, 2010).

42 **Americans go abroad for health care**: The calculation is based on a 2008 esti-mate of Americans' travel abroad for health care at "Medical Tourism Statistics and Facts," Health-Tourism.com, www.health-tourism.com/medical-tourism/ statistics/ (accessed November 4, 2010).

42 **average hourly earnings**: "15 Mind-Blowing Facts About Wealth and Inequality in America," *Business Insider*, April 9, 2010, www.businessinsider.com/15-charts -about-wealth-and-inequality-in-america-2010-4#the-gap-between-the-top-1-and -everyone-else-hasnt-been-this-bad-since-the-roaring-twenties-1 (accessed April 23, 2010).

42 **Since 1960, while tax rates**: Ibid.

42 **income gap in the United States**: Ibid.

42 **Of the thirty industrialized nations**: Ibid.

42 **Six banks**: Bill Moyers, "Six Banks Control 60% of Gross National Product—Is the US at the Mercy of an Unstoppable Oligarchy?" from *Bill Moyers Journal*

interview with Simon Johnson and James Kwak on their book *13 Bankers: The Wall Street Takeover and the Next Financial Meltdown*, republished in *AlterNet*, April 23, 2010, www.alternet.org/story/146528 (accessed April 23, 2010).

43 **Les Leopold . . .While [the abuse** Don Hazen, Les Leopold, and Bruce E. Levine, "Are Progressives Depressed or Too Privileged to Produce Social Change? Or Are We Just Failing to Organize Effectively," *AlterNet*, January 7, 2010, www.alternet.org/story/144982 (accessed January 7, 2010).

Chapter 3: Prelude to Battle

48 **learned helplessness experiment**: Martin E. Seligman, *Helplessness: On Depression, Development, and Death* (San Francisco: W. H. Freeman, 1975), 21–44.

54 **April 2009 CBS/New York Times Poll**: "Cuba," CBS News/New York Times Poll, April 22–26, 2009, PollingReport.com, www.pollingreport.com/cuba.htm (accessed April 28, 2010).

54 **Noam Chomsky points out**: Noam Chomsky, "The Unipolar Moment and the Obama Era," *Z Magazine*, March 2010, 23–29.

56 **MKULTRA**: John Marks, *The Search for the "Manchurian Candidate": The CIA and Mind Control* (New York: McGraw-Hill, 1980); "25 Years of Nightmares: Victims of CIA-Funded Mind Experiments Seek Damages from the Agency," *Washington Post*, July 28, 1985, and "The CIA and the Evil Doctor," *New York Times*, November 7, 1988, both in Peter R. Breggin, *Toxic Psychiatry* (New York: St. Martin's Press, 1991), 436.

56 **these drugs disconnect them from their emotions**: Robert Whitaker, *Anatomy of an Epidemic: Magic Bullets, Psychiatric Drugs, and the Astonishing Rise of Mental Illness in America* (New York: Crown Publishers, 2010), said of children on ADHD amphetamine drugs: "[They show] a marked drug-related increase in solitary play and a corresponding reduction in their initiation of social interaction . . . [and] reduced curiosity about the environment"; "[they] become passive, submissive and socially withdrawn"; "[they] seem zombie-like," 219–224.

58 **"Imagine Being Allergic to People"**: Carl Elliott, "How to Brand a Disease— and Sell a Cure," CNN.com, October 11, 2010, http://edition.cnn.com/2010/OPINION/10/11/elliott.branding.disease (accessed October 12, 2010).

59 **Mark Crispin Miller**: Edward Bernays, *Propaganda* (1928, reprinted with Miller introduction, New York: Ig Publishing, 2005), 11.

59 **Walter Lippmann**: Ibid., 12, 16.

60 **In 2009, the Nielsen Company**: Taylor Gandossy, "TV Viewing at 'All-Time High,' Nielsen Says," CNN.com/entertainment, February 24, 2009, www.cnn.com/2009/SHOWBIZ/TV/02/24/us.video.nielsen (accessed April 7, 2010).

60 **Researchers report that children in North America**: Chris Rowan, "Unplug— Don't Drug: A Critical Look at the Influence of Technology on Child Behavior

with an Alternative Way of Responding Other than Evaluation and Drugging," *Ethical Human Psychology and Psychiatry* 12, no. 1 (2010), 60–68.

61 **10 percent of American homes**: Robert D. Putnam, *Bowling Alone: The Collapse and Revival of American Community* (New York: Touchstone, 2000), 221.

61 **more than 99 percent**: Norman Herr, "Television Statistics," *The Sourcebook for Teaching Science*, www.csun.edu/science/health/docs/tv&health.html (accessed May 2, 2010).

61 **The TV set is turned on**: Ibid.

61 **Two-thirds of Americans**: Ibid.

61 **About 40 percent of Americans' leisure time**: Putnam, *Bowling Alone*, 222.

61 **Husbands and wives**: Ibid., 224.

61 **NOP World, a market research organization**: "Leisure Time Around the World," *First Glimpse* 2, no. 8 (September 1, 2005), 24–25, www.firstglimpsemag.com/Editorial/article.asp?article=articles/2005/y0208/05y08/05y08.asp&guid (accessed May 2, 2010—site discontinued).

61 **Another cross-cultural comparison . . . NationMaster.com**: "Television Viewing (Most Recent) by Country," NationMaster.com, 2010, www.nationmaster.com/red/graph/med_tel_vie-media-television-viewing&b_printable=1 (accessed May 1, 2010). Figures for European countries are from Andries van den Broek, "Leisure Across Europe," paper to International Association for Time Use Research, Annual Conference, Lisbon, 2002, which compared fourteen populations; the American figure is from Sanchez-Tabernero, "Media Concentration in Europe"; the Australian figure is from Australian Commercial Television 1986–1995, Bureau of Transport and Communication Economics, AGPS, Canberra, 1996.

62 **channels owned by six corporations**: "Ownership Chart: The Big Six," FreePress.net, www.freepress.net/ownership/chart/main (accessed May 2, 2010).

62 **primary pacifying agent**: Jerry Mander, *Four Arguments for the Elimination of Television* (San Francisco: HarperCollins, 1978); Bruce E. Levine, *Commonsense Rebellion: Taking Back Your Life from Drugs, Shrinks, Corporations, and a World Gone Crazy* (New York: Continuum, 2001), 216–225.

63 **viewers' brainwaves slow down**: Mander, *Four Arguments for the Elimination of Television*, 208–211.

65 **2000 US census**: Jacqueline Olds and Richard S. Schwartz, *The Lonely American: Drifting Apart in the Twenty-first Century* (Boston: Beacon Press, 2009), 2.

66 ***American Sociological Review***: Miller McPherson, et al., "Social Isolation in America: Changes in Core Discussion Networks Over Two Decades," *American Sociological Review* 71 (2006), 353–375.

66 **Robert Putnam's book *Bowling Alone***: Robert D. Putnam, *Bowling Alone: The Collapse and Revival of American Community* (New York: Touchstone, 2000).

67 **William Vega**: William A. Vega, et al., "Lifetime Prevalence of *DSM-III-R*

Psychiatric Disorders Among Urban and Rural Mexican Americans in California," *Archives of General Psychiatry* 55 (1998), 771–778. Vega quote in Patricia McBroom, "As Mexican Immigrants Adapt to American Society, Their Mental Illness Rates Increase Dramatically," *Berkeleyan*, October 21, 1998, www .berkeley.edu/news/berkeleyan/1998/1021/immigrant.html (accessed January 3, 2010).

67 **John T. Cacioppo**: Johannah Cornblatt, "Lonely Planet," *Newsweek* Web exclusive, August 21, 2009, www.newsweek.com/id/213088 (accessed February 24, 2010). Also see John T. Cacioppo and William Patrick, *Loneliness: Human Nature and the Need for Social Connection* (New York: W. W. Norton, 2008).

67 **Michael J. Bugeja**: Cornblatt, "Lonely Planet." Also see Michael J. Bugeja, *Interpersonal Divide: The Search for Community in a Technological Age* (New York: Oxford University Press, 2005).

68 **Stanford study**: News item in *Psychology Today*, July–August 2000, 14.

70 **Jdimytai Damour**: Bruce E. Levine, "Fundamentalist Consumerism and an Insane Society," *Z Magazine*, February 2009, 13–14.

73 **How did fundamentalist consumerism come into existence?**: Jeremy Rifkin, *The End of Work: The Decline of the Global Labor Force and the Dawn of the Post-Market Era* (New York: Putnam, 1995), 19–25.

73 **Edward Bernays**: Edward Bernays, *Propaganda* (1928, reprinted with Miller introduction, New York: Ig Publishing, 2005), 37, 127.

75 **David Brancaccio**: David Brancaccio, "Student Loan Sinkhole?" *NOW*, originally broadcast on June 19, 2009, and repeated December 25, 2009, www.pbs.org/ now/shows/525/index.html (accessed December 26, 2009).

76 **along with a couple of others**: Nan Mooney, "College Loan Slavery: Student Debt Is Getting Way Out of Hand," *AlterNet*, November 12, 2008, www.alternet .org/economy/106445 (accessed January 13, 2010).

77 **68.6 percent attended college**: "College Enrollment and Work Activity of 2009 High School Graduates," Bureau of Labor Statistics, US Department of Labor, www.bls.gov/news.release/hsgec.nr0.htm (accessed January 14, 2010).

77 **half of all college students didn't graduate**: Anya Kamenetz, *DIY U: Edupunks, Edupreneurs, and the Coming Transformation of Higher Education* (White River Junction, VT: Chelsea Green Publishing, 2010), viii.

77 **30 percent . . . eventually get a four-year college degree**: Ibid., 19.

77 **three times the rate of general inflation**: Data sources listed in John Uebersax, "College Tuition: Inflation or Hyperinflation," citing Bureau of Labor Statistics and College Board, *Satyagraha*, July 14, 2009, http://satyagraha.wordpress .com/2009/07/14/college-tuition-hyperinflation (accessed January 15, 2010).

77 **The cost, on average . . . 55 percent of their income**: Kamenetz, *DIY U*, 51.

77 **less than one-half . . . public university graduates**: "Student Debt," Pew Charitable Trust, www.pewtrusts.org/our_work_detail.aspx?id=98 (accessed January 15, 2010); "Student Debt: A Rising Challenge for Nonprofit Employers,"

American Humanics, www.humanics.org/site/c.omL2KiN4LvH/b.2157139/k.7378/ Student_Debt__Internships_Initiative.htm (accessed January 15, 2010).

78 **The average amount of undergraduate student debt**: Brancaccio, "Student Loan Sinkhole?"; Kamenetz, *DIY U*, 8.

78 **those with a master's degree . . . over $87,000**: "Student Loan Debt Statistics," American Student Assistance, www.asa.org/policy/resources/stats/default.aspx (accessed January 15, 2010).

78 **graduates of medical school**: "Medical Student Debt," American Medical Association, www.ama-assn.org/ama/pub/about-ama/our-people/member-groups -sections/medical-student-section/advocacy-policy/medical-student-debt.shtml (accessed January 15, 2010).

78 **Half of college students . . . credit cards**: "Student Loan Debt Statistics," American Student Assistance, www.asa.org/policy/resources/stats/default.aspx (accessed January 15, 2010).

78 **"Student Debt and the Spirit of Indenture"**: Jeffrey J. Williams, "Student Debt and the Spirit of Indenture," *Dissent Magazine*, Fall 2008 www.dissentmagazine .org/article/?article=1303Fall%202008 (accessed January 15, 2010).

79 **according to some studies**: Ibid.

80 **Do citizens of all nations**: "Comparison of Tuition Costs of Higher Education Around the World," HubPages.com, http://hubpages.com/hub/Comparison-of -cost-of-higher-education-around-the-world (accessed January 16, 2010); "Study in Iran: Educational System," ArabianCampus.com, www.arabiancampus.com/ studyiniran/edusys.htm (accessed January 16, 2010); Re Vica, "Iran," www .virtualcampuses.eu/index.php/Iran#Iran_education_system (accessed January 16, 2010).

80 **in Mexico, the "flagship" of the public university system**: "Global Examination of Post-Secondary Education: Cost Recovery Models," Ontario Undergraduate Student Alliance, March 2010, www.ousa.ca/wordpress/ wp-content/uploads/2010/06/Global-Examination-of-Post-Secondary-Education -Cost-Recovery-Models.pdf (accessed April 1, 2010); David Bacon, "The Poor Fight for Their University, The Rich Go Elsewhere," David Bacon Stories and Photographs, February 19, 1999, http://dbacon.igc.org/Mexico/26UniversityFight .htm (accessed April 1, 2010).

82 **Lewis Maltby**: Lewis Maltby, "Your Boss Can Secretly Film You in the Bathroom—The Countless Ways You Are Losing Privacy at Work," *AlterNet*, April 18, 2010, www.alternet.org/story/146047 (accessed April 18, 2010); Lewis Maltby, *Can They Do That?: Retaking Our Fundamental Rights in the Workplace* (New York: Penguin, 2009).

82 **Heidi Arace and Norma Yetsko . . . personal blogs**: Arace and Yetsko in Tatiana Morales, "Fired for Sending E-mail," *Early Show*, CBS News, August 24, 2004, www.cbsnews.com/stories/2004/08/17/earlyshow/living/ caught/main636589.shtml (accessed October 7, 2010); Fulmer and policies

on personal blogs in Jim Rendon, "10 Things Human Resources Won't Say," *SmartMoney Magazine*, April 22, 2010, www.smartmoney.com/personal-finance/employment/10-things-human-resources-wont-tell-you/?page=all (accessed October 7, 2010).

84 **Union members make more money**: Bureau of Labor Statistics, US Department of Labor, "Union Members Summary," January 22, 2010, www.bls.gov/news.release/union2.nr0.htm (accessed March 22, 2010); other BLS in Drum Major Institute, "The Middle-Class Squeeze 2008: A Drum Major Institute for Public Policy Overview," www.drummajorinstitute.org/library/report.php?ID=74 (accessed March 22, 2010).

84 **autoworkers in Flint, Michigan**: Vivian M. Baulch and Patricia Zacharias, "The Historic 1936–37 Flint Auto Plant Strikes," *Detroit News*, June 23, 1997, http://apps.detnews.com/apps/history/index.php?id=115 (accessed March 23, 2010).

84 **35 percent percent of American employees**: BLS, "Union Members Summary."

84 **union membership in the private sector**: Ibid.

85 **Of the 107.5 million**: Calculations to exclude managerial positions based on ibid., table 3, "Union Affiliation of Employed Wage and Salary Workers by Occupation and Industry," www.bls.gov/news.release/union2.t03.htm (accessed October 8, 2010).

85 **David Macaray**: David Macaray, "Three Big Reasons for the Decline of Labor Unions," *CounterPunch*, January 10, 2010, www.counterpunch.org/macaray01102008.html (accessed January 10, 2010).

87 **unauthorized "wildcat" strikes**: David Stratman, *We CAN Change the World: The Real Meaning of Everyday Life* (Boston: New Democracy Books, 1991), 120.

90 **We know now that Government**: Franklin D. Roosevelt, "Franklin Roosevelt's Address Announcing the Second New Deal, October 31, 1936," *Our Documents*, http://docs.fdrlibrary.marist.edu/od2ndst.html (accessed February 12, 2010).

91 **Barack Obama's response**: Julianna Goldman and Ian Katz "Obama Doesn't 'Begrudge' Bonuses for Blankfein, Dimon," February 10, 2010, www.bloomberg.com/apps/news?pid=newsarchive&sid=aKGZkktzkA1A&pos=1 (accessed February 11, 2010); *Wall Street Journal*, February 10, 2010, http://blogs.wsj.com/washwire/2010/02/10/obama-and-those-bonuses/tab/print (accessed Februay 11, 2010).

91 **Americans were asked in 1975**: Putnam, *Bowling Alone*, 272–273.

91 **In 1900, only 1 percent**: Ben Wattenberg, from the PBS show *The First Measured Century*, July 26, 2000, www.pbs.org/fmc/book/14business6.htm (accessed April 30, 2010).

92 **Greenspan in the 1950s**: "Three Women Who Launched a Movement," Cato Institute, www.cato.org/special/threewomen/rand.html (accessed February 26, 2010).

92 **Other admirers of Rand's philosophy**: Mark Ames, "Ayn Rand, Hugely Popular Author and Inspiration to Right-Wing Leaders, Was a Big Admirer of Serial

Killer," *AlterNet*, February 26, 2010, www.alternet.org/books/145819 (accessed February 26, 2010); Christopher Cox, "Times People," February 26, 2010, http://topics.nytimes.com/top/reference/timestopics/people/c/christopher_cox/index.html (accessed February 26, 2010).

92 **Rand ends *Atlas Shrugged***: Ayn Rand, *Atlas Shrugged* (New York: Random House, 1957), 1168.

94 **Bob Dylan and his son Jakob . . . Rolling Stones**: Edward Helmore, "Old Rockers Don't Die, They Just Sing for Microsoft," Guardian.co.uk, November 26, 2000, www.guardian.co.uk/world/2000/nov/26/theobserver (accessed February 27, 2010).

94 **the entire list**: "Rock Star! (Brought to You by Huge Advertiser!)," *Miller-McCune*, November 4, 2008, www.miller-mccune.com/media/rock-star-brought-to-you-by-huge-advertiser-4137 (accessed October 19, 2010).

95 **The highest percentage increase . . . Bush**: George W. Bush, "The President's Budget: Transcript of President Bush's Message to Congress on His Budget Proposal," *New York Times*, February 28, 2001, www.nytimes.com/2001/02/28/us/president-s-budget-transcript-president-bush-s-message-congress-his-budget.html?pagewanted=1 (accessed March 3, 2010).

95 **We'll invest in innovative programs . . . . Obama**: Barack Obama, "Remarks of President Barack Obama—As Prepared for Delivery Address to Joint Session of Congress," February 24, 2009, www.whitehouse.gov/the_press_office/remarks-of-president-barack-obama-address-to-joint-session-of-congress (accessed March 3, 2010).

95 **The truth is that schools . . . Gatto**: John Taylor Gatto, "Why Schools Don't Educate," text of a speech by John Taylor Gatto accepting the New York City Teacher of the Year Award on January 31, 1990, www.naturalchild.org/guest/john_gatto.html (accessed March 4, 2010).

96 **"The primordial task of the schools" . . . Bennett**: Stratman, *We CAN Change the World*, 62.

96 **The aim of public education . . . Mencken**: H. L. Mencken, review of *The Goslings: A Study of the American School*, by Upton Sinclair. *The American Mercury*, April 1924.

97 **"breed and train a standardized citizenry"**: Quoted in John Taylor Gatto, "How Public Education Cripples Our Kids, and Why," *Harper's*, September 2003, 33–38, also at www.spinninglobe.net/againstschool.htm (accessed March 5, 2010).

97 **John Holt noted**: In Ronald Gross and Beatrice Gross, editors, *Radical School Reform* (New York: Simon & Schuster, 1969), 75.

98 **Once a man or woman . . . Illich**: Ivan Illich, *Deschooling Society* (New York: Harper & Row, 1970), 39.

99 **Jonathan Kozol**: Jonathan Kozol, *The Night Is Dark and I Am Far from Home* (reprinted, New York: Bantam, 1975), 132–133, 61, 182–193.

101 **Today the function of psychiatry . . . Fromm**: Erich Fromm, *The Sane Society* (reprinted, New York: Fawcett World Library, 1955), 151.

102 **"Yet many psychiatrists"**: Ibid., 15.

102 **"An unhealthy society"**: Ibid., 71.

102 **a new mental disorder**: *Diagnostic and Statistical Manual of Mental Disorders*, 4th edition (Washington, DC: American Psychiatric Association, 1994), 94.

103 **A 2009 *Psychiatric Times* article**: Christopher K. Peters, "ADHD & ODD: Confronting the Challenges of Disruptive Behavior," *Psychiatric Times*, September 9, 2009, www.psychiatrictimes.com/adhd/content/article/10162/ 1452117 (accessed September 12, 2009).

103 **Recalling his childhood, Alinsky**: "A Candid Conversation with Saul Alinksy," *Playboy*, March 1972; reprinted in *The Progress Report*, "Interview with Saul Alinsky, Part 3," www.progress.org/2003/alinsky4.htm (accessed May 2, 2010).

104 **Studies show that most ADHD-diagnosed**: Thomas Armstrong, *The Myth of the ADD Child* (New York: Penguin, 1995), 13.

105 **these drugs make them "care less"**: Whitaker, *Anatomy of an Epidemic*, 222–224. Whitaker documents several studies and quotes several researchers, including Ohio State University psychologist Herbert Rie, who in 1978 studied twenty-eight "hyperactive children" for three months who were prescribed Ritalin, resulting in "little or no initiative or spontaneity . . . virtually no curiosity . . . unmistakably affectless, humorless, and apathetic"; Bowling Green psychologist Nancy Fiedler, who reported in 1983 that Ritalin reduced a child's "curiosity about the environment"; and a team of UCLA psychologists who in 1993 reported that children treated with ADHD drugs often become "passive, submissive" and "socially withdrawn." Whitaker quotes other researchers who describe medicated children with terms such as "zombie-like" and "distinctly subdued."

105 **"US dominates the ADHD market"**: Evelyn Pringle, "US Kids Represent Psychiatric Drug Goldmine," *Truthout*, December 12, 2009, www.truth-out .org/1213091 (accessed December 14, 2009).

105 **"Antipsychotics were the highest grossing class"**: Michael Bartholow, "Top 200 Prescription Drugs of 2009," *Pharmacy Times*, May 11, 2010, www.pharmacy times.com/issue/pharmacy/2010/May2010/RxFocusTopDrugs-0510 (accessed May 15, 2010).

105 **Among children receiving antipsychotic drugs**: Bridget M. Kuehn, "Studies Shed Light on Risks and Trends in Pediatric Antipsychotic Prescribing," *Journal of the American Medical Association* 303, no. 19 (2010), 1901–1903.

106 **Roland Chrisjohn**: Roland Chrisjohn, quoted at the International Center for the Study of Psychiatry Conference, June 13, 1999, Bethesda, MD.

108 **Dr. Benjamin Rush . . . labeled this illness "anarchia"**: Daniel J. Boorstin, *The Lost World of Thomas Jefferson* (Boston: Beacon, 1948), 182.

108 **Samuel Cartwright reported his discovery**: Samuel A. Cartwright, "Report on Diseases and Physical Peculiarities of the Negro Race," collected in *Health, Disease, and Illness: Concepts in Medicine*, edited by Arthur Kaplan, James

McCartney, and Dominic Sisti (Washington, DC: Georgetown University Press, 2004), 28–39; also see Stephen Jay Gould, *The Mismeasure of Man* (New York: W. W. Norton, 1981), 71, and Herb Kutchins and Stuart A. Kirk, *Making Us Crazy: DSM: The Psychiatric Bible and the Creation of Mental Disorders* (New York: Free Press, 1997), 210.

110 **Jon Stewart**: *The Daily Show with Jon Stewart*, August 9, 2007, www.thedaily show.com/watch/thu-august-9-2007/tal-ben-shahar (accessed April 18, 2010).

111 **John McKnight**: John McKnight, *The Careless Society: Community and Its Counterfeits* (New York: Basic Books, 1995).

111 **Populist historian Lawrence Goodwyn**: Lawrence Goodwyn, *The Populist Moment: A Short History of the Agrarian Revolt in America* (Oxford, London, New York: Oxford University Press, 1978), xix.

113 **David Halberstam's**: David Halberstam, *The Best and the Brightest* (New York: Random House, 1972).

118 **Who demands a standing army?**: William Jennings Bryan, "An Income Tax," 1894 speech to Congress, collected in *The Speeches of William Jennings Bryan, Volume 1* (New York: Funk and Wagnalls Company, 1909), 174.

119 **Michael Kazin**: Michael Kazin, *A Godly Hero: The Life of William Jennings Bryan* (New York: Alfred A. Knopf, 2006), 106, 70, 76.

Chapter 4: Energy to Do Battle

123 **Barbara Ehrenreich**: Barbara Ehrenreich, *Bright-Sided: How the Relentless Promotion of Positive Thinking Has Undermined America* (New York: Henry Holt and Company, 2009).

124 **Several classic studies show**: Bruce E. Levine, *Surviving America's Depression Epidemic: How to Find Morale, Energy, and Community in a World Gone Crazy* (White River Junction, VT: Chelsea Green Publishing, 2007), 21–22; Lauren B. Alloy and Lyn Y. Abramson, "Judgment of Contingency in Depressed and Nondepressed Students: Sadder but Wiser?" *Journal of Experimental Psychology: General* 108, no. 4 (1979), 441–485; Peter M. Lewinsohn, et al., "Social Competence and Depression: The Role of Illusory Self-Perceptions," *Journal of Abnormal Psychology* 89 (1980), 203–212.

125 **"God damn the US"**: Howard Zinn, *A People's History of the United States: 1492–Present* (New York: HarperPerennial, 1995), 307.

125 **Ralph Barton Perry's**: Ralph Barton Perry, *The Thought and Character of William James* (1935, reprinted New York: Harper & Row, 1964), 119–126.

125 **"Faith in a fact"**: William James, "The Will to Believe," in John J. McDermott, editor, *The Writings of William James* (Chicago: University of Chicago Press, 1977), 717–735.

128 **David Swanson . . .Levine finds solutions**: David Swanson, "No, We're Not a Broken People," *Let's Try Democracy*, December 30, 2009, www.davidswanson .org/node/2375 (accessed January 3, 2010).

128 **City Life/Vida Urbana has won victories**: *Bill Moyers Journal*, December 18, 2009, www.pbs.org/moyers/journal/12182009/transcript2.html (accessed December 19, 2009).

146 **Ignacio Martin-Baró**: Ignacio Martin-Baró, *Writings for a Liberation Psychology*, edited by Adrianne Aron and Shawn Corne (Cambridge, MA: Harvard University Press, 1994); murdered by the US-trained troops, 1; for other background on Martin-Baró, see the book's foreword by Elliot G. Mishler, vii–xii, and introduction by Aron and Corne, 1–11; Martin-Baró, "Toward a Liberation Psychology," 17–32.

147 **social workers, psychiatrists, and psychologists**: American Psychological Association, "How Many Practicing Psychologists Are There in the United States?," www.apa.org/support/about/psych/numbers-us.aspx#answer (accessed October 10, 2010); Bureau of Labor Statistics, *Occupational Outlook Handbook, 2010–11 Edition*, "Social Workers," www.bls.gov/oco/ocos060.htm#emply, and "Physicians and Surgeons," www.bls.gov/oco/ocos074.htm#emply (accessed October 10, 2010).

147 **US Surgeon General . . . 15 percent of adults**: US Department of Health and Human Services, *Mental Health: A Report of the Surgeon General*, chapter 2, "Overall Patterns of Use," 1999 www.surgeongeneral.gov/library/mentalhealth/chapter2/sec7.html#overall (accessed October 10, 2010).

152 **Rasmussen Reports poll**: Rasmussen Reports, "55% of Americans Are Populist, 7% Support the Political Class," March 20, 2009, www.rasmussen reports.com/public_content/politics/ideology/55_of_americans_are_populist_7 _support_the_political_class (accessed February 10, 2010). While Rasmussen polls have sometimes been criticized for polling methods, unconventional language in questions, and ideological bias, among twenty-three of the best-known polls, Rasmussen Reports was the most accurate poll of the 2008 presidential election and most accurate in battleground states in 2004 election according to Costas Panagopoulos, "Poll Accuracy in the 2008 Presidential Election," November 5, 2008, www.fordham.edu/images/academics/graduate _schools/gsas/elections_and_campaign_/poll%20accuracy%20in%20the%20 2008%20presidential%20election.pdf; David Kenner and William Saletan, "Let's Go to the Audiotape: Who Nailed the Election Results? Automated Pollsters," *Slate*, December 9, 2004. *Slate* said: "Before the election, we publicly doubted and privately derided Rasmussen and SurveyUSA, which used recorded voices to read their poll questions . . . Look who's laughing now. Rasmussen and SurveyUSA beat most of their human competitors in the battleground states, often by large margins," www.slate.com/id/2110860 (accessed February 10, 2010).

153 **52 percent of Democrats**: Calculations based on Rasmussen Reports, "55% of Americans Are Populist"; Rasmussen Reports, "Partisan Trends," http://www .rasmussenreports.com/public_content/archive/mood_of_america_archive/ partisan_trends/summary_of_party_affiliation, October 1, 2010 (accessed

October 11, 2010); and Census Bureau, "Population Estimates: Resident Population: National Population Estimates for the 2000s: Monthly Postcensal Resident Population, by Single Year of Age, Sex, Race, and Hispanic Origin: 1/1/2009 to 6/1/2009," www.census.gov/popest/national/asrh/2009-nat-res.html (accessed October 11, 2010). Rasmussen reports that the entire "populist pie" is divided in this manner: 37 percent are Republicans, 36 percent are Democrats, and 27 percent are not affiliated with either major party; using these party affiliation statistics of March 2009, calculations show 52 percent of the "Democrat pie" are populists, 62 percent of the "Republican pie" are populists, and 51 percent of those not affiliated with either major party were populists (e.g., the 36 percent of Democrats in the populist pie equaled approximately 45.9 million Democrats, which is approximately 52 percent of 88.6 million Democrats).

154 **As historian Lawrence Goodwyn notes**: Lawrence Goodwyn, *The Populist Moment: A Short History of the Agrarian Revolt in America* (Oxford, London, New York: Oxford University Press, 1978), xxiii.

159 **Christmas Eve and Christmas Day in 1914**: Thomas Vinciguerra, "The Truce of Christmas, 1914," *New York Times*, December 25, 2005, www.nytimes .com/2005/12/25/weekinreview/25word.ready.html (accessed May 1, 2010).

160 **with increasing savagery**: Bertie Felstead, "The Last Known Survivor of No-Man's-Land Football Died on July 22nd, Aged 106," *Economist*, August 2, 2001, www.economist.com/obituary/displaystory.cfm?story_id=718781 (accessed May 1, 2010; access requires subscription).

160 **A major point of David Stratman's book**: David Stratman, *We CAN Change the World: The Real Meaning of Everyday Life* (Boston: New Democracy Books, 1991), 262.

162 **The Detroit News described**: Vivian M. Baulch and Patricia Zacharias, "The Historic 1936–37 Flint Auto Plant Strikes," *Detroit News*, June 23, 1997, http:// apps.detnews.com/apps/history/index.php?id=115 (accessed March 23, 2010).

163 **New York Letter Carriers, Branch 36 Web site**: "1970 Postal Strike," New York Letter Carriers, Branch 36 Web site, www.nylcbr36.org/history.htm (accessed March 25, 2010).

164 **Vincent Sombrotto**: "1970 Postal Strike," New York Letter Carriers, Branch 36 Web site.

Chapter 5: Winning the Battle

167 **Their efforts, halting and disjointed**: Lawrence Goodwyn, *The Populist Moment: A Short History of the Agrarian Revolt in America* (Oxford, London, New York: Oxford University Press, 1978), viii.

167 **One myth about mass political insurgency**: Ibid., x.

167 **Goodwyn describes a necessary sequence**: Ibid., xvii–xxiv.

168 **They created a mechanism called "bulking"**: Ibid., 30.

168 **More cooperative ideas came about**: Howard Zinn, *A People's History of the United States: 1492–Present* (New York: HarperPerennial, 1995), 281.

170 **Populists were unable to sustain**: Ibid., 281; Goodwyn, *The Populist Moment*, 80–84.

170 **"This conclusion, of course"**: Goodwyn, *The Populist Moment*, 284.

171 **The courthouses, they believed**: Ibid., 288.

172 **"A community cannot persist"**: Ibid., 307.

172 **"In folklore, it came to be remembered"**: Ibid., 310.

173 **Helen Keller**: Daniela Gioseffi, editor, *Women on War: An International Anthology of Writings from Antiquity to the Present* (New York: The Feminist Press, 2003), xxxviii.

175 **If you can control a people's economy"**: Wendell Berry, "Conserving Forest Communities," collected in *Another Turn of the Crank* (Berkeley, CA: Counterpoint, 1996), 34–35.

176 **"the nature of disruptive power"**: Frances Fox Piven, *Challenging Authority: How Ordinary People Change America* (Lanham, MD: Rowman & Littlefield Publishers, 2006).

176 **ordinary people exercise power**: Ibid., 1.

177 **Saul Alinsky put it bluntly**: James Ridgeway, "Seeing Bobby Kennedy in Barack Obama," *Mother Jones*, June 5, 2008, http://motherjones.com/politics/2008/06/seeing-bobby-kennedy-barack-obama (accessed May 10, 2010).

177 **colonial crowds in Boston**: Piven, *Challenging Authority*, 44–45.

177 **Shays' Rebellion**: Ibid., 49.

178 **Gabriel Prosser . . . Nat Turner**: Ibid., 71.

178 **"What was perhaps the most . . . Underground Railroad"**: Ibid., 72.

178 **Liberty Party . . . William Lloyd Garrison**: Ibid., 73–74.

179 **many of them felt desperate . . . large labor strikes**: Ibid., 88.

179 **relief programs reaching 22 percent**: Ibid., 86–87.

180 **"to wall off from electoral influence"**: Ibid., 112.

181 **in July 2010 in Iran**: Ramin Mostaghim and Borzou Daragahi, "Iran Merchants and Tax Collectors End Standoff," *Los Angeles Times*, July 18, 2010, http://articles.latimes.com/2010/jul/18/world/la-fg-iran-economy-20100718 (accessed July 19, 2010).

182 **Research shows that significantly depressed parents**: Michael D. Yapko, *Hand-Me-Down Blues: How to Stop Depression from Spreading in Families* (New York: St. Martin's Press, 1999), 156–161.

183 **other significant protests in 150 other cities**: Sue Chan, "Massive Anti-War Outpouring," CBS News, February 15, 2003, www.cbsnews.com/stories/2003/02/16/iraq/main540782.shtml (accessed October 12, 2010).

186 **City Life states: We organize blockades, vigils**: City Life Web site, "Programs and Campaigns: Bank Organizing: Post-Foreclosure Eviction Defense Campaign," www.clvu.org/program_campaings.pdf (accessed January 10, 2010).

186 **Steve Meacham**: *Bill Moyers Journal*, December 18, 2009, www.pbs.org/moyers/journal/12182009/transcript2.html (accessed January 10, 2010).

187 **Neighborhood Assistance Corporation of America (NACA)**: Neighborhood Assistance Corporation of America Web site, www.naca.com/index_main.jsp (accessed January 12, 2010).

187 **Bruce Marks**: Jenifer McKim, "Taking Bank Chiefs to Task to Save Homes," *Boston Globe*, August 30, 2009, www.boston.com/business/articles/2009/08/30/ taking_bank_chiefs_to_task_to_save_homes (accessed September 21, 2010).

187 **NACA demonstrated at the Greenwich**: John Christoffersen, "Housing Group Stages Protests at Banking Executives' Homes," Associated Press (reported in *USA Today*), March 9, 2009, www.usatoday.com/money/economy/housing/2009 -02-09-housing-protest_N.htm (accessed January 12, 2010).

188 **JPMorgan Chase reneged**: Bruce Watson, "Chase Backlash: 1,000 Homeowners Protest at Bank's Manhattan HQ," www.dailyfinance.com/story/ company-news/chase-protests-1-000-homeowner-protest-at-banks-manhattan- head/19280812 (accessed January 12, 2010).

188 **Each one of us . . . Mumford**: Lewis Mumford, *The Myth of the Machine: The Pentagon of Power* (New York: Harcourt Brace Jovanovich, 1970), 433.

191 **Fellowship of Intentional Communities**: Fellowship of Intentional Communities Web site, www.ic.org; "Intentional Communities Directory," http:// directory.ic.org/; http://directory.ic.org/iclist/community_type.php (accessed April 5, 2010).

191 **Scott Nearing . . . *The Good Life***: Helen Nearing and Scott Nearing, *The Good Life* (New York: Shocken Books, 1970).

191 **Harlan Hubbard**: Wendell Berry, *Harlan Hubbard: Life and Work* (Lexington: University Press of Kentucky, 1990).

192 **World Wide Opportunities on Organic Farms**: World Wide Opportunities on Organic Farms Web site, www.wwoof.org (accessed April 6, 2010).

193 **Alaskan Independence Party**: Alaskan Independence Party Web site, "Introduction," www.akip.org/introduction.html (accessed April 6, 2010).

193 **Vermont's secessionist movement**: Christopher Ketcham, "The Secessionist Campaign for the Republic of Vermont," *Time*, January 31, 2010, www.time.com/ time/nation/article/0,8599,1957743,00.html (accessed April 6, 2010).

193 **Kirkpatrick Sale**: Bruce E. Levine, "Secession and Sanity: An Interview with Kirkpatrick Sale," *Z Magazine*, October 2006, 44–47.

195 **The College Board in 2010 reported**: College Board, "What It Costs to Go to College," www.collegeboard.com/student/pay/add-it-up/4494.html (accessed March 29, 2010).

195 **at Ohio State University**: Ohio State Web site, "Estimated Costs for U.S. Students," http://gradadmissions.osu.edu/Costs.html (accessed March 29, 2010).

196 **Massachusetts Institute of Technology**: MIT Open Courseware, http://ocw .mit.edu/OcwWeb/web/home/home/index.htm (accessed March 30, 2010).

196 **"7.012 Introduction to Biology"**: Introduction to Biology, MIT Open Courseware, http://ocw.mit.edu/courses/biology/7-012-introduction-to-biology -fall-2004 (accessed March 30, 2010).

197 **Work College Consortium . . . Robin Taffler**: Anya Kamenetz, *DIY U: Edupunks, Edupreneurs, and the Coming Transformation of Higher Education* (White River Junction, VT: Chelsea Green Publishing, 2010), 77.

198 **Western Governors University (WGU)**: Western Governors University Web site, www.wgu.edu (accessed March 20, 2010).

198 **"[WGU] has earned . . . once a week in class"**: Kathleen Kingsbury, "Go Western, Young Man," *Time*, November 13, 2008, www.time.com/time/magazine/article/0,9171,1858876,00.html (accessed March 20, 2010).

198 **Anya Kamenetz's**: Kamenetz, *DIY U.*

199 **AmeriCorps**: AmeriCorps Web site, www.americorps.gov (accessed March 21, 2010).

200 **"a business entity that is owned"**: US Federation of Worker Cooperatives, "What Is a Worker Cooperative?," www.usworker.coop/system/files/What%20is%20WC_1.pdf (accessed April 7, 2010).

200 **Union Cab's**: "About Us," Union Cab Cooperative of Madison Web site, www.unioncab.com/opencms/opencms/about_us (accessed April 7, 2010).

201 **Alvarado Street Bakery**: Alvarado Street Bakery, "About Us," www.alvaradostreetbakery.com/about_us.php (accessed April 7, 2010).

201 **according to a report by Petaluma's . . . Ronnie Bell**: Jeremy Hay, "Michael Moore's New Film Puts Spotlight on Petaluma Company," *Press Democrat*, October 1, 2009, www.pressdemocrat.com/article/20091001/ARTICLES/910019908 (accessed April 7, 2010).

202 **Coulee Region Organic Produce Pool (CROPP)**: CROPP Web site, www.farmers.coop/our-story/our-history (accessed April 9, 2010).

202 **Travis Forgues**: CROPP Web site, "Travis Forgues," www.farmers.coop/our-story/meet-the-owners/travis-and-amy-forgues (accessed April 9, 2010).

203 **"Co-ops are formed"**: "About Co-Ops," National Cooperative Business Association Web site, www.ncba.coop/ncba/about-co-ops (accessed April 7, 2010).

204 **Louis Proyect**: Louis Proyect, "Are Worker-Owned Companies an Alterative to Capitalism?" Unrepentant Marxist Web site, September 29, 2009, http://louisproyect.wordpress.com/2009/09/29/are-worker-owned-companies-an-alterative-to-capitalism (accessed April 7, 2010).

205 **Kent Nerburn's**: Kent Nerburn, *Chief Joseph and the Flight of the Nez Perce: The Untold Story of an American Tragedy* (San Francisco: HarperCollins, 2005): Chief Joseph quote, 267–268; unnamed contemporary Nez Perce quote, xx.

207 **Lincoln . . . The slaves of the South**: Joshua Wolf Shenk, *Lincoln's Melancholy: How Depression Challenged a President and Fueled His Greatness* (Boston: Houghton Mifflin, 2005), 146–147.

ACKNOWLEDGMENTS

My thanks to Lydia Sargent at Z *Magazine*, Jeffrey St. Clair at *CounterPunch*, Don Hazen and Jan Frel at *AlterNet*, and numerous other Internet sites for publishing the articles that led directly to this book. Owing to voluminous reader feedback, I had an even better sense of what was troubling Americans, and so I want to thank all those readers for taking the time to respond with their thoughts and experiences.

Chelsea Green Publishing is not a subsidiary of a giant corporation, which makes it quite different from most other publishers large enough to get their books in stores and on best-seller lists. Thanks to publisher Margo Baldwin, its primary force of energy for more than twenty-five years, Chelsea Green has remained decidedly outside the corporatocracy, not basing its publishing decisions solely on the financial bottom line. On this project, I also want to thank the entire Chelsea Green staff, including editor in chief Joni Praded and senior editor Susan Warner for their valuable input and their enthusiasm. I especially want to thank developmental editor Jonathan Teller-Elsberg, who threw all of himself into this project, tackling the manuscript several times, offering hundreds of suggestions that improved the book in innumerable ways, and always making himself available to mix it up with me to improve the quality of this book.

Major morale boosters for this project were Rhoda Bates, Lewis Kamrass, Aaron Lichtenberg, and Liz Lichtenberg, and I am deeply grateful to them. I also want to acknowledge several other people who provided me with energy and inspiration: Nathan Chamberlin, Tom Gelwicks, Mike Mercier, Steve Clark, Dave Stratman, David Oaks, and Robert Whitaker.

Last, my wife, who had the unenviable task of being the first to edit the original manuscript. Once again, as she has done for my previous three books, she started the editorial ball rolling with many excellent suggestions that made the book clearer and more inclusive. While she doesn't seek public acknowledgments, the people who love her enjoy seeing her acknowledged, so she goes along with it. Thanks, Bon.

INDEX

Abolitionist Movement, 178–79, 180, 206, 207–8
abuse syndrome, 43–46, 49–51, 131–36
advertising and marketing
    alienation from humanity from, 72
    of drugs, 6–7, 58
    in Obama campaign, 15, 31
    vs. propaganda and public relations, 73
    role in fundamentalist consumerism, 73–75
    on television, 64
Afghanistan War (2001–), 21–24, 30, 184
AFL-CIO, 26, 28, 34
Ahmadinejad, Mahmoud, 19, 37–38, 181, 207
air traffic controllers strike (1981), 85
air travel, bureaucratization of, 69
Alaskan Independence Party, 193
alienation from humanity, 9, 72, 101–2
Alinsky, Saul, 103, 122, 177
alliances, forging of, 152–58
altruism, 129–30, 139, 154, 158
Alvarado Street Bakery, 201
American Federation of State, County and Municipal Employees, 28
American Psychiatric Association, 102
American Revolution, 161, 176, 177, 180
Americans for Prosperity, 37
American Tobacco Company, 74–75
AmeriCorps, 199
Amish people, 190, 191
amphetamines, 56, 96, 105, 107
anarchia, 108
anarchism, 149–52
Anderson, John, 21
anesthetization, depression and apathy as, 50, 126
anger
    as energizer, 11, 194
    political exploitation of, 31
    in Tea Party movement, 35, 36, 37
anti-authoritarianism. See also noncompliance with authority
    and anarchism, 149–52
    and comfortable-afflicted continuum, 9–11
    vs. elitism, 8
    and illegal drug use, 57
    and mental illness labeling, 149–52
    pathologization of, 108
antipsychotic drugs, 6–7, 105–6, 138

apathy. See demoralization; passivity
Arace, Heidi, 82
Atlas Shrugged (Rand), 92–93
attention deficit hyperactivity disorder (ADHD), 56, 103, 104–5
Attkisson, Sharyl, 7
authoritarian/hierarchical systems
    acceptance by independent media, 14
    vs. anarchism, 149
    and desire for tensionlessness, 143, 144
    in education, 96, 97
    and elitism, 111, 160
    and individual self-respect, 140
    military as, 160
    and practical anarchism, 149–50
    and "problem children", 107, 108
    in television programming, 64
    and violent rebellion, 113–14, 177–78, 188

Bank of America, 42, 186, 187
battered people's syndrome, healing from, 131–36
Battle of Seattle (1999), 16–17, 188
behaviorism vs. cognitive psychology, 110
belief in possibility for change
    and critical thinking, 125
    energizing nature of, 2–3, 121
    historic examples of, 207–9
    importance of self-respect and self-confidence, 121, 171–72
Bell, Ronnie, 201
Bennett, William, 96, 97
Ben-Shahar, Tal, 110
Bernays, Edward, 59, 73–74
Berry, Wendell, 175
Big Pharma. See pharmaceutical-industrial complex
Blankfein, Lloyd, 91
boarding schools, fear in, 54
Boston, Massachusetts, City Life/Vida Urbana work, 186
Boston Community Capital, 186
Boston Tea Party (1773), 177
Brancaccio, David, 75
Brave New World (Huxley), 56
breaking a population, 1–4, 13–16, 69–75. See also demoralization; psychology of breaking a population

bribes, 53–55
Britain
  and American Revolution, 177
  Christmas Truce incident, 159–61
  Iraq war protests, 183
  television viewing, 61–62
brokenness. See demoralization; passivity
Brown, John, 178
Bryan, William Jennings, 119, 170, 172
Bugeja, Michael J., 67–68
Bush, George H. W., 6
Bush, George W.
  on education, 95
  election of, 18, 21, 43, 162
  industrial complexes involvement, 5, 6, 25, 30
  Iraq war involvement, 22
  Tea Party anger with, 35

Cacioppo, John T., 67
Calderón, Felipe, 19
Cameron, Ewen, 56
campaign financing, 4–5, 7
campaign messages, 14–15
Canada, health care system in, 41–42
capitalism
  and anarchism, 150–51
  and concentration of economic power, 154
  fundamentalist, 69
Cartwright, Samuel, 108
Center for Economic and Policy Research, 40
Chávez, César, 86
chickenhawks, 115
children. See also educational system
  anarchism in, 149–52
  development of self-respect in, 141, 142
  parental surveillance of, 83
  resentment in, 142, 144, 145
  separation from parents, 190
  time spent on technology, 60–61
Chomsky, Noam, 54–55
Chrisjohn, Roland, 106–7
Christmas Truce (World War I), 159–61
CIA (Central Intelligence Agency), 56, 74
cigarettes, and advertising/propaganda, 74–75
Citigroup, 42, 187
City Life/Vida Urbana, 16, 128–30, 186–87
civil disobedience, 15, 16, 37
civil rights movement, 185, 206
Civil War (1861-1865), small victories in, 161
class wars, 152, 155, 156, 175
Clinton, Bill, 35, 76, 85

CNN, 21
Coalition for the Good of All (Mexico), 19
cognitive dissonance, 51–52
cognitive psychology vs. behaviorism, 110
Cohn & Wolfe, 58
collective self-confidence
  as building block of energy, 3–4
  Great Populist Revolt effects, 171–73
  and healing from abusive relationships, 136
  importance of successes in, 171–72, 204
  money-centrism destruction of, 90
  role in democracy, 112
  solidarity role in, 161–65
college. See higher education
College Board, 195
Collomb, Bertrand, 17
comfortable-afflicted continuum, 9–11
Common Sense (Paine), 148
communication skills, and social isolation, 137
Communications Workers of America, 28
communism, fundamentalist, 69
Communist Party, 59, 208
community
  decline in, 66
  as energizer, 129–30
  methods for building, 136–40
  need for, in democracy, 111
  psychiatric survivor community, 138–39
  and social skills, 137, 138, 139
competition, as human trait, 154
compliance with authority. See also
noncompliance with authority
  and abuse syndrome, 51, 55
  drugs used for, 105
  and educational system, 97–100, 142
  of mental health professionals, 106, 132
  and self-respect, 142
compromises
  de-energizing nature of, 128, 180
  helpfulness vs. harmfulness of, 205–7
  by populists, 155
  by union leaders, 87, 88–89
conscientizacao, 134
consent to be governed, 59
conservatives
  on drugs used for compliance, 107
  hypocrisy of, 115
  as term of division, 8, 115
consumer cooperatives, 203
consumerism
  and alienation from humanity, 72
  history of, 73–75

and money-centrism, 89–94, 200
and moneyism, 89–94, 184, 185–86
in music, 94
role in breaking a population, 69–75
and television, 64
Coolidge, Calvin, 74, 174
cooperation, as human trait, 154
cooperatives
    in Great Populist Revolt, 168, 169, 171–72
    types of, 200–203
co-opting and bastardization, 59
corporate media. *See* mainstream media
corporatocracy
    overview, 4–8
    potential vulnerability of, 8, 208–9
corruption, 86–87
Cox, Christopher, 92
credit card debt, of college students, 78
credit systems, in Great Populist Revolt,
    169–70
criminalization of noncompliance, 57, 108, 181
critical consciousness, 134
critical thinking, 64, 122–27, 134
crop lien system, 166
CROPP (Coulee Region Organic Produce
    Pool), 202–3
Cuba, US sanctions against, 54–55
cults, 52–53
cynicism, role of, 173

Daily Show, 110
Damour, Jdimytai, 70
Daniels, Mitch, 5, 6
Debs, Eugene, 173
debt
    credit card, 78
    student loans, 75–81, 194–200
defense spending, 30. *See also* military-
    industrial complex
democracy and democratic movements
    Bernays view of, 74
    comfort with conflict, 143–45
    vs. elitism, 2, 111
    in families, 143–45
    initiation of, 3
    mental health services role, 147–48
    needs of, 64, 171
    and population size, 192
    in the workplace, 200–203
Democratic Party
    co-opting of name, 59
    elitists in, 155

Populists alliance with, 170, 172
    vs. Republican Party, 116, 117–19, 155–56
    special interests served by, 116
    vs. Tea Party, 35, 36
    Vietnam War involvement, 112–13
demoralization
    and campaign messages, 14–15
    and disruption tactics, 182
    of helpers, 127–28
    vs. other explanations of passivity, 43–46
    as source of inaction, 11–12
    from student-loan debt, 75–77
depression
    from abuse, 50
    and critical thinking, 124–27
    and disruption tactics, 182
    and learned helplessness, 49
Dimon, Jamie, 91
disorganized vs. organized resistance, 43–44
disruptive behavior. *See also* noncompliance
    with authority
    drugs used to control, 105–6, 107
    in families, 144, 150–51
    tactics for, 176–82
    withdrawal from power systems as, 194
disruptive disorders, 103, 104, 176
distrust, overcoming, 158–61
divide and conquer strategy
    magnitude of change to work for, 204
    overview, 8–12
    in political system, 8, 115, 118, 152–58
    and protest demonstration effectiveness,
    185
    television role in, 64
    used against Native Americans, 107
    used by activists, 188
    ways to overcome, 4, 8, 207–9
Don'tGo (organization), 37
Douglass, Frederick, 122
Douglass, Jason, 76
drapetomania, 108
drugs. *See* amphetamines; antipsychotic drugs;
    psychotropic drugs
Dylan, Bob, 94
dysaesthesia aethiopis, 108

economic crisis (2008–), 24–26
economic sanctions, for breaking a population,
    54–55
educational system
    boarding schools, 54
    and development of self-respect, 142

effect on family relationships, 144–45
elitism training, 109–12
medication of students, 56, 57–58
powerlessness taught by, 95–100
role of, 96
education reform movement, 9
egomaniacs, 113–14, 115
Ehrenreich, Barbara, 123–24
Eisenhower, Dwight, 5, 29, 123
electoral politics
    and abolitionist movement, 178
    differing populist views of, 173–75
    Great Populist Revolt failure in, 170–73
    and learned helplessness, 115–20
electroshock learned helplessness experiment,
48–49
Eli Lilly and Company, 6–7
elites
    defined, 7
    differing populist views of, 155–56
elitism
    vs. anti-authoritarianism, 8
    vs. democracy, 2, 111
    and hypocrisy, 114–15
    and jargon, 110
    vs. populism, 152–53
    training in, 109–12
e-mail communication, 68
Emergency Economic Stabilization Act
(2008), 24
Emerson, Ralph Waldo, 47, 120
empathy, 10–11, 130
employer surveillance, normalization of, 82–83
employment, and development of self-respect,
143
energy for action, 121–65
    building blocks of, 2–3
    collective self-confidence role, 121, 161–65
    combating social isolation, 136–40
    commercialization of, 94
    creating respectful relationships, 143–45
    and critical thinking, 122–27
    cycle of, 3
    de-energizing nature of compromises, 180
    forging alliances, 152–58
    fuels for, 127–31
    healing from abuse syndrome, 131–36
    individual self-respect role, 121, 140–43
    and liberation psychology, 145–52
    and morale, 122–27
    overcoming distrust, 158–61
    in secession movements, 193–94

and small victories, 128, 161–65, 171–72,
    178, 204
energy-industrial complex, 5, 30, 184
Europe
    Iraq war protests in, 22
    paid leave in, 40
    television viewing in, 61–62
evictions, activism on, 16, 128–30, 186–88
expatriates, as seceders, 192

Facebook, 67
Fair Labor Standards Act, 179
families, and self-respect, 143–45. See also
    children; parents
fatalism, liberation from, 134, 146
fear
    for breaking a population, 53–55
    from educational system, 99
    from health care system, 41
    from loss of self-reliance, 72
    from surveillance, 82, 83
    and television viewing, 64
Fernandez, Orlando, 39
financial-industrial complex, 5
Flint, Michigan, sit-down strike (1936-37),
    84, 162–63
Flowers, Margaret, 16
foreclosures, activism on, 16, 128–30, 186–88
Forgues, Travis, 202–3
"The Fox and the Grapes" (fable), 52
Fox News, 35
France
    higher education costs, 80
    retirement age protests, 33–34
FreedomWorks, 37
free time/leisure time
    decline in, 73, 98
    lack of, in cults, 53
    paid holidays, 40
    and television viewing, 61, 64
Freire, Paulo, 134, 146
Frey, William, 187
Fromm, Erich, 8, 101–2
Fugitive Slave Act (1850), 178–79
Fulmer, Nate, 82
fundamentalist capitalism, 69
fundamentalist communism, 69
fundamentalist consumerism, 69–71. See also
    consumerism

Garrison, William Lloyd, 178, 180
Gatto, John Taylor, 9, 95

General Electric, 26, 74
General Motors, 74, 84, 162–63
Germany
    Christmas Truce incident, 159–61
    higher education costs in, 80
    paid leave in, 40
give-backs, 89
GlaxoSmithKline, 58
globalization
    and decline in unions, 85
    Seattle protests, 16–17, 188
    Tea Party opposition to, 36, 37
Goldman Sachs, 42, 91
Gomez, Juan, 39
Goodwin, Stephan, 46
Goodwyn, Lawrence
    on populists, 154, 167, 168, 170, 172
    on self-respect and self-confidence, 3,
        111–12, 140
Gore, Al, 18, 21
government
    differing populist views of, 155, 170–71
    as scapegoat for corporatocracy, 155
    vs. unions, 85–86
Gramsci, Antonio, 125
Great Depression, disruptive tactics during,
    179
Great Populist Revolt, 166–73
Green Party, 14, 20–21, 162
Greenspan, Alan, 92
Greenwich Financial Services, 187
Griffiths, Melonie, 129
gun control, 157–58
Guthrie, Woody, 122

Harding, Warren, 174
Harper's Ferry raid of 1859, 178
Health Care for America, 28
health care reform, 27–29, 31, 41, 184
health care system, US vs. other countries,
    41–42
Heguy, Adriana, 90
helplessness, learned. *See* learned helplessness
Herbert, Bob, 13
higher education. *See also* student-loan debt
    alternatives to, 196–200
    bureaucratization of, 100
    costs of, 77, 195–96
    decline in student activism, 15
    US vs. other countries, 42
Hill, Joe, 124
Hillel the Elder (scholar), 158

Hoang, Kathy, 23
Hoffa, Jimmy, 86
Holt, John, 97
Homeland Security Act, 6
Hoover, Herbert, 174
HR 4437 (illegal immigration), 38, 184–85
Hubbard, Anna, 191–92
Hubbard, Harlan, 191–92
Huxley, Aldous, 56
hypocrisy, 57, 93, 112–15

ignorance, assumption of, 10–11
illegal drugs, criminalization of users, 57
illegal immigration demonstrations, 38–40,
    184–85
Illich, Ivan, 98
immigration
    demonstrations on, 38–40, 184–85
    Mexican American assimilation study, 67
    as secession from original society, 190
inaction. *See* passivity
indentured servitude, 75–81, 194–200
independent media, 14
individual self-respect
    and bribes, 55
    as building block of energy, 3–4
    and electoral politics involvement, 174
    and empowerment, 140–43
    Great Populist Revolt effects, 171, 172–73
    and healing from abusive relationships,
        136
    and loss of self-reliance, 71–72
    money-centrism destruction of, 90
    role in alliances, 158
    role in democracy, 111–12
    role of families, 143–45
    and small victories, 204
industrial complexes, 5, 31. *See also specific
    types*
inflation, 41, 77
integrity
    and compromises, 205–7
    and individual self-respect, 140–41, 143
    and normalization of manipulativeness, 75
    and union compromises, 88–89
    weakness from loss of, 55
intelligence tests, 109
intentional communities, 190–91
International Monetary Fund (IMF), 17
Internet
    increased use of, 60–61
    online universities, 198, 199

vs. real social connectedness, 67–68
surveillance uses, 82, 83, 99
interpersonal psychotherapy, 110
Iran
  higher education costs, 80
  presidential election of 2009, 19
  tax protests, 37–38, 181–82, 206–7
Iraq War (2003–), 22–24, 30, 183–84
Iversen, Gerald, 123
Izumi, Alisa, 198

Jackson, Jesse, 26
James, William, 124–25
jargon, and elitism, 110
Johnson, Lyndon Baines, 113
Joseph (Nez Perce chief), 205–6
JPMorgan Chase, 42, 91, 187, 188

Kamenetz, Anya, 198
Kansas-Nebraska Act (1854), 192
Kazin, Michael, 119
Keller, Helen, 173
Kinser, Kevin, 198
Klein, Ezra, 31
Koch Industries, 37
Kohn, Alfie, 9
Kovach, Therese, 77
Kozol, Jonathan, 99–100

labeling
  for breaking a population, 57–58
  of disruptive tactics, 181
  and mental illness, 101, 104, 109, 149
  of secession movements, 192
Latino Americans, illegal immigration
  demonstrations, 38–40, 184–85
laziness, as reason for passivity, 44–45
learned helplessness
  and abusive relationships, 133–34
  for breaking a population, 48–49
  educational system role, 95–100
  electoral system role, 115–20
  overview, 1–4
leftist anarchists, 150
leftist populists, 36, 154, 157
Leopold, Les, 43
liberals, 107, 114–15. See also progressives
liberation psychology, 145–52
libertarian anarchy, 151
libertarian populists, 154, 157
Liberty Clover Worker's Brigade, 201
Liberty Party, 178

lies
  in abusive relationships, 133, 135
  and corporate media, 112–15
  as technique for breaking a population,
    58–59
Limbaugh, Rush, 92
Lincoln, Abraham, 207–8
Lippmann, Walter, 59
Livestock Commission of Chicago, 169
living alone, increase in, 65–66
Logan, Perry, 29
London, Iraq war protest in, 22
loneliness. See social isolation
Looking Glass (Nez Perce chief), 206
López Obrador, Andrés Manuel, 19–20
Los Angeles, California, illegal immigration
  demonstrations, 38, 39, 184
Ludd, Joshua, 99
Lugar, Richard, 6

Macaray, David, 85–86
Mack, John, 187
Madrid, Spain, Iraq war protest in, 22
Mafia principle, and Cuba, 55
mainstream media
  Afghanistan war coverage, 24
  concentrated power of, 62
  dismissal of populist movements, 14
  lies from, 112–15
  as part of corporatocracy, 7, 8
  presidential election coverage, 17–18
  Seattle protest coverage, 16–17
  secession movement labels, 192
Malcolm X, 122
Maltby, Lewis, 82, 83
Mander, Jerry, 63–64
manipulativeness
  of advertising, 64, 72, 73–75
  of mental health profession, 101, 102, 111
  of television, 63–65
market anarchy, 151
Marks, Bruce, 187
marriage, dissolution of, 189–90
Marshall, George C., 122
Martin-Baró, Ignacio, 146–47, 148, 149
Martinez, Robert, 39
McCain, John, 30, 36
McKnight, John, 111
McNamara, Robert, 113
Meacham, Steve, 129, 130, 186
media. See independent media; mainstream
  media

Medicare prescription drug law, 5
Mencken, H. L., 96, 97
Mennonite people, 190, 191
mental health professionals
    abusive training environments, 131–32
    compliance of, 106, 132
    and elitism training, 109–12
    political actions of, 147–48
mental health reform movement, 8–9, 108–9,
    138–39
mental illness
    noncompliance as, 100–109, 149–52
    psychiatric survivor community, 138–39
Mexican American immigrants, 67
Mexico
    higher education costs, 80
    presidential election of 2006, 19–20
    television viewing, 61
military-industrial complex, 5, 30, 160, 184
Miller, Mark Crispin, 59
Mills, C. Wright, 89
Milwaukee, Wisconsin, illegal immigration
    demonstrations, 39
MindFreedom, 138, 139
MKULTRA project, 56
money-centrism, 89–94, 200
moneyism, 89–94, 184, 185–86
morale, and energy for action, 122–27. *See also*
    demoralization
morality, as energizer, 128, 129, 130, 180
Morgan Stanley, 42, 187
Mousavi, Mir-Hossein, 19
movement educating, 167, 168–70
movement forming, 167
movement politicization, 167, 170–71
movement recruiting, 167–68
Moyers, Bill, 13, 23, 32–33
Mumford, Lewis, 189
music, commercialization of, 94
mutual nature of dependency, 181–82, 183
MySpace, 67

NAACP, 34
Nader, Ralph, 20–21
NAFTA (North American Free Trade
    Agreement), 36, 37, 80, 85
National Autonomous University of Mexico
    (UNAM), 80
National Cooperative Business Association
    (NCBA), 203
National Council of La Raza, 34
National Day of Action (immigration), 39

National Farmers Alliance and Industrial
    Union, 167, 168, 169, 171, 172
National Gay and Lesbian Task Force, 34
National Labor Relations Act, 179
National Physicians Alliance, 28
National Security Agency (NSA), 82
National Tea Party Convention (2010), 36–37
Native Americans, 107, 205–6
Nazism, 54
Nearing, Helen, 191
Nearing, Scott, 191
Neighborhood Assistance Corporation of
    American (NACA), 187–88
neocon con men, 115
Nerburn, Kent, 205, 206
neurotransmitters, and psychotropic drugs, 56
New York City
    Iraq war protests, 22, 23, 183
    postal worker wildcat strike, 87, 163–65
    project developments, 114–15
    teacher strike, 95
    Wall Street bailout protest, 26
New York Mets, 161–62
Nez Perce flight, 205–6
1984 (Orwell), 53, 59
Nixon, Richard, 29, 87, 113, 163, 164
noncompliance with authority. *See also*
    compliance with authority
    criminalization of, 57, 108, 181
    medication of students for, 96
    as mental illness, 100–109
    punishment of, 97
normalization
    of manipulativeness in advertising, 75
    of selfishness, 90, 92, 93
    of surveillance, 82–83

Oaks, David, 138
Obama, Barack
    campaign and election of, 14–15, 29–31,
        115–16
    on education, 95
    and financial-industrial complex, 5, 91
    health care reform, 29, 31
    leftist anger with, 35, 43
    propaganda about, 156
    troop increases, 21
    Wall Street bailout support, 25, 30
objectification, for breaking a population,
    57–58
Obrador, Andrés Manuel López, 19–20
Occupational Health and Safety Act (1970), 86

O'Neil, Eric, 17
One Nation Working Together protest, 34
online universities, 198, 199
open education movement, 197, 198
oppositional defiant disorder (ODD), 102–4, 105
Orange Revolution (Ukraine), 19
Organic Valley, 202
Organization for Economic Cooperation and Development (OECD), 42
organized religion and moneyism, 93–94
organized vs. disorganized resistance, 43–44
Orwell, George, 53, 59
Overby, Jimmy, 70

pain
    from abuse, 50
    and comfortable-afflicted continuum, 9–11
    from critical thinking, 124–27
    demoralization from, 11–12
    and encouraged drug use, 56–57
Paine, Tom, 148
Palin, Sarah, 36–37, 193
parents
    depression in, 182
    educational system pressures on, 144–45
    paid leave for, 41
    relationships with anarchist children, 151–52
    separation from children, 190
    surveillance of children, 83
passive aggression, 104–5, 176
passivity
    and assumption of ignorance, 10
    causes for vs. evidence of, 47
    and comfortable-afflicted continuum, 10–11
    from demoralization, 11–12, 43–46
    and depression, 50, 126–27
    from disorganization, 43–44
    from drugs, 105–6
    and lack of information, 23–24
    socialization of, 98
    from student-loan debt, 81
    widespread nature of, 13–16
pathologization of noncompliance with authority, 57–58, 100–109, 181
Paulson, Henry, 5
Paxil, 58
People for the American Way, 34
People's Party, 14, 170, 172
Perot, Ross, 21

Perry, Ralph Barton, 125
pessimism and critical thinking, 125–26
pharmaceutical-industrial complex, 5–7, 48, 56–58, 105, 184
Pharmaceutical Research and Manufacturers of America (PhRMA), 6
Piven, Frances Fox, 176, 178, 180
Poland, Solidarity organization in, 208
political parties. See also electoral politics; specific parties
    compromises by, 180
    divisiveness of, 8, 115, 118, 152–58
    two-party system, 14
political sanctions, for breaking a population, 54–55
population size, and democracy, 192
Populist Movement (1800s), 3, 154, 166–73
populists
    defined, 152
    differences among, 153–54
    leftist, 36, 154, 157
    libertarian, 154, 157
    need for unity among, 8, 152–58
    vs. Tea Partiers, 36
positive thinking vs. morale, 123–24, 125
postal workers, resistance by, 15, 87–88, 163–65
Procter & Gamble, 74
producer cooperatives, 202–3
Professional Air Traffic Controllers Organization, 85
Progressive/American Labor Party, 20
Progressive Party, 14
progressives. See also liberals; specific organizations
    and learned helplessness, 116
    umbrella demonstration, 34
    and Wall Street bailout, 26
project developments (housing), 114–15
propaganda
    in abusive relationships, 133, 135
    vs. advertising and public relations, 73
    for breaking a population, 58–59
    role in fundamentalist consumerism, 73–75
Propaganda (Bernays), 59, 73–74
protest demonstration effectiveness, 182–88. See also specific incidents
Proyect, Louis, 204
psychiatric survivor community, 138–39
psychology of breaking a population
    abuse syndrome, 43–46, 49–51, 131–36
    cognitive dissonance, 51–52

drugs, 55–57
   fear, punishment and bribes, 53–55
   labeling and objectification, 57–58
   learned helplessness, 48–49
   lies and propaganda, 58–59
   social isolation and surveillance, 52–53,
      68–69
psychotropic drugs, 55–57, 138
public relations, 73, 186–87
Pullman strike (1894), 179
punishment
   of noncompliance with authority, 97
   as technique for breaking a population,
      53–55
purchasing cooperatives, 203
Putnam, Robert, 66

Rand, Ayn, 92–93
Randolph, A. Philip, 86
Reagan, Ronald, 85
Reich, Robert, 29
relationship boundaries, 134, 136
religion and spirituality, 69–70, 93–94
Republican Party
   co-opting of name, 59
   vs. Democratic Party, 116, 117–19, 155
   elitists in, 155
   vs. Tea Party, 35, 36–37
   Vietnam War involvement, 112, 113
Republic Windows and Doors sit-in, 32, 33
resentment
   of assumption of ignorance, 10–11
   in children, 142, 144, 145, 151–52
resiliency, 142–43
resistance to domination. *See also*
noncompliance with authority
   importance of morale building, 126–27
   measures of, 13–16
   timidity of, 40, 43
Restoring Honor event (2010), 36
Reuters, 26, 27
Reuther, Walter, 86
risk-taking
   in disruption tactics, 180
   in higher education alternatives, 199–200
   and level of commitment, 15
   student-loan debt dampening of, 81
   truth-telling as, 148
Rockefeller, John D., 74
Rolling Stones, 94
Rome, Italy, Iraq war protest in, 22
Roosevelt, Theodore, 14, 90–91

Rudolph, Robert, 7
Rush, Benjamin, 108

Sale, Kirkpatrick, 193–94
sanctions, for breaking a population, 54–55
San Diego, California, illegal immigration
   demonstrations, 39
Sanford, Mark, 92
schools. *See* educational system
Seattle, Washington protests (1999), 16–17,
   188
secession/withdrawal from power systems,
   188–94
Second Vermont Republic, 193
self-absorption, 72–73, 141
self-discipline, 142
self-education, 196, 199
self-forgiveness, 133, 135, 136
self-help groups, 67
selfishness, 89–94, 154
self-reliance, loss of, 71–72
self-respect. *See* individual self-respect
Service Employees International Union, 28
Sewald, Josef, 159–60
sexuality, labeling of, 57
Shaker people, 190, 191
shame, in victims of abuse, 133, 134–35
shared services cooperatives, 203
Shays, Daniel, 177
Shays' Rebellion, 177
Sherman, William Tecumseh, 208
shock experiment on learned helplessness,
   48–49
Sierra Club, 34
single-payer health care, 27–28, 184
sit-down strike of 1936-37 (Flint, Michigan),
   84, 162–63
slave revolts, 178
slavery
   abolition of, 178–79, 180, 206, 207–8
   pathologization of rebellious behavior, 108
small victories, importance of
   in abolitionist movement, 178
   and collective self-confidence, 171–72
   and compromises, 180
   differing views of, 204–7
   for morale, 128
   and solidarity, 161–65
social anxiety disorder, 58
social capital, 66
social isolation
   for breaking a population, 52–53, 68–69

increase in, 65–69
methods for combating, 136–40
from technology, 65–69
from television, 62–63, 64
Socialist Party, 14
social networking, 67
Social Security establishment, 179
social skills training (SST), 137
solidarity
    as energizer, 129–30
    and overcoming distrust, 158–61
    role in collective self-confidence, 161–65
Solidarity (Poland), 208
soma (fictional drug), 56
Sombrotto, Vincent, 164–65
soul matters and anarchism, 151–52
Southern United States
    Confederacy in, 161, 192, 208
    corporate support for change in, 185
    emigration from, 190
    racial apartheid in, 180, 190
    slavery in, 108, 178–79, 180, 206, 207–8
Soviet Union collapse, 208
Spain, Iraq war protests in, 22
spirituality and moneyism, 93–94
spoiledness, as reason for passivity, 44–45
sports, collective self-confidence in, 161–62
Stanford University, 68
Stevens, John Paul, 18
Stewart, Jon, 110
stimulants, 56, 96, 105, 107
Stockholm syndrome, 50–51
stock market investment, 91–92
Stone, I. F., 127, 128
strategies for action, 166–209
    belief in possibility for change, 2–3, 121,
        125, 171–72, 207–9
    disruption tactics, 176–82
    Great Populist Revolt lessons, 166–73
    higher education alternatives, 194–200
    and modern electoral politics, 173–75
    protest demonstrations, 182–88
    secession/dissolution/withdrawal, 188–94
    small victories and compromises, 204–7
    workplace democracy, 200–203
Stratman, David, 160–61
strikes
    Flint sit-down strike, 84, 162–63
    during Great Depression, 179
    Iranian merchants, 37–38, 181–82, 206–7
    New York City teachers, 95
    postal workers, 87–88, 163–65

Pullman workers, 179
    Taft-Hartley Act restrictions on, 85
student-loan debt, 75–81, 194–200
Students for a Democratic Society, 113
stupidity, as reason for passivity, 44–45
successes. See small victories, importance of
Summer, Lawrence, 5
surveillance, 52–53, 82–83
Swanson, David, 128
Sweeney, John, 26
Szasz, Thomas, 8

Taffler, Robin, 197
Taft, William, 14
Taft-Hartley Act of 1947, 85
Tarfon (Rabbi), 127
Taurel, Sidney, 6
Tauzin, Billy, 5–6
taxes, 37–38, 40–43, 181–82, 206–7
Taxpayer March on Washington (2009), 36
Teamsters Union, 87
Tea Party movement, 26, 34–38, 177
technology
    adverse effects of, 60–65
    and normalization of surveillance, 82–83
    vs. real social connectedness, 65–69
television
    adverse effects of, 60–65
    as evidence vs. cause of passivity, 47–48
    need for control of, 64–65
tension and conflict
    and cognitive dissonance, 51–52
    comfort with, 121–22, 143–45
    and compliance with authority, 106
    role of families, 143–45
    and withdrawal/secession, 189–90
Texas Exchange, 169
texting, 67–68
Thomas, Clarence, 92
tobacco companies, 74–75
TransAtlantic Business Dialogue (TABD), 17
Troubled Assets Relief Program, 24
Trumka, Richard, 32–33
truth-telling, as energizer, 148
Turner, Nat, 178
tweeting, 67–68

Ukraine, presidential election of 2004, 19
Underground Railroad, 178
unemployment rates, 31–32
Union Cab Cooperative, 200
unions. See also specific unions

compromises by, 88
decline in, 83–89
health care reform protest, 28
lack of activism in, 31–34
use of disruptive tactics, 179, 180
Wall Street bailout protests, 26
worker/leader conflict, 86, 87, 181
United Auto Workers (UAW), 84, 162–63
United Fruit Company, 74
United States presidential elections
1896, 119, 170, 172
1996, 20–21
2000, 17–21, 43, 162
2008, 14–15, 29–31
United States Social Forum (2010), 16
US Federation of Worker Cooperatives, 200, 201

values
and integrity, 88–89, 141, 205
and self-respect, 141, 143
of Tea Party, 35
Vari, Bruce, 26
Vega, William, 67
Ventura, Jesse, 117
Vermont
producer cooperatives, 202, 203
secession movements, 193
victim mentality, 134, 152
victories. *See* small victories, importance of
Vietnam War (1965-1975), 21, 112–13, 161
violence
anti-authoritarian views on, 151
in disruption tactics, 176–78
against government, 113, 114
voter turnout
and learned helplessness, 116–17
as measure of resistance, 14, 174
US presidential elections, 17, 29–30, 119

wages
college graduate increase in, 79–80, 81, 195
fall in, 42

Wallace, George, 21
Wallace, Henry, 20
Wall Street bailout (2008), 24–26
Walmart employee death, 70
Washington, DC
Afghanistan war protests, 21
health care reform protest, 28
illegal immigration protests, 39
Iraq war protests, 23
One Nation Working Together protest, 34
Tea Party events, 36
World Bank/IMF protests, 17
Weathermen (activist group), 113–14
Weaver, James, 170
Wedeberg, Jim, 202
Weingarten, Randi, 26
Wells Fargo, 42, 187
White Bird (Nez Perce chief), 206
Williams, Jeffrey, 78
Wolin, Neal, 5
women's suffrage, 173–74
Work College Consortium, 197, 198–99
work colleges, 197
worker cooperatives, 200–201
workers. *See also* unions
and loss of power, 83–89
morale in, 123
unemployment rates, 31–32
workplace democracy, 200–203
World Bank, 17
World Trade Organization (WTO), 16–17, 188
World War I (1914-1918), 58–59, 73, 159–61

Yanukovych, Viktor, 19
Yetsko, Norma, 82
Yippies, 113
Yushchenko, Viktor, 19

Zinn, Howard, 13, 23–24
zombification, 61, 63, 64
Zyprexa, 6–7

ABOUT THE AUTHOR

AARON LICHTENBERG

BRUCE E. LEVINE is the author of *Surviving America's Depression Epidemic* and *Commonsense Rebellion*. He is a regular contributor to *The Huffington Post*, *CounterPunch*, *AlterNet*, and *Z Magazine*, and his articles and interviews have been published in *Adbusters*, *The Ecologist*, *High Times*, and numerous other magazines. Dr. Levine, a practicing clinical psychologist often at odds with the mainstream of his profession, also gives talks and workshops. His Web site is brucelevine.net.